W9-ADW-335

REVERSE DICTIONARY SERIES

ABBREVIATIONS

A
REVERSE
GUIDE

DEDICATION

For Evan Thompson and David Rosenbaum,
my colleagues in reference

ABBREVIATIONS;

A REVERSE GUIDE TO STANDARD AND GENERALLY ACCEPTED ABBREVIATED FORMS

First Edition

Compiled and Edited by

Stephen Rybicki

Reference Librarian,
Macomb County Community College
Warren, Michigan

The Pierian Press
Ann Arbor, Michigan
1971

Library of Congress Catalog Card Number: 74-143239
International Standard Book Number: 87650-010-6

© Copyright 1971, The Pierian Press
All Rights Reserved

PREFACE

PURPOSE

As early as 1962, the American Library Association's New Reference Tools Committee recognized the need for a reverse approach to standard abbreviations. Over the years an ever-expanding list of initialese has only compounded this need. As a companion volume to all other abbreviation dictionaries presently available (Shankle, Schwartz, De Sola, etc.), it is hoped that the word-abbreviations approach offered herein will serve to further standardize and control this unwieldy field.

SCOPE

The scope of this work, like its purpose, is fully revealed by its title. Every effort has been made to include all "standard and generally accepted" abbreviations. Additionally, many new and not-so-standard initialisms have been listed because of their immediate social or technological significance, together with occasional reference to more obscure organizations and institutions.

ARRANGEMENT

Entries are arranged alphabetically, letter by letter, disregarding initial articles. 'Mc' is filed as if spelled 'Mac.' Abbreviations have been recorded as accurately and faithfully as possible, so that inconsistencies in form and punctuation should first be attributed to the original source rather than to this writer. Where apparent repetition occurs, or where an abbreviation differs only by way of a period or capital letter, variant forms have actually been included as a matter of course. The purpose again has been to aid in the establishment of a standard of usage based upon a concensus of established sources, inasmuch as existing rules for abbreviation vary and are largely disregarded.

62260

INDEX

An index to the abbreviations has been appended, providing
the traditional approach to abbreviations in addition to the reverse
approach. Abbreviations consisting only of symbols are listed
first, followed by abbreviations starting with or consisting only
of numbers. Alpha abbreviations are entered last and comprise the
great majority of the index. Arrangement of alpha abbreviations
is letter by letter. When the same set of letters appears in variant forms, abbreviations without punctuation preceed abbreviations
with punctuation, and within those confines, lower case abbreviations
preceed upper case. Numbers appearing within alpha abbreviations
are filed as if spelled out. Citations for each abbreviation consist
of page and line numbers.

ACKNOWLEDGEMENTS

I wish to thank my wife Clarice for her understanding support
during the long months required to complete this project. Thanks
also to friend and publisher, C. Edward Wall, for his continual
help, prodding, and patience. Special appreciation to Don Schoening
of Giffles and Associates, and to his wife, Marion, who provided the
numerous architectural and building initialisms. Finally, thanks
to my mother Mary for bringing me into the world, albeit in abbre-
viated form, and to my father Steven J. for keeping me here. And
to Jamie and Christina for just being.

In conclusion, the author invites suggestions for future
editions. Inquires, additions, or corrections may be sent to my
attention c/o Pierian Press, Ann Arbor, Michigan.

Stephen Rybicki

February 1971

```
a cappella - a capp                                           1
A one - A-1                                                   2
ab initio (from the beginning) - ab init.                     3
Ab Urbe Condita (From the Founding of the City of Rome) -     4
    A.U.C.                                                    5
abandoned - aband.                                            6
abandonment - abandmt.; abandt                                7
Abbot - Ab.                                                   8
abbreviated - abbr.; abbrev.                                  9
abbreviation - a.; ab.; abb.; abbr.; abbrev.                 10
abdicate - abd.                                              11
abdicated - abd.                                             12
abdomen - abdom.                                             13
abdominal - abdom.                                           14
Aberdeen - Aber.                                             15
Aberdeen and Rockfish (RR) - A&R                             16
aberration - aber.                                           17
ablative - abl.; ablat.                                      18
able-bodied seaman - A.B.                                    19
aboriginal - abo.                                            20
aborigine - abo.                                             21
Abort Guidance System - AGS                                  22
about (L, circa, circiter, cirum) - a.; ab.; (c; ca.; cir.;  23
    circ.)                                                   24
above (L, supra) - abv.; (sup.)                              25
above average (common stock rating) - A-                     26
above mean sea level - amsl                                  27
above sea level - asl                                        28
above-named - a.n.                                           29
Abraham - Abe; Abr.                                          30
abrasive - abr.; abrsv.                                      31
Abrasive Grain Association - AGA                             32
abridged - abr.                                              33
abridgment - abr.                                            34
abscissa - X                                                 35
absent - a; ab.; abs.                                        36
absent with leave - a.w.l.                                   37
absent without official leave - a.w.o.l.                     38
absente reo (the defendant being absent) - abs. re.          39
absolute - A; a; abs.; absol.                                40
absolute temperature - A; T                                  41
absolute zero - abs. z.                                      42
absolutely - absol.                                          43
absorbing - abs.                                             44
abstract - abs.; abstr.                                      45
abstracted - abstr.                                          46
abstracts - absts.                                           47
Abstracts of Instructional Materials in Vocational and       48
    Technical Education - AIM                                49
Abstracts of Research and Related Materials in Vocational    50
    and Technical Education - ARM                            51
abundant - abt.                                              52
abutment - abut.                                             53
Abyssinian - Abyss.                                          54
Academiae Americanae Socius (Fellow of the American Academy  55
    [of Arts and Sciences]) - A.A.S.                         56
```

1

```
academic - acad.                                                    1
Academy - Acad.                                                     2
Academy of American Poets - AAP                                     3
Academy of Science (Fr, Académie des Sciences) - ADS                4
Acadia - Acad.                                                      5
Acapulco - Acap.                                                    6
accelerando - accel.                                                7
accelerate - accel.                                                 8
acceleration - G, g                                                 9
accept - acc.; acpt.                                               10
acceptable quality level - AQL                                     11
acceptance - acpt.                                                 12
accepted - acc.                                                    13
access - acc.                                                      14
access area - AA                                                   15
access door - AD                                                   16
access panel - AP                                                  17
accessory - access.; accy.                                         18
Accessory power supply - APS                                       19
accident - acdt.                                                   20
accident & health - a&h                                            21
accommodation - accom.                                             22
accompaniment - accomp.                                            23
accompany - acmp.                                                  24
accomplish - accomp.                                               25
accord - acd.                                                      26
according - acc.                                                   27
according to (L, secundum) - sec.                                  28
according to art (L, secundum artem) - s.a.                        29
according to law (L, secundum legem) - sec. leg.                   30
according to nature (L, secundum naturam) - sec. nat.             31
according to rule (L, secundum regulam) - sec. reg.               32
according to value (L, ad valorem) - ad val.                      33
account - a/c; acc.; acct.                                         34
account current - A/C; a/c                                         35
account number - acct. no.                                         36
account of - a/o                                                   37
account sales - a/s                                                38
accountant - acct.                                                 39
accountant and auditor - acc & aud; Acct. & Aud.                   40
accounts payable - a.p.; a/cs pay.                                 41
accounts receivable - AR; a/cs rec.                                42
accrued - acrd.; accrd.                                            43
accrued interest - accrd. int.                                     44
accumulate - accum.                                                45
accumulative - accum.                                              46
accumulator - A                                                    47
accumulator extension - Q                                          48
accusative - acc.                                                  49
acetic - ace.                                                      50
acetone - acet.                                                    51
acetylene - acetl.                                                 52
achievement - achiev.                                              53
achievement age - AA; A.A.; aa                                     54
achievement quotient - AQ; A.Q.                                    55
acid number - AN; A.N.                                             56
```

2

```
acid value - AV; A.V.                                                1
acknowledge - ack.                                                   2
acknowledged - ack.                                                  3
acknowledgment - ack.; ackgt.                                        4
acoustic - acous.                                                    5
Acoustical Plaster - Ac. Plas.; Acst Plas                            6
acoustical tile - AT                                                 7
acoustics - acous.; acoust.                                          8
acquire - acq.                                                       9
acquisition(s) - acquis.                                            10
acquittal - acq.                                                    11
acre(s) - a.                                                        12
acreage - acrg.                                                     13
acrobat - acro.                                                     14
acrobatic - acro.                                                   15
acronym - acron.                                                    16
Acronym-Oriented Nuts - ACORNS                                      17
acrophobia - acro.                                                  18
acting - act.; Actg.; actg.                                         19
Acting Chief - Actg. Chf.                                           20
Acting Secretary - Actg. Sec.                                       21
actinium - Ac                                                       22
action - act.                                                       23
Action for Children's Television - ACT                              24
action time - A/T                                                   25
activate - actv.                                                    26
active - act.                                                       27
active duty - acdu.; ad                                             28
active leaf - A.L.                                                  29
actor - act.                                                        30
Actors' Equity Association - AEA                                    31
actress - act.                                                      32
Acts of the Apostles - Acts                                         33
actual - act.                                                       34
actual cash value - acv                                             35
actual count - act. ct.                                             36
actual cubic feet per minute - a.c.f./min.                          37
actual gross weight - agw                                           38
actual time of departure - atd                                      39
actual value - act. val.                                            40
actual weight - a/w                                                 41
actuate - act.                                                      42
ad finem (at the end, to one end) - ad fin.                         43
ad hunc locum (to this place, on this passage) - ad h.l.            44
ad infinitum (to infinity) - ad inf.                                45
ad initium (at the beginning) ad init.                              46
ad interim (in the meantime) - ad int.                              47
ad libitum (at pleasure) - ad lib.                                  48
ad locum (at the place) - ad loc.                                   49
ad valorem (according to the value - ad val.; a/v                   50
adagio (music) - adag.                                              51
adapted - adap.                                                     52
adapter - adpt.                                                     53
addendum - add.                                                     54
addition - add.; addn.                                              55
additional premium - a.p.                                           56
```

```
additions - addns.                                          1
add-or-subtract - AOS                                       2
address - adr.                                              3
address-indicating group - AIG                              4
addressed - addsd.                                          5
add-subtract - AS                                           6
Aden - Adn                                                  7
adenosine triphosphate - ATP                                8
adhesive - adh.                                             9
adjacent - adj.                                            10
adjective - a.; ad.; adj.                                  11
adjoining - adj.                                           12
adjoint - adj.                                             13
adjourned - adj.                                           14
adjunct - adj.                                             15
adjust - adj.                                              16
Adjusted (stock) - a                                       17
adjustment - adj.                                          18
adjutant - adj.; adjt.                                     19
Adjutant General's Department - AGD                        20
Adjutant General's Office - AGO                            21
administration - adm.; admin.                              22
administrative - adm.                                      23
administrative terminal system - ATS                       24
administrator - admr.; Admr.; admstr.                      25
administratrix - admrx.; Admx.; admx.                      26
Admiral - Adm.                                             27
Admiralty - Adm.                                           28
Admiralty Islands - AI                                     29
admission - adm.                                           30
Adolf - Adf.                                               31
adoption - adop                                            32
adrenalin - adren.                                         33
adreno-cortico-tropic hormone - ACTH                       34
Adrian - Adr                                               35
Adriatic - Adr                                             36
adult - a                                                  37
adulterate - adult.                                        38
adulteration - adult.                                      39
advance - adv.                                             40
advance charges - adv chgs; adv. chgs.                     41
advance freight - adv frt; adv. frt.                       42
Advanced Flying Unit - AFU                                 43
Advanced Research Projects Agency - ARPA                   44
advanced solid logic technology - ASLT                     45
advantage - ad                                             46
advent - Adv.; adv.                                        47
Advent Christian - AC                                      48
Adventist - Adv.                                           49
adventure - adven.                                         50
adventurer - adven.                                        51
adverb - ad.; adv.                                         52
adverbial - adv.; advbl.; advl.                            53
adverbially - adv.; advbl.                                 54
adverse - adv.                                             55
adverse possession - adv poss                              56
```

```
advertisement - ad; adv.; advt.                              1
advertisements - ads                                         2
advertising - advtg.                                         3
Advertising Federation of America - AFA                      4
advice - adv.                                                5
advise - adv.                                                6
advise of availability - ADAVAL                              7
advise shipping date - ADSHPDAT                              8
advise stock on hand - ADSTKOH                               9
Adviser - Adv.                                              10
Advisor - Adv.                                              11
advocate - Adv.; adv.                                       12
aerial - a                                                  13
aerial tuning inductance - A.T.I.; ati                      14
Aero Space Plane - ASP                                      15
Aerocondor - OD                                             16
Aeroflot - AFL                                              17
Aerolineas Argentinas - ARG                                 18
Aerolineas Peruanas - APSA                                  19
aerological - aerol                                         20
Aerological Officer - Aer Of                                21
aeronautical - Ae.; aero.                                   22
Aeronautical Engineer - Ae.E.; Aero E.                      23
aeronautics - aero.                                         24
Aeronaves de Mexico - AM                                    25
aerospace - aerosp.                                         26
Aerovias Naciona les de Colombia - AVN                      27
Aerovias Panama - APA                                       28
Aerovias Venezolanas - AVENSA                               29
aesthetic(s) - aesth(s)                                     30
aetatis (aged, of age) - ae.; aet.; aetat.                  31
affairs - aff.                                              32
affectionate - aff.                                         33
affidavit - afft; afft.                                     34
affiliated - affil.                                         35
affirmative - aff.; afirm.                                  36
affirmatively - aff.                                        37
affirming - aff.                                            38
Afghan(s) - Afg                                             39
Afghanistan - Afg; Afg.                                     40
aforesaid - afsd                                            41
Africa - Afr.                                               42
African-American - Afro-American                            43
African Methodist Episcopal - AME                           44
African Methodist Episcopal Zion - AMEZ                     45
African Negro - Afro-                                       46
after (L, post) - aft; (p.)                                 47
After Action Report - AAR                                   48
after death (L, post mortem) - P.M.                         49
after food - p.c.                                           50
after hatch - ah                                            51
after meals (L, post cibum) - p.c.                          52
afternoon (L, post meridiem) - aft; aftn.; (p.m.)           53
afterward - aftwd.                                          54
afterwards - aftwds.                                        55
again - agn.                                                56
```

```
against (L, contra, versus) - agst.; (con.; v.; vs.)        1
against all risks - AAR; aar                                 2
Agatha - Aggie                                               3
aged (L, aetatis) - ae.                                      4
agency - agcy.                                               5
Agency for International Development - AID                   6
agent - agt.                                                 7
(an) agent for the FBI - G-man                               8
agglomerate - aglm.                                          9
aggregate - aggr.                                           10
Agnes - Aggie                                               11
agnostic - agnos.                                           12
agnosticism - agnos.                                        13
agreement - agr.; agt.                                      14
agricultural - ag.; agr.; agric.                            15
Agricultural Adjustment Administration - AAA                16
Agricultural Adjustment Agency - AAA                        17
Agricultural & Mechanical College - A. & M. C.              18
Agricultural Engineer - Ag. E.                              19
Agricultural Research Service - ARS                         20
agriculture - ag.; agr.; agric.                             21
agriculturist - agric.                                      22
agronomy - agron.                                           23
agrostology - agros.                                        24
ahead - ahd.                                                25
Ahnapee and Western (Wis.) (RR) - A&W                       26
Aid for International Development - AID                      27
Aid to Dependent Children - ADC                             28
Aid to Families with Dependent Children - AFDC              29
Aide-de-Camp - ADC; A.D.C.; aide                            30
Air base - AB                                               31
Air Canada - AC                                             32
air conditioning - Air Cond                                 33
air cooled - a.c.; acld.                                    34
Air Corps - AC                                              35
Air Defense Identification Zone - ADIZ                      36
Air Defense Officer - ADO                                   37
Air Defense Position - ADP                                  38
Air Defense Research and Development Establishment - ADRDE  39
Air Distribution Institute - ADI                            40
air dried - ad                                              41
air express - airex                                         42
Air Filter Institute - AFI                                  43
Air Force - AF                                              44
Air Force Aid Society - AFAS                                45
Air Force Association - AFA                                 46
Air Force Base - AFB                                        47
Air Force Cross - AFC                                       48
Air Force Intelligence Officer - A-2                        49
Air Force Medal - AFM                                       50
Air Force of the Republic of Viet Nam - AFRVN               51
Air Force of the United States - AFUS                       52
Air Force Operations and Training Officer - A-3             53
Air Force Personnel Officer - A-1                           54
Air Force Supply Officer - A-4                              55
Air Force With Army - AFWA                                  56
```

```
Air Force With Navy - AFWN                                           1
Air France - AF                                                      2
Air Freight Forwarders Association - AFFA                            3
Air Headquarters - AHQ                                               4
air horsepower - ahp                                                 5
Air India - AI                                                       6
Air Mail - AM                                                        7
Air New Zealand - TE                                                 8
Air Parcel Post - APP                                                9
air speed indicator - a.s.i.                                        10
air temperature - TT                                                11
air to air missile - AAM                                            12
air to ground missile - AGM                                         13
Air West - RW                                                       14
airborne - abn.                                                     15
aircraft - acft.                                                    16
Aircraft (Bell Telephone) - A                                       17
Aircraft Carrier - Acft.C.                                          18
aircraft depot - A Dpo                                              19
Aircraft Industries Association of America - AIAA                   20
Aircraft Warning Service - AWS                                      21
Aircraftwoman - ACW                                                 22
airdrome - ad; adrm; Adrm.                                          23
airfield - afld                                                     24
Air-India - AI                                                      25
airlift - alft                                                      26
airman - amn.; an.                                                  27
airman basic - Airman                                               28
airman first class - Airman 1c; Alc.                                29
airman second class - Airman 2c                                     30
airman third class - Airman 3c                                      31
Airplane - Ap                                                       32
airport - aprt                                                      33
air-sea rescue - asr                                                34
airship - ashp.                                                     35
airtight - at.                                                      36
airway - awy                                                        37
Akron - Akr                                                         38
Akron, Canton & Youngstown (RR) - AC&Y                              39
Alabama - Ala.                                                      40
Alabama, Tennessee and Northern (RR) - AT&N                         41
alabamine - Ab                                                      42
Alan - Al                                                           43
alarm - alm                                                         44
Alaska - Alsk.                                                      45
Alaska Airlines - ASA                                               46
Alaska Coastal Airlines - AK                                        47
Alaska-Canada - AlCan                                               48
Albania - Alb.                                                      49
Albanian - Alb.                                                     50
Albert - Al                                                         51
Alberta (Can.) - Alb.                                               52
Alberta - Alta.                                                     53
Albrecht - Albr.                                                    54
Albuquerque - Albq                                                  55
Albus (white, a liturgical color) - Alb.                            56
```

```
alchemy - alch.                                                        1
Alcoholics Anonymous - AA; A.A.                                        2
alcove - A                                                             3
Alderman - Ald.; aldm.                                                 4
Aleutian - Aleut                                                       5
Alex - Al                                                              6
Alexander - Al; Alex                                                   7
Alexian Brothers - C.F.A.                                              8
Alfonso - Alf.                                                         9
Alfred - Al; Alf.                                                     10
algae - alg                                                           11
algebra - alg.                                                        12
algebraic - alg.                                                      13
algebraic compiler - ALCOM                                            14
algebraic computer - ALCOM                                            15
Algeria - Alg.                                                        16
algorithmic language - ALGOL                                          17
alia, alii (other things, other persons) - al.                        18
alias - al                                                            19
alignment - align.                                                    20
Alitalia - AZ                                                         21
alkali - alk.                                                         22
All Okay - A.O.K.                                                     23
all rail - AR; ar; a.r.                                               24
all risks - AR; ar; a.r.                                              25
all water - A/W; a/w; a.w.                                            26
Allegheny Airlines - AL                                               27
Allen - Al                                                            28
allergy - alg; all.; All.                                             29
alley - al                                                            30
Allied - Al                                                           31
Allied Expeditionary Force - AEF                                      32
Allied Headquarters - AHQ                                             33
Allied Military Government - AMG                                      34
allocate - alloc                                                      35
allocation - alloc                                                    36
allotment - alot; Almt; almt.                                         37
Allotted - Alot                                                       38
allowance - alw.                                                      39
allowance (horse racing) - Alw.                                       40
allowance stake (horse racing) - Alw. S.                              41
allowances - alws.                                                    42
alloy - aly                                                           43
allusion - allus.                                                     44
allusive - allus.                                                     45
almanac(s) - Almc.                                                    46
Aloha Airlines - TS                                                   47
along - alg                                                           48
Alpha Methyl 3, 4-Methylenedioxyphenethylamine - MDA                  49
(the) alphabet - ABC's                                                50
Alphabetic numeric - Alphameric                                       51
alphabetical - alpha                                                  52
Alphonse - Alph.                                                      53
Alphonso - Alph.                                                      54
Alsace-Lorraine - Al.-L.                                              55
also known as - a.k.a.                                                56
```

```
alteration - alt.; alter.                                         1
alternate - alt.                                                  2
alternate days - alt. dieb.                                       3
alternate hours - alt. hor.                                       4
alternating - alt.                                                5
alternating continuous waves - acw                                6
alternating current - AC; A-C; A.-C.; A.C.                        7
alternating current/direct current - ac/dc                        8
alternative - alt.                                                9
altimeter - altm                                                 10
altitude - alt.                                                  11
alto - alt.                                                      12
aluminum - al; Al.                                               13
Aluminum Acoustical Panels - Al. Ac. Pan.                        14
Aluminum Acoustical Pans - Al. Ac. P.                            15
Aluminum Balustor - Al. Bal.                                     16
Aluminum Company of America - Alcoa                              17
Aluminum Hand Railing - Al. H. Rail                              18
Aluminum Siding - Al. Sid.                                       19
Aluminum Siding Painted - Al. Sid./Pt.                           20
Alvin - Al                                                       21
always afloat - a.a.                                             22
amalgam - aaa; a.a.a.; amal.                                     23
amalgamate - amal.                                               24
amalgamated - amal.                                              25
Amalgamated Clothing Workers of America - ACWA                   26
Amalgamated Engineering Union - AEU                              27
amalgamation - amal.                                             28
amateur - a; amat                                                29
Amateur Boxing Association - A.B.A.                              30
Amateur Fencers League of America - AFLA                         31
Amateur Hockey Association of the U.S. - AHAUS                   32
ambassador - Amb.                                                33
amber - amb                                                      34
ambiguity - ambig                                                35
ambiguous - ambig                                                36
ambulance - amb.                                                 37
Ambulance Corps - A.C.                                           38
amendment(s) - amdt.; amend.                                     39
America - Am.; Amer.                                             40
American - Am.; Amer.                                            41
American Academy of Arts and Letters - AAAL; A.A.A.L.            42
American Academy of Arts and Sciences - AAAS; A.A.A.S.           43
American Airlines - AA                                           44
American Association for the Advancement of Science -            45
    A.A.A.S.                                                     46
American Association of Junior Colleges - AAJC                   47
American Association of Law Libraries - AALL                     48
American Association of School Librarians - AASL                 49
American Association of University Professors - A.A.U.P.         50
American Automobile Association - A.A.A.                         51
American Ballet Theatre - ABT                                    52
American Bar Association - ABA; A.B.A.                           53
American Basketball Association - ABA                            54
American Bible Society - A.B.S.                                  55
American Booksellers Association - ABA                           56
```

```
American Bowlers Association - A.B.A.                                    1
American Broadcasting Company - ABC                                      2
American Cancer Society - ACS                                            3
American Catholic Who's Who - ACWW                                       4
American Ceramic Society - ACS                                           5
American Chain of Warehouses - ACW                                       6
American Civil Liberties Union - ACLU; A.C.L.U.                          7
American Cloak and Suit Manufacturers Association - ACSMA                8
American College Dictionary - ACD                                        9
American College of Radiology - ACR; A.C.R.                             10
American College Test - ACT                                             11
American Concrete Institute - ACI                                       12
American Congregational Union - ACU                                     13
American Congress of Surveying and Mapping - ACSM                       14
American Cotton Shippers Association - ACSA                             15
American Council of Venture Clubs - ACVC                                16
American Dairy Association - ADA                                        17
American Dairy Science Association - ADSA                               18
American Decisions - Am. Dec.                                           19
American Dehydrators Association - ADA                                  20
American Dental Association - ADA; A.D.A.                               21
American Dental Trade Association - ADTA                                22
American Depositary Receipts - ADR                                      23
American Diabetes Association - ADA                                     24
American Dialect Society - ADS; A.D.S.                                  25
American Die Casting Institute - ADCI                                   26
American Dietetic Association - ADA                                     27
American Distilling Company - ADC                                       28
American Documentary Films - ADF                                        29
American Documentation Institute - ADI                                  30
American Drug Manufacturers Association - ADMA                          31
American Economic Foundation - AEF                                      32
American Educational Theatre Association - AETA                         33
American Electrochemical Society - AES                                  34
American Electroplaters Society - AES                                   35
American Engineering Standards Committee - AESC                         36
American Ethnological Society - AES                                     37
American Eugenics Society - AES                                         38
American Expeditionary Forces - AEF; A.E.F.                             39
American Fair Trade Council - AFTC                                      40
American Farm Bureau Federation - AFBF                                  41
American Farm Economic Association - AFEA                               42
American Federation of Grain Millers - AFGM                             43
American Federation of International Institutes - AFII                  44
American Federation of Labor - AFL; A.F.L.; A.F. of L.                  45
American Federation of Labor and Congress of Industrial                 46
    Organizations - AFL-CIO                                             47
American Federation of Musicians - AFM                                  48
American Federation of Radio Artists - AFRA                             49
American Federation of Soroptimist Clubs - AFSC                         50
American Federation of State, County, and Municipal                     51
    Employees - AFSCME                                                  52
American Federation of Teachers - AFT                                   53
American Federation of the Physically Handicapped - AFPH                54
American Field Service - AFS                                            55
American Fisheries Society - AFS                                        56
```

American Flight Strips Association - AFSA   1
American Folklore Society - AFS   2
American Football League - AFL   3
American Foreign Insurance Association - AFIA   4
American Foreign Law Association - AFLA   5
American Forest Products Industries - AFPI   6
American Foundation for Homeopathy - AFH   7
American Foundation for Mental Hygiene - AFMH   8
American Foundation for Pharmaceutical Education - AFPE   9
American Foundation for Tropical Medicine - AFTM   10
American Foundrymen's Association - AFA   11
American French - Am. Fr.   12
American Friends Service Committee - AFSC   13
American Gas Association - AGA   14
American Gas Institute - A.G.I.   15
American Gem Society - AGS   16
American Genetic Association - AGA   17
American Geological Institute - AGI   18
American Glassware Association - AGA   19
American Guild of Organists - AGO   20
American Hardware Manufacturers Association - AHMA   21
American Hearing Society - AHS   22
American Heart Association - AHA   23
American Helicopter Society - AHS   24
American Heritage Foundation - AHF   25
American Historical Association - AHA   26
American history - Amer. Hist.   27
American Hobby Federation - AHF   28
American Hockey League - AHL   29
American Home Missionary Society - AHMS   30
American Honey Institute - AHI   31
American Horse Shows Association - AHSA   32
American Horticultural Society - AHS   33
American Hospital Association - AHA   34
American Hotel Association - AHA   35
American Humane Society - AHS   36
American Independent Party - A.I.P.   37
American Indian - Am. Ind.; Amer. Ind.   38
American Institute - AI   39
American Institute of Accountants - AIA   40
American Institute of Architects - AIA; A.I.A.   41
American Institute of Baking - AIB   42
American Institute of Banking - AIB   43
American Institute of Chemists - AIC   44
American Institute of Electrical Engineers - AIEE   45
American Institute of Steel Construction - AISC   46
American Institute of Weights and Measures - A.I.W.M.   47
American International Association for Economic and Social   48
    Development - AIAESD   49
American Jewish Historical Society - AJHS   50
American Kennel Club - AKA   51
The American Language - Mencken   52
American Law Reports - A.L.R.   53
American League (baseball) - AL   54
American Legion - A.L.   55
American Library Association - ALA; A.L.A.   56

11

```
American Lutheran - AL                                          1
American Management Association - A.M.A.                        2
American Maritime Cases - A.M.C.                                3
American Medical Association - A.M.A.                           4
American Missionary Association - AMA                           5
American Motors Corporation - AMC                               6
American Negro Academy - A.N.A.                                 7
American Newspaper Publishers Association - ANPA                8
American Nurses' Association - A.N.A.                           9
American Ophthalmological Society - A.O.S.                     10
American Oriental Society - A.O.S.                             11
American Peace Society - A.P.S.                                12
American Pediatric Society - A.P.S.                           13
American Petroleum Institute - API; A.P.I.                    14
American Pharmaceutical Association - A.Ph.A.                 15
American Philological Association - A.P.A.                    16
American Philosophical Association - A.P.A.                   17
American Philosophical Society - A.P.S.                       18
American Psychological Association - APA; A.P.A.              19
American Psychological Society - A.P.S.                       20
American Raceways, Inc. - ARI                                 21
American Red Cross - ARC                                      22
American Reports - Am. Repts.                                 23
American Soccer Association - ASA                             24
American Society for Testing Materials - ASTM; A.S.T.M.       25
American Society of Civil Engineers - ASCE; A.S.C.E.         26
American Society of Composers, Authors, and Publishers -     27
    ASCAP                                                     28
American Society of Heating & Ventilating Engineers -        29
    A.S.H.V.E.                                                30
American Society of Mechanical Engineers - ASME; A.S.M.E.    31
American Society of Orthodontists - A.S.O.                    32
American Society of Refrigerating Engineers - ASRE           33
American Society of Travel Agents, Inc. -  ASTA              34
American Sociological Association - ASA                       35
American Spanish - Am. Sp.                                    36
American Standard - Amer Std                                  37
American Standards Association - ASA                          38
American Stock Exchange - Amex; ASE                           39
American Telephone & Telegraph - AT&T                         40
American Tennis Association - ATA                             41
American Veterans Committee - AVC                             42
American Veterans of World War II - AMVETS                    43
American Water Works Association - AWWA                        44
American Welding Society - AWS                                45
American Wire Gauge - AWG                                     46
American Youth Hostels - AYH; A.Y.H.                          47
American-English Usage - AEU                                  48
Americans for Democratic Action - ADA; A.D.A.                49
americium - Am                                               50
ammeter - am.                                                51
ammunition - ammo; amn.                                      52
among - amg.                                                 53
amorphous - amor                                             54
Amos - Am.                                                   55
amount - amt.                                                56
```

```
amount of precipitation - RR                                    1
ampere(s) - A; amp(s)                                           2
ampere turn - a.t.                                              3
ampere-hour - a.h.                                              4
amperes per square foot - a./s.f.; a.s.f.                       5
amphibian - amph.                                               6
amphibious - amph.                                              7
amphibious tractor - amtrac                                     8
amplified - ampl.                                               9
amplifier - ampl.                                              10
amplitude modulation - AM; A-M; A.-M.; A.M.                    11
Amsterdam - Amst.                                              12
anaesthesia - anaesth                                          13
anaesthesiologist - anaesth                                    14
Anales - An.                                                   15
analog computer - ANACOM                                       16
analog function generator - AFG                                17
analog translator - ANATRON                                    18
Analog-digital converter - ADC                                 19
analog-to-digit recorder - ADR                                 20
analogous - anal.                                              21
analogue to digital - A/D                                      22
analogy - anal.                                                23
analysis - anal.                                               24
Analysis & Solution - A&S                                      25
analytic - anal.                                               26
analytical - analyt.                                           27
analytical entries - anals                                     28
anarchism - anarch                                             29
anarchist - anarch                                             30
anarchy - anarch                                               31
Anatomical - Anat.                                             32
anatomical - anat.                                             33
anatomist - anat.                                              34
anatomy - anat.                                                35
anchor bolt - AB                                               36
anchorage - anch                                               37
anchors - anc's                                                38
anchors and chains proved - a&cp                               39
ancient - anc.                                                 40
Ancient Free and Accepted Masons - A.F.A.M.                    41
Ancient Mystical Order of Rosae Crucis (Rosicrusian Order) -   42
    A.M.O.R.C.                                                 43
Ancient Order of Hibernians - A.O.H.                           44
and (Ger, und) - &; u.                                         45
and elsewhere (L, et alibi) - et al.                           46
and husband - et vir.                                          47
and/or - a/or                                                  48
and others (L, et alii or aliae) - et al.                      49
and others, and so forth (L, et ceteri, ceterae or cetera) -   50
    etc.                                                       51
and so forth (L, et cetera) - etc.                             52
and the following (L, et sequens) - et seq.                    53
and the following (page) - f.; fo.; fol.                       54
and the following (pages) - ff.                                55
and those following (L, et sequentes) - et sqq.                56
```

13

```
andante (music) - and.                                          1
Andorra - And.                                                  2
Andromeda - And                                                 3
anecdote(s) - anec                                              4
angle - ang                                                     5
angle of incidence - i                                          6
Anglican - Angl                                                 7
Anglo-French - AF; Anglo-Fr.                                    8
Anglo-Indian - Anglo-Ind.                                       9
Anglo-Irish - Anglo-Ir.                                        10
Anglo-Latin - Anglo-L.                                         11
Anglo-Norman - Anglo-Norm.                                     12
Anglo-Norse - Anglo-N.                                         13
Anglo-Saxon - AS.                                              14
Angola - Ang.                                                  15
angstrom unit - A; A.U.; a.u.                                  16
angstrom units - AU; A.U.                                      17
angular - ang.                                                 18
angular position digitizer - APD                               19
animal - anl                                                   20
animal husbandry - an. hus.                                    21
animal protein factor - apf                                    22
animated - anim.                                               23
animato (music) - anim.                                        24
Ann Arbor (RR) - AA                                            25
Annalen - Ann.                                                 26
annales (annals) - ann.                                        27
annals - ann.                                                  28
Annam - An                                                     29
Annamese - An                                                  30
annealed - anld                                                31
annex - anx                                                    32
anniversary - anniv.                                           33
anno (in the year) - an.                                       34
anno ante Christum (in the year before Christ) - A.A.C.        35
anno Domini (in the year of our Lord) - A.D.                   36
anno inventionis (in the year of the discovery) - A.I.         37
Annus mirabilis (the wonderful year [1666]) - A.M.             38
Anno mundi (year of the World) - A.M.                          39
annotated - annot; annot.                                      40
annotations - annot.                                           41
annotator - annot.                                             42
announcement - ann                                             43
announcer - ann                                                44
annual - an.; ann.                                             45
Annual - Ann.                                                  46
annual report - ann. rep.                                      47
annual return - AR                                             48
annuity - ann.                                                 49
annuities - ann.                                               50
annulment - annul.                                             51
Annunciation - Annun.                                          52
annunciator - ANN                                              53
anodal closing odor - aco                                      54
anodal closing sound - acs                                     55
anode - A; a; an                                               56
```

14

```
anodize - anod                                                      1
anonymous - anon.                                                   2
another - anr.                                                      3
answer - A.; ans.                                                   4
an answer is requested (Fr, Répondez, s'il vous plaît) -            5
    R.S.V.P.                                                        6
Antarctic - Antarc                                                  7
Antarctica - Ant.; Antarc                                           8
ante Christum (before Christ) - A.C.                                9
ante diem (before the day) - a.d.                                  10
ante meridiem (before noon) - A.M.; a.m.                           11
antenna(s) - ant.                                                  12
anterior - ant.                                                    13
anthology - anthol.                                                14
anthropological - anthrop.                                         15
anthropological - anthropol.                                       16
anthropology - anthrop.                                            17
anti gas - ag                                                      18
antiaircraft - AA; aa                                              19
antiaircraft artillery - AAA                                       20
anti-ballistic missile - ABM                                       21
anticipated - ant.                                                 22
anticipated freight - ant. frt.                                    23
antifriction bearing - afb                                         24
Antifriction Bearing Manufacturers Association - AFBMA             25
Antila (the air pump) - Ant                                        26
antilogarithm - antilog                                            27
antimony (L, stibium) - SB                                         28
antipersonnel - apers                                              29
antiphon - ant.                                                    30
antiquarian - antiq.                                               31
Antiquariorum Regiae Societalis Socius (Fellow of the Royal        32
    Society of Antiquaries) - A.R.S.S.                             33
antiquary - antiq.                                                 34
antique - ant.                                                     35
antiquities - antiq.                                               36
Antiquity - Antiq.                                                 37
antitank - A.Tk.                                                   38
anti-tuberculosis vaccine (bacillus Calmette-Guérin) - BCG         39
antonym - ant.                                                     40
Antwerp - Ant                                                      41
any good brand - agb                                               42
any quantity - AQ                                                  43
Anzeiger - Anz.                                                    44
aortic second sound - $A_2$                                        45
Apache (RR) - A                                                    46
Apalachicola Northern (RR) - AN                                    47
apartment - apt.                                                   48
apartments - apts.                                                 49
aphetic - aph.                                                     50
Apocalypse - Ap                                                    51
Apocalypse of Baruch - Apoc. Bar.                                  52
Apocalypse of Moses - Apoc. Mos.                                   53
Apollo Lunar Hand Tools - ALHT                                     54
Apollo Lunar Surface Close-up Camera - ALSCC                       55
Apostle - Ap.                                                      56
```

apostrophe - ap; apos   1
Appalachian Hardwood Manufacturers Incorporated - AHMI   2
apparatus - app.; appar.   3
apparel - app   4
apparent - app.; appar.   5
apparently - appar.   6
appeal - app   7
Appellate - App.   8
appellate - app.   9
Appellate Division - App. Div.   10
appendage - app   11
appended - app   12
appendices - app.; appx.   13
appendix - app.; appx.   14
appendixes - apps.   15
appetite - app   16
appetizer(s) - app   17
applause - app   18
applicable - appl.   19
application - appln.   20
applied - app.; appl.   21
appoint - appt.   22
appointed - app.; apptd.   23
appointment - appt.; appmt.   24
appositive - appos.   25
apprehended - app   26
apprentice - app.; appr.   27
apprentice allowance of 5 lbs. (horse racing) - X.   28
approach - app   29
approbation - appro.   30
appropriate - app   31
appropriation - app   32
approval - app.; appval.   33
approved - appd.   34
approximate - approx.   35
approximately - approx.; aprxly.   36
April - Ap.; Apl.; Apr.   37
Apus (the Bird of Paradise) - Aps   38
aquarium - aquar   39
Aquarius (the Water Bearer) - Aqr   40
aqueduct - aque   41
Aquila (the Eagle) - Aql   42
Ara (the Altar) - Ara   43
Arabic - Ar.   44
Aramaic - Aram.   45
arbitrary - arb   46
arbitration - arb; arbtrn.   47
arbitrator - arbtror.   48
arboriculture - arbor.   49
arc - a   50
arcade - arc.   51
archaeological - archaeol.   52
archaeology - archaeol.   53
archaic - arch.   54
archaism - arch.   55
archbishop - Abp.   56

```
Archdeacon - Archd.                                            1
archdeacon - archd.                                            2
Archdiocesan Development Fund - ADF                            3
Archduke - Archd.                                              4
archduke - archd.                                              5
archeological - archeo                                         6
Archeological Institute of America - AIA                       7
archeologist - archeo                                          8
archeology - archeo; archeol.                                  9
archery - arch.                                                10
archipelago - arch.                                            11
architect - arch.                                              12
architectural - arch.                                          13
Architectural Aluminum Trade - A.A.T.                          14
Architectural Metals Trade - A.M.T.                            15
architectural terra cotta - ATC                                16
architecture - arch.                                           17
architecture - archit.                                         18
Archiv - Arch.                                                 19
archival - archi                                               20
archive - archi                                                21
archivist - archi                                              22
Archivio - Arch.                                               23
Archivolt - AR                                                 24
Arctic - Arc.                                                  25
Arctic Ocean - Arc O                                           26
are (100 sq. meters) - a                                       27
area - A; a                                                    28
area drain - AD                                                29
Area Ecuador Airlines - AREA                                   30
area forecast - arfor                                          31
Argentina - Arg.; Argent.                                      32
Argentina, Brazil, and Chile - ABC                             33
argentum - Ar.                                                 34
Argo (Ship Argo) - Arg                                         35
argon - A                                                      36
argument(s) - arg.                                             37
Aries (the Ram) - Ari                                          38
Aristophanes - Aristoph.                                       39
Aristotle - Arist.                                             40
arithmetic - arith.                                            41
arithmetic and logic unit - ALU                                42
arithmetic factor register - D                                 43
arithmetical - arith.                                          44
Arizona - Ariz.                                                45
Arkansas - Ark.                                                46
Arkansas and Louisiana Missouri (RR) - A&LM                    47
armament - armt.                                               48
armature - arm.                                                49
Armed Forces Information and Education Division - AFIED         50
Armed Forces Press Service - AFPS                              51
Armed Forces Radio Service - AFRS                              52
Armed Forces Special Weapons Project - AFSWP                   53
Armenian - Armen.                                              54
armored - Armd.; armd.                                         55
armored brigade - Armd. Brig.                                  56
```

```
armored division - Armd. Div.                                     1
armored fighting vehicle - AFV                                    2
Armoric - Arm.                                                    3
arms and armor - armor.                                           4
Arms Control and Disarmament Agency - ACDA                        5
Army - A                                                          6
army agent - Ar. Agt.                                             7
Army Air Forces - AAF                                             8
Army Educational Corps - AEC                                      9
Army Exchange Service - AES                                      10
Army Field Forces - AFF                                          11
Army Ground Forces - AGF                                         12
Army Headquarters - AHQ                                          13
Army Hospital Corps - AHC                                        14
Army of the Republic of Vietnam - ARVN                          15
Army of the United States - AUS                                 16
Army package power reactor - APPR                               17
Army Post Office - APO                                           18
Army Regulations - AR                                            19
Army Service Number - A.S.N.                                     20
Arnold - Arn                                                     21
aromatic - arom                                                  22
aromatic radical - Ar                                            23
arrange - arr.                                                   24
arranged - arr.                                                  25
arrest - ar                                                      26
arrival - ar.; arr.                                              27
arrival notice - a.n.; arr.n.                                    28
arrive(s) - ar.; arr.                                            29
arrived - arr.                                                   30
arsenal - ars.                                                   31
Arsenic - As                                                     32
Arthur - Art                                                     33
article - art.                                                   34
articles - arts.                                                 35
Articles of War - AW                                             36
artificial - art.                                                37
Artificial Flower Manufacturers Board of Trade - AFMBT          38
artificial insemination donor - aid                             39
artificially - art.                                              40
artillery - Arty.; arty.                                         41
Artillery Corps - Arty. C.                                       42
artisan - art.                                                   43
artist - art.                                                    44
as above (L, ut supra) - ut sup.                                 45
as circumstances may require (L, pro renata) - p.r.n.           46
as directed (medical) - e.m.p.                                   47
as directed (L, ut dictum) - ut dict.                            48
as if he had said (L, quasi dixisset) - q.d.                    49
as if one should say (L, quasi dicat) - q.d.                    50
as if said (L, quasi dictum) - q.d.                             51
as much as is sufficient (medical) - q.s.                       52
as much as seems good (L, quantum placet) - q.pl.              53
as much as will suffice (L, quantum sufficit) - q.s.           54
as much as you like (L, quantum vis) - q.v.                     55
as much as you please (L, quantum libet) - q.l.                56
```

```
as much as you please (L, quantum placet) - q.pl.        1
as much as you will (L, quantum vis) - q.v.              2
as soon as possible - asap                               3
asbestos - asb.                                          4
asbestos board - AB                                      5
asbestos millboard - AMB                                 6
asbestos roof shingle - ARS                              7
Ascent Propulsion System - APS                           8
Aschheim-Zondek test for pregnancy - A.Z.                9
Ashley, Drew and Northern (RR) - AD&N                   10
Asked Price - A                                         11
asphalt - asph.                                         12
asphalt tile - A.T.; Asph.T.                            13
asphalt tile base - ATB                                 14
asphalt tile edge strip - A.T.E.S.                      15
asphyxia - asphy                                        16
assault - aslt                                          17
assault and battery - a&b                               18
Assault Section (Sturmabteilung) - S.A.                 19
assemble - assem.                                       20
assembler - asmblr.                                     21
Assemblies of God - AG                                  22
assembly - asm.; assy; assy.                            23
assembly fixture - asfx                                 24
assembly layout - aslo                                  25
assented - asst.; asstd.; ast.                          26
assessed - assd.                                        27
assessment - assmt.; asst.; ast.                        28
assessment paid - a.p.                                  29
assigned - Asgd; asgd.; assnd.                          30
assignment - asg; asgmt.                                31
assimilated - assim.                                    32
assistant - asst.                                       33
assistant chief - Asst. Chf.                            34
Assistant Chief of Staff - AC/S; AC of S                35
assistant librarian - Asst. Lib.                        36
assistant secretary - asst. sec.                        37
assistant surgeon - Asst. Surg.                         38
assists - a.                                            39
assists (baseball) - a.                                 40
assists (ice hockey) - A                                41
associate - asso.; assoc.                               42
Associate in Business Administration - A.B.A.           43
Associate in General Education - A.G.E.                 44
Associate in Home Economics - A.H.E.                    45
Associate in Industrial Education - A.I.Ed.             46
Associate Justice - A.J.                                47
Associate Royal Institute of British Architects - A.R.I.B.A.  48
associated - assoc.                                     49
Associated Equipment Distributors - AED                 50
Associated General Contractors of America - AGCA        51
Associated Press - AP                                   52
associated with - assoc. w.                             53
association - assn.; assoc.                             54
Association - Assoc.                                     55
Association for Women Psychologists - AWP               56
```

```
Association of American Railroads - AAR                        1
Association of Black Students - ABS                            2
Association of Casualty and Surety Companies - ACSC            3
Association of Catholic Trade Unionists - ACTU; A.C.T.U.       4
Association of College Unions - ACU                            5
Association of Colleges and Secondary Schools for Negroes -    6
   ACSSN                                                       7
Association of Collegiate Schools of Architecture - ACSA       8
Association of Collegiate Schools of Nursing - ACSN            9
Association of Food and Drug Officials of the United States - 10
   AFDOUS                                                     11
Association of Food Distributors - AFD                        12
assorted - asstd.                                             13
assortment - asmt.                                            14
Assumptionist Fathers - A.A.                                  15
assurance - ass.                                              16
assured - assd.                                               17
Assyria - Ass.                                                18
Assyrian - Assyr.                                             19
astigmatism - As; ast.                                        20
astrologer - astrol.                                          21
astrological - astrol.                                        22
astrology - astrol.                                           23
astronaut - astro                                             24
Astronaut maneuvering unit - AMU                              25
astronautics - astro                                          26
astronomer - astr.; astron.                                   27
astronomical - astr.; astron.                                 28
Astronomical - Astron.                                        29
Astronomical Unit - A.U.                                      30
astronomy - astr.; astron.                                    31
astrophysical - astrophys.                                    32
astrophysics - astrophys.                                     33
asylum - asy.                                                 34
asymmetric - asym.                                            35
asymmetrical - asym.                                          36
at - a                                                        37
at a later date - ald                                         38
at bat (baseball) - ab.                                       39
at bedtime (medical) - h.s.                                   40
at bedtime (L, hora decubitus) - hor. decub.                  41
at buyer's risk (L, caveat emptor) - c.e.                     42
at night (L, nocte) - n.; noct.                               43
at one end, to one end (L, ad finem) - ad fin.                44
at or to the place (L, ad locum) - ad loc.                    45
at once - stat.                                               46
at pleasure, as needed (L, ad libitum) - ad lib.              47
at the beginning (L, ad initium) - ad init.                   48
at the end (L, in fine) - in f.                               49
at the outset (L, in limine) - in lim.                        50
at the place (L, ad locum) - ad loc.                          51
at this time (L, hoc tempore) - h.t.                          52
at will - ad lib.                                             53
Atchison Topeka and Santa Fe (RR) - AT&SF                     54
atheism - ath                                                 55
atheist - ath                                                 56
```

```
Athens - Ath                                                    1
athlete - athl.                                                 2
athletic - ath; athl.                                           3
athletic association - AA                                       4
athletic club - AC                                              5
Athletic Goods Manufacturers Association - AGMA                 6
athwartship - athw.                                             7
Atlanta - Atl.                                                  8
Atlanta and St. Andrews Bay (RR) - A&SAB                        9
Atlanta and West Point (RR) - A&WP                             10
Atlantic - Atl.                                                11
Atlantic and East Carolina (RR) - A&EC                         12
Atlantic and Pacific - A&P                                     13
Atlantic and Western (N.C.) (RR) - A&W                         14
Atlantic Charter - A.C.                                        15
Atlantic Coast Line (RR) - A.C.L.                              16
Atlantic Ocean - Atl. O.                                       17
Atlantic Standard Time - A.S.T.                                18
Atlantic Time - A.T.                                           19
Atlas Basic Language (computer) - ABL                          20
atmosphere - a.; at.; atm.                                     21
atmospheres absolute - a.; atm.; atma.                         22
atmospheric - at.                                              23
atmospheric pressure - atm press; PPP                          24
atmospheric temperature absolute - ata                         25
atomic - at.                                                   26
atomic, biological, and chemical - ABC                         27
atomic bomb - A-bomb                                           28
Atomic Energy Commission - AEC                                 29
atomic explosion - at. xpl.                                    30
atomic mass unit - amu; a.m.u.                                 31
atomic number - at.no.; Z                                      32
atomic percent - a/o                                           33
atomic volume - at.vol.                                        34
atomic volume control - acv; a.c.v.                            35
atomic warfare - AW                                            36
atomic weight - at.wt.                                         37
attaché - Att.                                                 38
attached - att.; atchd.                                        39
attack - atk; atk.                                             40
attendant - atdt.                                              41
attention - att.; atten.; attn.                                42
Attic - Att                                                    43
attorney - att.; atty.                                         44
Attorney General - Atty. Gen.                                  45
attribute - attrib.                                            46
attributive - attrib.                                          47
attributively - attrib.                                        48
Auburn University - AU                                         49
audio frequency - AF; A-F; A.-F.; A.F.; af; a.f.               50
audio response unit - ARU                                      51
audio-visual - AV                                              52
Audio-Visual Center - AVC                                      53
audit - a; aud.                                                54
auditor - aud.                                                 55
Auditor General - Aud. Gen.                                    56
```

```
augment - aug.                                                        1
augmentative - aug.; augm.                                            2
augmented - aug.; augm.                                               3
augmented target docking adapter - ATDA                               4
August - Ag.; Aug.                                                    5
Augustan - August.                                                    6
Augustinian Friars - O.S.A.                                           7
Augustus - August.                                                    8
aujourd'hui (today) - auj                                             9
Auriga (the Charioteer) - Aur                                        10
Austin - Aust.                                                       11
Australia - Austl.                                                   12
Australian - Austl.                                                  13
Australian Capital Territory - ACT                                   14
Australian Council of Trade Unions - ACTU                            15
Austria - Aus.                                                       16
Austrian - Aust.                                                     17
authentic - auth.                                                    18
authenticity - auth.                                                 19
author - au.; auth.                                                  20
authority - auth.                                                    21
authorization - auth.                                                22
authorized - auth.                                                   23
Authorized Version - AV                                              24
Authorized Version (of the Bible) - A.V.                             25
authors - auths.                                                     26
author's alteration - aa                                             27
Autocycle Union - ACU                                                28
autograph - autog                                                    29
autograph document signed - ads; a.d.s.                              30
autograph letter - A.L.; a.l.                                        31
autograph letter signed - a.l.s.                                     32
autograph note signed - a.n.s.                                       33
autograph postcard signed - a.p.s.                                   34
auto-manual - A/M                                                    35
automated batch mixing (computer) - ABM                              36
automatic - aut.; auto.                                              37
automatic brightness control - abc                                   38
Automatic Car Wash Association International - ACWAI                  39
automatic checkout and readiness equipment - ACRE                    40
automatic computer - AC                                              41
Automatic Computer-Controlled Electronic Scanning System -           42
   ACCESS                                                            43
automatic data acquisition - ADA                                     44
automatic data exchange - ADX                                        45
automatic data processing - ADP                                      46
automatic data processing center - ADPC                              47
automatic data processing system - ADPS                              48
automatic digital data acquisition and recording - ADDAR             49
automatic digital on-line instrumentation system - ADONIS            50
automatic display and plotting systems - ADAPS                       51
automatic drafting machine - ADMA                                    52
automatic frequency control - AFC; A.F.C.; afc                       53
automatic gain control - AGC; A.G.C.; agc                            54
automatic output control - AOC                                       55
automatic pass compensation - Abc                                    56
```

```
automatic picture transmission - APT                                    1
automatic pilot - autopilot                                             2
automatic program unit, high-speed - APUHS                              3
automatic program unit, low-speed - APULS                               4
automatic programmed checkout equipment - APCHE                         5
automatic ratio control - ARC                                           6
automatic reporting telephone - ART                                     7
automatic self-verification - ASV                                       8
automatic send receive - ASR                                            9
automatic servo plotter - ASP                                          10
automatic switching panel - ASP                                        11
automatic teleprinter exchange service - TEX                           12
automatic teletypewriter exchange service - TELEX                      13
automatic ticketing - AT                                               14
automatic volume control - A.V.C.; a-v-c; avc                          15
automatic washing machine - awm                                        16
automation - automtn                                                   17
automobile - auto.                                                     18
automotive - auto.                                                     19
Automotive Electric Association - AEA                                   20
autonomic nervous system - A.N.S.                                      21
autonomous - auton                                                     22
Autonomous Soviet Socialist Republic - ASSR                            23
autonomy - auton                                                       24
autopilot control - a/o ctl                                            25
autopsy - autop                                                        26
auxiliary - aux.                                                       27
auxiliary power plant - APP                                            28
auxiliary power supply - APS                                           29
auxiliary report - XREP                                                30
auxiliary verb - aux. v.                                               31
availability - aval                                                    32
available - aval                                                       33
Ave Maria - A.M.                                                       34
Avenue - Av.; Ave.                                                     35
average - av.; avg.                                                    36
average (common stock rating) - B+                                     37
average deviation - ad                                                 38
average length - avl                                                   39
average sample number - ASN                                            40
average width - avw                                                    41
Aviateca - GU                                                          42
aviation - avn.                                                        43
Aviation Distributors and Manufacturers Association - ADMA             44
aviator - av                                                           45
avoirdupois - av.; avdp.; avoir.                                       46
award - awd                                                            47
awkward - awk.; k                                                      48
awning - awn                                                           49
axes - ax.                                                             50
axiom - ax.                                                            51
axis - a; ax.                                                          52
azimuth - az.                                                          53
Azores - Az                                                            54
Azores Islands - Az. Is.                                               55
Aztec - Az                                                             56
```

23

```
azure - a; az.                                                      1
baby - b                                                            2
Babylonian - Bab.                                                   3
bachelor - bach.                                                    4
Bachelor of Accounting - B.Acc.                                     5
Bachelor of Agriculture - B.Ag.                                     6
Bachelor of Applied Arts - B.A.A.                                   7
Bachelor of Applied Mathematics - B.A.M.                            8
Bachelor of Applied Science - B.A.S.                                9
Bachelor of Architecture - B.Ar.; B.Arch.                          10
Bachelor of Arts (L, Artium Baccalaureus) - A.B.                   11
Bachelor of Arts in Education - A.B.Ed.                            12
Bachelor of Arts in Music - B.A.M.                                 13
Bachelor of Business Administration - B.B.A.                       14
Bachelor of Canon Law - J.C.B.                                     15
Bachelor of Chemical Engineering - B.C.E.; B.Ch.E.                 16
Bachelor of Chemistry - B.C.                                       17
Bachelor of Christian Education - B.C.E.                           18
Bachelor of Church Music - B.C.M.                                  19
Bachelor of Civil Engineering - B.C.E.                             20
Bachelor of Civil Law (L, Juris Civilis Baccalaureus) -           21
   B.C.L.; (J.C.B.)                                                22
Bachelor of Dental Surgery - B.D.S.                                23
Bachelor of Divinity - B.D.                                        24
Bachelor of Education - B.E.; Ed.B.                                25
Bachelor of Electrical Engineering - B.E.E.                        26
Bachelor of Engineering - B.E.                                     27
Bachelor of Engineering Physics - B.E.P.                           28
Bachelor of Fine Arts - B.F.A.                                     29
Bachelor of Journalism - B.J.                                      30
Bachelor of Laws (L, Legum Baccalaureus) - B.L.; (LL.B.)          31
Bachelor of Letters (L, Literarum Baccalaureus) - B.Litt.;        32
   (L.B.); Litt.B.                                                 33
Bachelor of Library Science - B.L.S.                               34
Bachelor of Literature - B.Lit.; Lit.B.                           35
Bachelor of Mechanical Engineering - B.M.E.                        36
Bachelor of Medicine (L, Medicinae Baccalaureus) - B.M.;          37
   (M.B.)                                                          38
Bachelor of Metallurgy - B.Met.                                    39
Bachelor of Mining Engineering - B.M.E.                            40
Bachelor of Music (L, Musical Baccalaureus) - B.Mus.;             41
   (Mus.B.; Mus.Bac.)                                              42
Bachelor of Pedagogy - B.Pd.; Pd.B.                               43
Bachelor of Podiatrics - Pe.B.                                    44
Bachelor of Pharmacy - B.P.; Phar.B.                              45
Bachelor of Philosophy (L, Philosophiae Baccalaureus) -           46
   B.Phil.; (Ph.B.)                                                47
Bachelor of Physical Education - B.P.E.                            48
Bachelor of Public Health - B.P.H.                                 49
Bachelor of Sacred Theology (L, Sacrae Theologiae                 50
   Baccalaureus) - S.T.B.                                          51
Bachelor of Science (L, Scientiae Baccalaureus) - B.S.;           52
   B.Sc.; (S.B.; Sc.B.)                                            53
Bachelor of Science in Agriculture - B.S.A.                       54
Bachelor of Science in Chemical Engineering - B.S. in Ch.E.       55
Bachelor of Science in Library Service - B.S. in L.S.             56
```

Bachelor of Scientific Agriculture - B.S.A.   1
Bachelor of Surgery - B.S.; C.B.   2
Bachelor of Theology (L, Scientiae Theologicae Baccalaureus)   3
    B.T.; B.Th.; (S.T.B.)   4
Bachelor of Veterinary Science - B.V.Sc.   5
bacilli - bac   6
bacillus - B; b; bac   7
bacillus of Calmette and Guérin - B.C.G.   8
Back (football) - B   9
Back (Polo) - B   10
back dividends - b.d.   11
back electromotive force - BEMF; B.E.M.F.   12
back feed - BF   13
back focal length - BFL; B.F.L.   14
back order - b.o.   15
back to back - B/B   16
back water valve - BWV   17
background - bkgd   18
backset - bs   19
backward (skating direction) - B   20
bacon, lettuce, and tomato (sandwich) - blt   21
bacteria - bac; bact.   22
bacteriologist - bac   23
bacteriology - bac   24
Bacteriology - Bacteriol.   25
bad conduct discharge - bcd   26
bag - bg.   27
baggage - bag.   28
baggageman - bgmn   29
Baghdad - Bag   30
Bahama Islands - B.I.; Ba.Is.   31
Bahamas Airways - BH   32
bail bond - BB   33
bakery - bak; bkry   34
Bakteriologie - Bakteriol.   35
balance - bal.; blc.   36
Balance Forwarded - B.F.   37
balance sheet - b.s.   38
balanced inductor logical element - BILE   39
balancing - bal.   40
Balboa - Balb   41
balcony - bal   42
bale(s) - bl.   43
balk (baseball) - BK   44
ball bearing - b.b.   45
ballast - ball.   46
Balling - B.   47
ballistic missile early warning system - BMEWS   48
balloon - bln.   49
baloney - bal   50
balsam - bals.   51
Baltic - Balt.; Bltc.   52
Baltimore - Balt.   53
Baltimore and Annapolis (Md.)(RR) - B&A   54
Baltimore and Eastern (RR) - B&E   55
Baltimore and Ohio (RR) - B&O   56

```
baluster - bals.                                                   1
band - bd.                                                         2
Bangkok - Bank                                                     3
Bangor - Bng                                                       4
Bangor and Aroostook (Me.)(RR) - B&A                               5
bank - bk.                                                         6
bank book - b.b.                                                   7
bank clearings - bank clgs.                                        8
bank debits - bank debs.                                           9
bank draft - B/D                                                  10
Bank for International Settlements - BIS                          11
bank post bill - b.p.b.                                           12
banking - bkg.                                                    13
bankrupt - bkpt.                                                  14
Baptist - Bapt.                                                   15
baptized - bapt.; bp.                                             16
Barbados - Barb.                                                  17
Barbara - Bab                                                     18
barbarian - barb.                                                 19
barbecue - barb.; bar-b-q; B.B.Q.                                 20
barber - barb.                                                    21
Barcelona - Barc; Bcl                                             22
bare and painted - b.&p.                                          23
baritone - barit.                                                 24
Barium - Ba                                                       25
bark - bk.                                                        26
Barnard - Barn                                                    27
barometer - bar.                                                  28
Baronet - Bart.; Bt.                                              29
Baroque - Bar                                                     30
barracks - bks.                                                   31
Barre and Chelsea (N.H.-Vt.)(RR) - B&C                            32
barrel - bbl.                                                     33
barrel(s) - bl.                                                   34
barrels - bbls.                                                   35
barrels per charge day - b./c.d.                                  36
barrels per day - b/d; bbls/day; bpd; b.p.d.                      37
barrels per stream day - b.p.s.d.                                 38
barrister - bar.; barr.                                           39
Baruch - Bar                                                      40
basal metabolic rate - BMR                                        41
basal metabolism rate - B.M.R.                                    42
base -b                                                           43
base and increment - b&i                                          44
base/box (tin) - bb.                                              45
base helix angle - bha                                            46
base hit (scoring) - -                                            47
base hits (baseball) - h.                                         48
base line - ba; b.l.                                              49
base on balls (baseball) - BB                                     50
base unit - bu                                                    51
basement - basm't; bsmt.                                          52
basic - bsc                                                       53
basic automatic checkout equipment - BACE                        54
basic display unit - BDU                                          55
basic level automation of data through electronics - BLADE       56
```

```
basic message switching center - BSC                              1
basic sediment and water - BS&W; B.S.&W.; b.s.&w.                 2
basic-transient diode logic - BTDL                                3
Basilian Fathers - C.S.B.                                         4
Basilica - Bas                                                    5
basket - bkt.; bsk.                                               6
Basque - Bsq                                                      7
bass - b.                                                         8
bass clarinet - b.c.                                              9
basso - b.                                                       10
bassoon - bass.                                                  11
bastard - bstd                                                   12
Basutoland - Bas.                                                13
Batelle Memorial Institute - BMI                                14
bathroom - B                                                    15
bathtub - BT; bt                                                16
Baton Rouge - Bat Rou                                           17
battalion - batn.; bn.                                          18
batter - batt                                                   19
batteries - batt                                                20
battery - bat.; batty; bty.                                     21
battery charger - bat. chg.                                     22
battery charging - bat. chg.                                    23
Battery orders - Bty O                                          24
battle - bat.                                                   25
battle dress - b.d.                                             26
Baumé - B.                                                      27
Baumé or Beaumé - Bé.                                           28
bay - B.; b.                                                    29
Bay-colored (horse racing) - b.                                 30
Baylor University - BU                                          31
beachhead - bhd                                                 32
beacon - bcn                                                    33
beaded one side - b.s.                                          34
beagle(s) - bgl(s)                                              35
beam - bm.                                                      36
bearing - brg.                                                  37
bearing bronze - bbz                                            38
bearing weight loss - BWL; B.W.L.                               39
beat-frequency oscillator - BFO                                 40
Beatrice - Bea                                                  41
beautiful - beaut                                               42
Beaver, Mead and Engelwood (RR) - BM&E                          43
because - bec.                                                  44
Bechuanaland - Bech.                                            45
bed - bd.                                                       46
bed and board - b&b                                             47
beds - bds.                                                     48
before - bef.                                                   49
before Christ (L, ante Christum) - (A.C.); B.C.; b.c.           50
before depletion (stock) - b                                    51
before meals (L, ante cibum) - a.c.                             52
before noon (L, ante meridiem) - A.M.; a.m.                     53
Before the Christian Era - BCE                                  54
before the day (L, ante diem) - a.d.                            55
beginning and end - b.&e.                                       56
```

```
beginning of tape - BOT                                          1
behavior - behav.                                                2
behavioral - behav.                                              3
Beiträge - Beitr.                                                4
Belfast & Moosehead Lake (RR) - B&ML                             5
Belgian - Bel.                                                   6
Belgian francs - FB                                              7
Belgian Congo - BC                                               8
Belgium - Bel.                                                   9
bell and flange - B&F                                           10
bell and spigot - B&S                                           11
below (L, infra) - bel.;  (inf.)                                12
below average (common stock rating) - B                         13
below ground level - bgl                                        14
Belt Railway Chicago (RR) - BRC                                 15
Ben Jonson - B.Jon.                                             16
benchboard - bnchbd                                            17
benchmar - bm                                                  18
bending moment - M                                             19
Benedict - Ben; Bened.                                         20
beneficiary - bfcy                                             21
Benevolent and Protective Order of Elks - B.P.O.E.             22
Bengal - Beng.                                                 23
Bengali - Beng.                                                24
Benjamin - Ben; Benj.                                          25
bent - bt.                                                     26
benzedrine - benz                                              27
benzene - Bz.                                                  28
benzine - benz                                                 29
bequeathed - beqd.                                             30
bequest - beqt.                                                31
Berichte - Ber.                                                32
Berkeley - Berk                                                33
Berlin - Ber.                                                  34
Bernard - Bern.                                                35
berth - bth                                                    36
berth terms - b.t.                                             37
Bertram - Bert.                                                38
Beryllium - Be                                                 39
Bessemer - Bess.                                               40
Bessemer and Lake Erie (RR) - B&LE                             41
best (L, optimus) - opt.                                       42
best - XXXX                                                    43
Best game (billiards) - BG                                     44
better - btr.                                                  45
Better Government Association (Chgo.) - BGA                    46
between - betw.; btwn.                                          47
bevel - bev.                                                   48
beleved - bev.                                                 49
beveled edge - be.                                             50
beverage - bev                                                 51
Beverly - Bev                                                  52
Bhutan - Bhu.                                                  53
Bible - B.                                                     54
Biblical - Bib.                                                55
biblical - bib.                                                56
```

```
bibliographer - bib.; bibliog.                                          1
bibliographical - bibl.; biblio.; bibliog.                              2
bibliographical footnote - bibl. fn.                                    3
bibliography - bib.; bibliog.                                           4
Biblioteca Nacional - Bib Nac                                           5
Bibliotheque Nationale - Bib Nat                                        6
bicarbonate of soda - bicarb.                                           7
bicuspid - b                                                            8
bicycle - bcl                                                           9
bicyclist - bclt                                                       10
Bid Price - B                                                          11
bidet - B; bdt.                                                        12
biennial - bien                                                        13
big man on campus - BMOC                                               14
big woman on campus - BWOC                                             15
bikini - biki                                                          16
bilateral - bilat                                                      17
bilateral iterative network - BITN                                     18
bill for collection - B/C                                              19
bill of entry - B/E; b/e                                               20
bill of exchange - B/E; b/e; B.E.; b.e.                                21
Bill of Health - BH                                                    22
bill of lading - B.L.; b.l.; B/L; b/l                                  23
bill of lading attached - B/L Att.                                     24
bill of material - B/m, b/m                                            25
bill of parcels - B/P                                                  26
bill of sale - B/S, b/s; b.s.                                          27
bill rendered - b.rend.                                                28
Bill to 3rd No. (Bell Telephone) - B                                   29
billed at - b/a                                                        30
billet - bil                                                           31
billion electron volts - Bev.; bev.; b.e.v.                            32
bills discounted - b.d.                                                33
bills of lading - Bs/L                                                 34
bills payable - B/P, b.p.; b.pay.                                      35
bills receivable - B.R.; B/R; b.r.; b.rec.                             36
bi-monthly - bi-m.                                                     37
binary - bin.                                                          38
binary add - BA                                                        39
binary asymmetric channel - BAC                                        40
binary code - BC                                                       41
binary code frequency shift keying - BCFSK                             42
binary decimal counter - BDC                                           43
binary digit(s) - bit(s)                                               44
binary information exchange - BIX                                      45
binary number system - BN                                              46
binary subtract - BS                                                   47
binary symmetric independent channel - BSIC                            48
binary-coded decimal/binary - BCD/B                                    49
binary-coded decimal/quarternary - BCD/Q                               50
binary-coded octal - BCO                                               51
binary-to-decimal - BIDEC                                              52
binary-to-decimal decoder - BDD                                        53
binding - bdg.; bndg.                                                  54
binoculars - binocs                                                    55
Bioastronautical Orbiting Space Station - BOSS                         56
```

```
Biochemical - Biochem.                                              1
biographer - biog.                                                  2
biographical - biog.                                                3
biography - biog.                                                   4
Biological - Biol.                                                  5
biological - biol.                                                  6
Biological Abstracts - Biol Abstr                                   7
biological chemistry - biochem.                                     8
biological satellite - BIOS                                         9
biological warfare - biowar                                        10
Biologie - Biol.                                                   11
Biologique - Biol.                                                 12
biologist - biol.                                                  13
biology - biol.                                                    14
biomedical - biomed                                                15
biophysical - biophys                                              16
Birch - Bir.                                                       17
Birmingham - B'ham; Birm.                                          18
birthplace - bp; bpl.                                              19
bishop (L, pontifex) - Bp.; bp.; (P.)                              20
Bismarck - Bis                                                     21
Bismark Archipelago - Bis. Arch.                                   22
Bismuth - Bi                                                       23
bistable magnetic core - BIMAG                                     24
bit (computer) - B                                                 25
bits per inch - BPI                                                26
bits per second - BPS                                              27
bituminous - b; bitum.                                             28
bivariant function generator - BIVAR                               29
black - b; bk; blk.                                                30
Black Afro Militant Movement - BAAM                                31
black and white - B/W                                              32
Black Caucus of the American Library Association - BCALA           33
black letter - B.L.                                                34
Black Panther Party - B.P.P.                                       35
Black Panther Party Newspaper - B.P.P.News                         36
blackout - bo                                                      37
blacksmith - blksmith                                              38
blanket - blnkt                                                    39
blanking - BL                                                      40
Blatchford's Prize Cases - Blatch. Pr. Cas.                        41
blend of - b.                                                      42
blended - b.                                                       43
Blessed - Bl.                                                      44
Blessed Sacrament - B.S.                                           45
Blessed Virgin Mary - B.V.M.                                       46
blind approach - ba                                                47
blinkers (horse racing) - b.                                       48
blizzard - bliz                                                    49
Block - Bl.                                                        50
block - bl.; blk.                                                  51
blocking - blkg.                                                   52
Block Liquid Cement Enameled - Bl./Liq.C.E.                        53
Block-Painted - Bl./Pt.                                            54
Block-Plastic Painted - Bl./Pl.Pt.                                 55
blood - bld                                                        56
```

```
blood pressure - B.P.; b.p.                              1
blood urea nitrogen - BUN                                2
blood-alcohol test (drunk driving) - b-a test            3
blouse - blou                                            4
blower - blo                                             5
blow-off - BO                                            6
blue - b; bl.                                            7
Blue Book - B.B.                                         8
Blue Ridge (RR) - BR                                     9
blueprint - BP                                          10
bluestone - BS                                          11
bluish - B                                              12
bluish green - bG                                       13
blunt end first - b.e.f.                                14
B'nai B'rith - BB                                       15
board - bd.                                             16
board foot - bd.ft.; fbm                                17
board measure - b.m.                                    18
Board of Supervisors - Bd of Sup                        19
Board of Trade - B.O.T.                                 20
board, room, and tuition - BRT                          21
boards - bds.                                           22
boat - bt.                                              23
boatswain - bos'n.                                      24
Boccaccio - Boc                                         25
Bodleian Library - Bodl Lib                             26
body odor - BO                                          27
body of law (L, corpus juris) - C.J.                    28
Bogatá - Bog                                            29
Bohemia - Bohem.                                        30
Bohemian - Bohem.                                       31
boil - coq.                                             32
boiler - BLR                                            33
boiler feed - BF                                        34
boiler horsepower - boiler h.p.                         35
boiler house - BH                                       36
boiler room - BR                                        37
boiling point - b.p.                                    38
boiling water (L, aqua bulliens) - aq. bull.            39
boldface - bf                                           40
Bolivia - Bol.                                          41
Bolivian - Bol.                                         42
bolster - bols                                          43
bolts - bt                                              44
bombardier - Bdr.; bmdr.                                45
Bombay - Bom                                            46
bond - bd.                                              47
bond rights - bd. rts.                                  48
bonded goods - B/G                                      49
bonding - bond.                                         50
bonds - bds.                                            51
book - b.                                               52
book(s) - bk.(s.)                                       53
book (L, liber) - L; lib.                               54
book (Fr, tome) - t.                                    55
book shelves - bk sh                                    56
```

31

```
book value - B/v; b.v.                                          1
bookbinder - bkbndr.                                            2
bookbinding - bkbdg.; bkbndg.                                   3
bookkeeper - bkpr.                                              4
bookkeeping - bkg.; bkpg.                                       5
booklet(s) - bklet.(s)                                          6
Books in Print - BIP                                            7
booster - bstr                                                  8
Boötes (the Herdsman) - Boo                                     9
Bordeaux - Bdx                                                 10
boring - bor                                                   11
boring bar - bobr                                              12
born - b.                                                      13
born (Ger, geboren) - geb.                                     14
born (L, natus) - n.                                          /15
Boron - B                                                      16
boron - bor.                                                   17
Borough - Bor.                                                 18
borough - bor.; boro                                           19
borrowed light - blt                                           20
Boston - Bos.; Bost.                                           21
Boston and Maine (RR) - B&M                                    22
Boston College - BC                                            23
Boston Public Library - BPL                                    24
Boston Red Sox - Bosox                                         25
Boston Stock Exchange - BSE; BO                                26
Boston's Massachusetts General Hospital - MGH                  27
Botanical - Bot.                                               28
botanical - bot.                                               29
Botanisches - Bot.                                             30
botanist - bot.                                                31
Botany - Bot.                                                  32
botany - bot.                                                  33
both ways - B.W.                                               34
bottle - bot.; btl.                                            35
bottles - btls.                                                36
bottom - bot.; bott.                                           37
bottom chord - B.C.                                            38
bought - bgt.; bt.                                             39
Boulevard - Blvd.                                              40
boulevard - blvd.; boul.                                       41
bound - bd.; bnd.                                              42
bound in boards - bds.                                         43
boundary - bd.; bdy.; bndy.                                    44
bowel movement - bm; b.m.                                      45
bowled (cricket) - b.                                          46
bowling - bwg.                                                 46
box - bx.                                                      47
box office - BO; b.o.                                          48
boxed - bxd.                                                   49
boxes - bxs.                                                   50
Boy Scouts of America - BSA; B.S.A.                            51
bracing - brcg.                                                52
bracket - bkt.; brkt.                                          53
Bradley University - BU                                        54
brake - bk                                                     55
brake horsepower - BHP; B.H.P.; bhp; b.h.p.                    56
```

```
brake horsepower-hour - bhp-hr                    1
brakeman - brkmn                                  2
branch - br.                                      3
branch and store instruction - BSI               4
branch no group - BNG                             5
branch office - B.O.; b.o.                        6
branch or skip on condition - BSI                7
branch output interrupt - BOI                    8
brand - br.                                       9
Brandeis University - BU                         10
brandy and soda - b.&s.                          11
Braniff International Airways - BN               12
brass - b.; brs.                                 13
brass steeple tips - bst                         14
brassiere - bra                                  15
brazier - braz                                   16
Brazil - Braz.                                   17
Brazilian - Braz.                                18
brazing - brzg.                                  19
bread and water - b&w                            20
breadth - b.                                     21
break request signal - BRS                       22
breakfast-lunch - brunch                         23
breaking and entering - b&e                      24
breakwater - bkw                                 25
breech loading - b.l.; B.L.                      26
breezing (horse racing) - b.                     27
Brethren - Br.                                   28
Breton - Bret.                                   29
brevet - Bvt.; bvt.                              30
brevetted - bvt.                                 31
brevier - brev.                                  32
brewer - brew.                                   33
brewing - brew.                                  34
brick - bk.; brk.                                35
Brick-Ceramic Glazed - Br./Cer.G.                36
Brick-Common - Br.Com.                           37
bricklayer - brklyr.                             38
Brick, Common-Painted - Br.Com./Pt.              39
bridge - b; br.                                  40
brief - br.; brf.                                41
brig - br.                                       42
Brigade - Brig.                                  43
brigade command - bg.c.                          44
Brigadier - Brig.                                45
brigadier general - Brig. Gen.                   46
bright - brt                                     47
Brigitte Bardot - BB                             48
brine return (pipe) - br.                        49
brine supply (pipe) - b.                         50
brinell hardness - bh                            51
Brinell hardness - B.H.N.                        52
bring your own - byo                             53
bring your own beer - byob                       54
bring your own booze - byob                      55
bring your own girl - byog                       56
```

```
Bristol - Brist                                                  1
British - Br.; Brit.                                             2
British Academy - BA                                             3
British Admiralty - BA                                           4
British Broadcasting Corporation - BBC                           5
British Columbia - B.C.                                          6
British Documents - Brit. Doc.                                   7
British Guiana - Br. Gu.                                         8
British Honduras - BH; B. Hond.; Br. Hond.                       9
British Meteorological Research Flight - MRF                    10
British Museum - B.M.                                           11
British Overseas Airways Corp. - BOAC                           12
British Pharmacopoeia (L, Pharmacopoeia Britannica) - P.B.      13
British standard - Br. std.                                     14
British standard gage - BSG                                     15
British thermal unit - B.T.U.; B.t.u.                           16
British West Indian Airways - BWIA                              17
British West Indies - B.W.I.                                    18
broach - bro                                                    19
broadcast - bcst                                                20
broadcast control - BC                                          21
Broadway - Bway.                                                22
broken - bkn.; brk.                                             23
broker - brok                                                   24
brokerage - brok                                                25
Bromine - Br.                                                   26
bronze - br.; brnz.                                             27
bronzing - brnz.                                                28
Brooklyn - Bklyn                                                29
Brooklyn Bridge - Bklyn Brdg                                    30
Brooklyn Public Library - BPL                                   31
broom closet - BC                                               32
brother - b.; bro.                                              33
Brotherhood - B.                                                34
Brotherhood of Railway and Airline Clerks - BRAC               35
Brothers - Bros.                                                36
Brothers of Charity - C.F.C.                                    37
Brothers of Christian Instruction - F.I.C.                      38
Brothers of Saint Francis Xavier - C.F.X.                       39
Brothers of Saint John of God - O.S.J.D.                        40
Brothers of the Christian Schools - F.S.C.                      41
Brothers of the Sacred Heart - S.C.                             42
brought - brt.                                                  43
brought down - B/d                                              44
brought forward- B/F; b.f.; brt.fwd.                            45
brown - br.; brn.                                               46
Brown & Sharpe gauge - B&S ga                                   47
Brown University - BU                                           48
brownish orange - brO                                           49
brownish pink - brPk                                            50
(Brunauer, Emmett, Teller) catalyst surface area - BET;         51
     B.E.T.                                                     52
Brunei - Bru.                                                   53
Bruno - Bru.                                                    54
Brunswick - Bruns.                                              55
brush holder - brh                                              56
```

```
Brussels - Brux.                                        1
Bucharest - Buchar.                                     2
Bucknell University - BU                                3
buckram - buck.                                         4
Budapest - Bdp; Buda                                    5
Buddha - Bud.                                           6
Buddhism - Bud.; Budd.                                  7
Buddhist - Bud.; Budd.                                  8
budget - bud.                                           9
Buffalo - Bfo                                          10
buffer address register - BAR                          11
buffer control word - BCW                              12
buffer module - BM                                     13
bugler - bglr                                          14
builder - bldr.                                        15
builder's risk - b.r.                                  16
build-in place components - BIPCO                      17
Building - Bldg.                                       18
building - bldg.                                       19
building line - BL                                     20
built - blt.                                           21
built-in - blt-in                                      22
built-in-test - BIT                                    23
bulb angle - BA                                        24
Bulgaria - Bul.                                        25
Bulgarian - Bulg.                                      26
bulk - blk.                                            27
bulkhead - bhd.; blkd.                                 28
bulldozer - bdzr                                       29
bullet tips - blt                                      30
bulletin - bull.                                       31
Bulletin - Bull.                                       32
bulletin board - bb; bull. bd.                         33
bulletins - bulls.                                     34
bulwark - bwk                                          35
bunch - bch.                                           36
bunches - bchs.                                        37
bundle - bd.; bdle.                                    38
bundle(s) - bd(s)                                      39
a bundle (L, fasciculus) - fasc.                       40
Bureau - Bur.                                          41
bureau - bur.; buro                                    42
Bureau of Agricultural Economics - BAE                 43
Bureau of Employees' Compensation - BEC                44
Bureau of Labor Statistics - BLS                       45
Bureau of Standards - BS                               46
bureaucracy - bur.; bur'cy                             47
burgess - bug.                                         48
burglar alarm - ba                                     49
burgomaster - burg                                     50
buried (L, sepultus) - S.                              51
burlap - brlp                                          52
burlesque - burl.                                      53
Burma - Bur.                                           54
burner - bnr                                           55
burning rate - BR; B.R.                                56
```

```
burnish - bnh                                                     1
bursar - Burs                                                     2
burst - brst                                                      3
bushel(s) - bu.; bus.; bush.                                      4
business - bus.                                                   5
business administration - bizad                                  6
Business and Defense Services Administration - BDSA              7
Business Directed Study - BDS                                    8
butcher - butch.                                                  9
butter - but.                                                    10
buttock - btk.                                                   11
button - btn.; but.                                              12
buyer's option - b.o.                                            13
buzzer - buz.; bz.                                               14
by (as 2' x 4') - x                                              15
by authority of the office (L, ex officio) - ex off.            16
by, for (L, per) - p.                                            17
by the hundred (L, per centum) - per cent; per ct.              18
by weight (L, pondere) - p.                                      19
by-pass - bp; byp                                                20
Byzantine - Byz.                                                 21
cab over engine - coe                                            22
cabal - cab                                                      23
cabbage - cab                                                    24
cabin - cab                                                      25
cabinet - cab.; cabt.                                            26
cabinetmaker - cbtmkr.                                           27
cabinetwork - cabwk.                                             28
cable - ca; cab; cbl                                             29
cable letter - LC                                                30
Cable Television - CATV                                          31
cable transfer - C.T.                                            32
cadastral - cad.                                                 33
cadaver - cad.; cdv.                                             34
caddie - cad.                                                    35
cadence - cad.                                                   36
cadenza - cad.                                                   37
cadet - cad.                                                     38
Cadillac - Cad                                                   39
cadmium - cad.                                                   40
Cadmium - Cd                                                     41
cadmium plate - cd pl                                            42
Caelum (the Burin) - Cae                                         43
Caesar - Cs.                                                     44
Caesar Chavez - CC                                               45
Caesium - Cs                                                     46
cafeteria - caf                                                  47
caffeine - caf                                                   48
Cairo - Cai                                                      49
Cains - C.                                                       50
calcimine - C                                                    51
Calcium - Ca                                                     52
calcium - cal.                                                   53
calculate - calc                                                 54
calculation - calc                                               55
calculator - CC                                                  56
```

```
calculus - calc                                            1
Calcutta - Calc                                            2
Caledonia - Caled                                          3
Caledonian - Caled                                         4
calendar - cal.                                            5
calf (bookbinding) - cf.                                   6
caliber - cal.                                             7
calibrate - calbr                                          8
calibrated airspeed - cas                                  9
calibrated altitude - ca                                  10
calibration - cab; calbr                                  11
California - Calif.                                        12
calking - clkg                                            13
call for help - SOS                                       14
call indicator - CI                                       15
call request - CR                                         16
call waiting - CW                                         17
called - cld.                                             18
called line - CLD                                         19
calling line - CLG                                        20
call-in-time - CIT                                        21
calorie, large - Cal.                                     22
calorie, small - cal.                                     23
Calvin - Calv.                                            24
Calvinist - Calv.                                         25
cam plate readout - CPR                                   26
Camas Prairie (RR) - CAP                                  27
Cambodia - Cambod                                         28
Cambodian - Cambod                                        29
Cambria and Indiana (RR) - C&I                            30
Cambridge History of American Literature - CHAL           31
Cambridge History of English Literature - CHEL            32
Cambridge University - C.U.                               33
Camelopardalis (the Giraffe) - Cam                        34
Cameroun - Cam.                                           35
Camp Fire Girls - CFG                                     36
The Campaign Against Pollution - CAP                      37
camouflage - cam.                                         38
can - c.                                                  39
Canada - Can.                                             40
Canadian - Can.                                           41
Canadian Broadcasting Corporation - CBC                   42
Canadian Football League - CFL                            43
Canadian French - Canad. Fr.                              44
Canadian National (RR) - CN                               45
Canadian Pacific (RR) - CP                                46
Canadian Pacific Airlines - CP                            47
Canadian Standard Freeness - CSF; C.S.F.                  48
Canadian Stock Exchange - Can.; CS                        49
canal - can.                                              50
Canal Zone - C.Z.                                         51
Canary Islands - Can. Is.                                 52
cancel - can.; canc.                                      53
cancelled - can.; canc.                                   54
cancellation - can.; canc.                                55
Cancer (the Crab) - Cnc                                   56
```

```
candela - cd                                              1
candelabra - cand.                                        2
candidate - cand                                          3
candle - c                                                4
candle hour(s) - ch                                       5
candle power - c.p.                                       6
candle-hour - c.-h.                                       7
candlepower - cp.                                         8
candlepower seconds - c.p.s.                              9
Canes Venatici (the Hunting Dogs) - CVn                  10
canine - c.                                              11
Canis Major (the Greater Dog) - CMa                      12
Canis Minor (the Lesser Dog) - CMi                       13
canister - can.                                          14
canned - cd.                                             15
cannon - can.                                            16
canoeing (Canadian type) - C                             17
canon - can.                                             18
canopy - can                                             19
Cantabrigiensis (of Cambridge) - Cantab.                 20
cantaloupes - cants                                      21
Canterbury - Cant.                                       22
Canticle of Canticles - Ct                               23
Canticles - Cant.                                        24
canto - can.                                             25
Canton & Carthage (RR) - C&C                             26
Cantonese - Cant.                                        27
canvas - canv                                            28
capacitance - C                                          29
capacitive reactance - $X_C$                             30
capacitor - C; CAP                                       31
capacitor-resistor-diode network - CRD                   32
capacity - c.; cap.; cy.; k.                             33
Cape - C.                                                34
Cape Breton - CB                                         35
Cape Kennedy - C.K.                                      36
Cape Verde Islands - CVI; C.V.Is.                        37
capital - cap.                                           38
capital asset - ca                                       39
capital letter - cap.                                    40
capital letters - caps.                                  41
capitalize - cap.                                        42
capitals - caps.                                         43
Capricornus (the Goat) - Cap                             44
caps and small caps - c. and s.c.                        45
capsule - cap.; caps.                                    46
capsule communicator - cap com                           47
capsule separation - cap sep                             48
capsules - caps.                                         49
Captain - Capt.                                          50
captain - capt.                                          51
captured air bubble - cab                                52
Capuchin Fathers - O.F.M. Cap                            53
caput - cap.                                              54
Caracas - Cas                                            55
carat (metric) - c; car.; k.; kt                         56
```

```
carbohydrate - C                                               1
carbon - C; carb                                               2
carbon copy - CC; cc; cc.; c.c.                                3
carbon dioxide - CO₂                                           4
carbon tetrachloride - carbontet                               5
Carboniferous - Carbonif                                       6
carburetor - carb                                              7
carcinoma - Ca.                                                8
card catalog - card cat.                                       9
card random access memory - CRAM                              10
cardamon - card.                                              11
cardinal - card.                                              12
cardiology - cardiol                                          13
cardiovascular - cardiov                                      14
card-programmed calculator - CPC                              15
cards - cds.                                                  16
cards per minute - CPM                                        17
care of - c/o; c.o.                                           18
Career Development Center - CDC                               19
cargo - cgo                                                   20
caretaker - crtkr.                                            21
Caribbean - Carib.                                            22
Caribbean Atlantic Airlines, Inc. - CBA                       23
Carina (the Keel [of Argo]) - Car                             24
Carleton - Car                                                25
carload - CL; cl.                                             26
car-load lot - C/L                                            27
Carmelite Fathers - O. Carm.                                  28
Carnegie Hall - CH                                            29
Carolina - Caro.                                              30
Carolina & Northwestern (N.C.-S.C.)(RR) - C&NW                31
Caroline - Caro.                                              32
Carpathian - Carp                                             33
carpenter - carp; carp.; cptr.                                34
carpentry - carp.                                             35
carpet - carp.                                                36
carpeting - carp.                                             37
carriage - carr.                                              38
carriage control - CC                                         39
carriage return - CR                                          40
carriage return contact - CRC                                 41
carried down - c/d; C/D                                       42
carried forward - c/f; C/F                                    43
carried over - c.o.; c/o                                      44
carrier - carr.; cxr;                                         45
carrier-to-interference ratio - C/I                           46
carrier-to-noise - C/N                                        47
carrier-to-noise power ratio - CNR                            48
Carson City - CC                                              49
cartage - ctg.; ctge.                                         50
Carte Blanche - CB                                            51
Carthage - Carth                                              52
Carthaginian - Carth                                          53
Carthusian - Carth                                            54
Carthusian Order - O. Cart.                                   55
cartographer - cart.; cartog.                                 56
```

```
cartography - cartog.;  crtog.                              1
carton - C; cart.; ctn.                                     2
cartridge - ctg                                             3
Casablanca - Csb                                            4
case - C; ca; cs.                                           5
case copy - CY                                              6
case harden - ch                                            7
cases - c/s                                                 8
cash - c.                                                   9
cash against disbursements - cad                           10
cash against documents - cad; c.v.d.                       11
cash before delivery - c.b.d.                              12
cashbook - c.b.                                            13
cash credit - c.c.                                         14
cash discount - c.d.                                       15
cash on delivery - COD; cod.; C.O.D.; c.o.d.               16
cash on shipment - C.O.S.; c.o.s.                          17
cash order - C.O.; c/o                                     18
cash with order - c.w.o.                                   19
Cashier - Cash.                                            20
cashier's check - c.c.                                     21
cash-on-hand - coh                                         22
Casimir - Cas                                              23
casing - csg                                               24
cask - ck.; csk.                                           25
casks - cks.                                               26
Cassiopeia - Cas                                           27
cast - c                                                   28
cast box strike - CBX                                      29
cast brass - CB                                            30
cast concrete - c conc                                     31
cast iron - c.i.                                           32
cast iron pipe - CIP                                       33
cast steel - cs                                            34
castatrographic failure rate - CFR                        35
casting - cstg                                             36
castle - cas                                               37
Castling on King's side - 0-0                              38
Castling on Queen's side - 0-0-0                           39
casual - cas.                                              40
Catalan - Cat                                              41
Catalina Airlines - CV                                     42
catalog - cat.                                             43
catalogue - cat.                                           44
Catalonia - Cat.                                           45
Catalonian - Catal.                                        46
catapult - cat.                                            47
catch basin - C.B.                                         48
catcher (baseball) - c.; 2                                 49
catechism - cat.                                           50
category - cat.                                            51
caterpillar tractor - cat.                                 52
cathedral - cath.                                          53
Catherine - Cath                                           54
catheter - cath                                            55
cathode - C; cath.                                         56
```

```
cathode ray - CR; C.R.                                          1
cathode ray tube - CRT; C.R.T.                                  2
cathode-ray tube indication - IP                                3
Catholic - C.; Cath.                                            4
Catholic Interracial Council - CIC                              5
Catholic Library Association - CLA                              6
Catholic Order of Foresters - C.O.F.                            7
Catholic Peace Fellowship - CPF                                 8
Catholic Periodical Index - CPI                                 9
Catholic Relief Services - CRS                                 10
Catholic Truth Society - C.T.S.                                11
Catholic Youth Organization - C.Y.O.                           12
Caucasian - Cau                                                13
caudal - c                                                     14
caught - ct.                                                   15
caught (cricket) - c.                                          16
caught stealing (baseball) - cs                                17
cauliflower - cauli                                            18
caulking - clkg.                                               19
causation - caus.                                              20
causative - caus.                                              21
caution - caut                                                 22
cavalier - cav.                                                23
cavalry - C; cav.                                              24
caveat emptor (let the buyer beware) - c.e.                    25
ceiling - clg.; ceil.                                          26
celebrate - cel.; celeb.                                       27
celebrated - cel.                                              28
celebration - celeb.                                           29
celebrities - celebs                                           30
celebrity - celeb                                              31
celery - cel                                                   32
celestial - C; cel                                             33
celibate - cel                                                 34
cellar - cel                                                   35
cellular - cel                                                 36
Celsius - C.; Cels.                                            37
Celtic - C.; Celt.                                             38
cement - cem.                                                  39
cement asbestos - cem a                                        40
cement asbestos board - cem ab                                 41
cement floor - cem fl                                          42
cement mortar - cem mort                                       43
cement plaster - cem plas                                      44
Cement Plaster - C. Plas.                                      45
Cement Plaster-Painted - C.Plas./Pt.                           46
cement water paint - cem p                                     47
cemetery - cem.                                                48
censor - cens                                                  49
censorship - cens                                              50
Census Bureau - CB                                             51
cent(s) - c.                                                   52
cent - ct.                                                     53
centare - ca.                                                  54
Centaurus (the Centaur) - Cen                                  55
centavo - ctvo.                                                56
```

41

```
centennial - cen; centen                                              1
center - cen.; ctr.                                                   2
center (basketball) - c.                                              3
center (football) - c.                                                4
center (ice hockey) - c.                                              5
center (lacrosse) - c.                                                6
Center - o                                                            7
center back (volleyball) - cb.                                        8
center back (water polo) - cb.                                        9
center field (baseball) - cf.                                        10
center fielder - 8                                                   11
Center for Ecological Action to Save the Environment - CEASE 12
center forward (field hockey) - cf.                                  13
center forward (soccer) - cf.                                        14
center halfback (field hockey) - ch.; CHB                            15
center halfback (soccer) - ch.; CHB                                  16
center line - CL                                                     17
centerline - c.l.                                                    18
center matched - CM                                                  19
center of bouyancy - c.b.                                            20
center of floatation - cf.                                           21
center of gravity - CG; C.G.; c.g.                                   22
center of pressure - c.p.                                            23
center to center - c/c                                               24
centers on - oc                                                      25
centiare - ca.                                                       26
Centigrade - C                                                       27
centigrade - c.; cent.; centig.                                      28
centigrade thermal unit - CTU                                        29
centigram - cg.; cgm.                                                30
centiliter - cl.                                                     31
centime(s) - c.                                                      32
centimeter - c.; cm.                                                 33
centimeter-gram-second - cgs; c.g.s.                                 34
centimeter-gram-second electromagnetic - cgsm                        35
centimeter-gram-second electrostatic - cgse                          36
centimeters - cm.                                                    37
centipose(s) - cp.; cpc.; cps.; cpse.                                38
centistoke - cs.; cst.; ck.                                          39
central - cen.; cent.; cntrl.                                        40
Central Accounting Office - CAO                                      41
central address memory - CAM                                         42
Central African Republic - Cen. Afr. Rep.                            43
Central Airlines - CN                                                44
Central America - Cen. Am.                                           45
Central Business District - CBD                                      46
central computer and sequencer - CC&S                                47
central control - CC                                                 48
central data-conversion equipment - CDCE                             49
central display unit - CDU                                           50
central exchange - CX                                                51
central file - CF                                                    52
central files - cf                                                   53
central filing - cf                                                  54
central index file - CIF                                             55
Central Indiana (RR) - CI                                            56
```

```
central input-output multiplexer - CIO                          1
central integration facility - CIF                              2
Central Intelligence Agency - CIA                               3
central logic unit - CLU                                        4
central nervous system - C.N.S.                                 5
Central News Agency - CNA                                       6
Central of Georgia (RR) - C of G                                7
Central of New Jersey (RR) - CNJ                                8
central processing system - CPS                                 9
central processing unit - CPU                                   10
central programmer and evaluator - CPE                          11
central standard time - CST; c.s.t.                             12
central terminal unit - CTU                                     13
central time - CT; c.t.                                         14
Central Treaty Organization - CENTO                             15
Central Vermont (RR) - CV                                       16
Centralblatt - Centralbl.                                       17
centralized traffic control - CTC; C.T.C.                       18
centrifugal - cent.                                             19
centrifugal force - cf.                                         20
cents - cts.                                                    21
centum (one hundred) - cent.                                    22
centum weight (hundred-weight) - cwt.                           23
centuries - cc; cent.                                           24
century - C; c.; cen.; cent.                                    25
Century Dictionary and Cyclopedia - Cent. Dict. & Cyclo.        26
Cepheus - Cep                                                   27
ceramic - cerm.                                                 28
ceramic mosaic tile - C.M.T.                                    29
Ceramic Veneer - Cer.Ver.                                       30
ceramics - ceram.                                               31
ceramic-wafer printed circuit - CPC                             32
cerebral palsy - CP                                             33
cerebrospinal fluid - C.S.F.                                    34
Cerium - Ce                                                     35
certificate - cert.; certif.; ct.; ctf.                         36
certificate of deposit - C/D; c.d.                              37
certificate of disability for discharge - CDD                   38
certificate of insurance - C/I                                  39
certificate stamped - ct. stp.                                  40
certificated - certif.                                          41
certificates - ctf.; ctfs.                                      42
certificates of deposit - c.o.d.                                43
certification - cert.; ct.; ctf.; certif.                       44
certified - cert.; ct.; ctf.                                    45
certified official government business - COGB                   46
certified public accountant - CPA                               47
certified teacher - C.T.                                        48
certify - cert.                                                 49
cervical - C; cerv                                              50
Cesium - Cs                                                     51
cesspool - cp                                                   52
Cetus (the Sea Monster or Whale) - Cet                          53
Ceylon - Ce; Cey.                                               54
chain - ch.; chn.                                               55
chain of command - chacom                                       56
```

```
chained sequential operation - CSO              1
chains - chs.                                   2
Chairman - Chm.                                 3
chairman - chm.; chmn.                          4
Chaldean - Ch.                                  5
Chaldee - Ch.                                   6
chaldron - chd                                  7
chalkboard - Ch.Bd.                             8
challenge - chal                                9
Chamaeleon- Cha                                10
chamber - chamb                                11
Chamber of Commerce - C.C.; C of C             12
chambers    chrs.                              13
chamfer - cham .                               14
chamfered - chfd.                              15
champion - cham; champ                         16
championship - champ                           17
chancellor - Chanc.                            18
chancery - Chanc.                              19
change - chg; chg.                             20
changed - chgd.                                21
changeover - chovr; CO                         22
changes - chgs.                                23
channel - chan; chnl                           24
channel address register - CAR                 25
channel address word - CAW                     26
channel and traffic control agency - CTCA      27
channel iron frame - cif                       28
channel status - CS                            29
chapel - chap.                                 30
Chaplain - Chap.                               31
chapter - c.; cap.; ch.; chap.                 32
chapters - cc.; chaps.                         33
character - char.                              34
characteristic(s) - char.                      35
characteristic independence - CI               36
characteristic of pressure change - a          37
characters per second - CPS                    38
charcoal - charc                               39
charge - chg.; chrg.                           40
charge account - chg. acct.                    41
charged - chgd.                                42
charges - chgs.                                43
charity - char                                 44
Charles - Chas                                 45
Charlestown - Chasn                            46
Charleston & Western Carolina (RR) - C&WC      47
charter - char.; chtr.                         48
chartered - chtrd.                             49
Chartered Accountant - C.A.                    50
chartered accountant - c.a.                    51
chartered freight - chtrd. frt.                52
Chartered Public Accountant - C.P.A.; c.p.a.   53
chassis - chas                                 54
chattel mortgage - chat mtg                    55
chauffeur - cfr.; chauf.                       56
```

```
check - ch.; CK; ck.                                                      1
check (chess) - Ch.                                                       2
check sorter - CS                                                         3
check valve - cv                                                          4
checked - chec                                                            5
checkered - chec; chkd                                                    6
checking operator - CKO                                                   7
checkout and automatic monitoring - CAM                                   8
checkout data processor - CDP                                             9
checks - chs.; cks.                                                      10
checkup - cu.                                                            11
chemical - Chem.; chem.                                                  12
Chemical Abstracts - Chem Abst                                           13
chemical and biological warfare - CBW                                    14
chemical, biological, radiological - cbr                                 15
Chemical Engineer - Ch.E.; Chem.E.                                       16
chemical oxygen demand - COD; C.O.D.                                     17
chemical stimulation of the brain - csb                                  18
chemical warfare - chem war                                              19
chemically pure - CP; C.P.; c.p.                                         20
Chemie - Chem.                                                           21
chemist - chem.                                                          22
chemistry - chem.                                                        23
cheque - chq                                                             24
Cherbourg - Chb                                                          25
Chesapeake and Ohio (RR) - C&O                                           26
Cheshire - Ches                                                          27
chess club - c.c.                                                        28
chest - ch.                                                              29
Chester - Chs.                                                           30
chestnut (color) - ch.                                                   31
Chevrolet - Chev                                                         32
Cheyenne - Chey                                                          33
Chicago - Cgo.; Chgo.; Chi.                                              34
Chicago & Eastern Illinois (RR) - C&EI                                   35
Chicago & Illinois Midland (RR) - C&IM                                   36
Chicago & NorthWestern (RR) - C&NW                                       37
Chicago & Western Indiana (RR) - C&WI                                    38
Chicago, Burlington & Quincy (RR) - CB&Q                                 39
Chicago Great Western (RR) - CGW                                         40
Chicago, Indianapolis & Louisville (RR) - CI&L                           41
Chicago, Milwaukee, St. Paul and Pacific (RR) - CMSP&P                   42
Chicago, Rock Island & Pacific (RR) - CRI&P                              43
Chicago White Sox - Chisox                                               44
chief - chf.                                                             45
chief accountant - c.a.                                                  46
Chief Justice - C.J.                                                     47
chief master sergeant - Chief M. Sgt.                                    48
Chief of Staff - C. of S.                                                49
Chief Petty Officer - CPO                                                50
chief petty officer - c.p.o.                                             51
chief value - c.v.                                                       52
chief warrant officer - CWO                                              53
child - c; ch.                                                           54
children - ch.                                                           55
Children's Television Workshop - CTW                                     56
```

45

```
Chile - Ch                                                          1
Chilean - Ch                                                        2
Chimie - Chim.                                                      3
chimpanzee - chimp                                                  4
china cabinet - ch cab                                              5
chinchilla - chin.                                                  6
Chinese - Chin.                                                     7
Chinese-Japanese - Sino-Jap.                                        8
chiropractor - chiro                                                9
chirurgiae magister (master of surgery) - C.M.                     10
chloride - chlor                                                   11
chlorine - chlor; Cl                                               12
chloroform - chl; chlor                                            13
chocolate - choc                                                   14
choice - ch                                                        15
choir - ch                                                         16
choke - ch                                                         17
choral - chor                                                      18
choreographer - chor                                               19
choreography - chor                                                20
chorus - chor                                                      21
choruses - chor                                                    22
Chosen - Cho                                                       23
Christ - P; XP; X; Xt.                                             24
Christian - X; Xn; Xtian                                           25
Christian & Missionary Alliance - CMA                              26
Christian Children's Fund - CCF                                    27
Christian Family Movement - CFM                                    28
Christian monogram (derived from the first two letters of          29
    Greek word for Christ) - XP                                    30
Christian Reformed - Christ Ref.                                   31
Christian Science - C.S.                                           32
Christian Science Monitor - CSM                                    33
Christianity - Xnty.; Xty.                                         34
Christmas - Xm.; Xmas                                              35
Christopher - Chris                                                 36
chromium - Cr                                                      37
chromium plate - Cr Pl                                             38
chromosome(s) - chromo(s)                                          39
chronicle - chron                                                  40
1 Chronicles - 1 Chr                                               41
2 Chronicles - 2 Chr                                               42
Chronicles - Chron                                                 43
chronological - chron.                                             44
chronology - chron.                                                45
chrysanthemums - mums                                              46
Chrysler - Chrys                                                   47
church - Ch.; ch.                                                  48
church history - Ch. Hist.                                         49
Church of the Brethren - CBr.                                      50
Church of Christ - CC                                              51
Church of England - C.E.                                           52
Church of God - CG                                                 53
Church of New Jerusalem - CNJ                                      54
Cicero - Cic.                                                      55
cigar - cig.                                                       56
```

```
cigarette - cig.                                              1
Cincinnati - Cin.                                             2
Cincinnati Stock Exchange - CIN; Ci                           3
cinder block - cin bl                                         4
cinema - cine                                                 5
cinnamon - cinna                                              6
cipher - cip                                                  7
circa (about) - c.; ca.; cir.                                 8
Circinus (the Compasses) - Cir                                9
circle - cir                                                 10
circuit - CIR; ckt                                           11
circuit breaker - cb; cir bkr                                12
circuit court - Circ. Ct.                                    13
Circuit Court of Appeals - C.C.A.                            14
circuit interrupter - CI                                     15
circuit judge - Circ. J.                                     16
circuit lineup - CLU                                         17
circuit net loss - CNL                                       18
circular - cir.; circ.                                       19
circular error probability - CEP                             20
circular mil - c.m.                                          21
circular mils - cir. mils                                    22
circular pitch - c.p.                                        23
circulating chilled or hot water flow - CH                   24
circulating chilled or hot water return - CHR                25
circulating water pump - CWP                                 26
circulation - circ.                                          27
circum - c.                                                  28
circumference - cir.; circ.; circum.                         29
circumscribe - circumscr.                                    30
cirrus - c                                                   31
Cistercian - Cist.                                           32
Cistercian Order - O. Cist.                                  33
Cistercians of the Common Observance - S.O. Cist.            34
Cistercians of the Strict Observance (Trapist) - O.C.S.O.    35
citation - cit.                                              36
cited - cit.                                                 37
citizen - cit.                                               38
Citizens Against Narcotics - CAN                             39
citizen's band (radio) - CB                                  40
citron - citr.                                               41
civil - civ.                                                 42
Civil Aeronautics Administration - CAA                       43
Civil Aeronautics Authority - CAA                            44
Civil Aeronautics Board - CAB                                45
Civil Air Patrol - CAP; C.A.P.                               46
Civil Air Transport - CAT                                    47
civil authorities - Civ. Auth.                               48
civil authority - ca                                         49
Civil Defense - CD                                           50
Civil Engineer - C.E.                                        51
Civil Police (Ardnungspolizei) - ORPO                        52
Civil Rights Commission - CRC                                53
Civil Service Commission - CSC; C.S.C.                       54
civilian - civ.                                              55
claim - cl.                                                  56
```

```
claiming race (horse racing) - Cl.                                    1
claims agent - C.A.                                                   2
Clarence - Clar                                                       3
Claretian Missionary Fathers - C.M.F.                                 4
clarification - clar                                                  5
clarinet - clar.                                                      6
class - CL; cl.                                                       7
classic - class.                                                      8
classical - class.                                                    9
classics - class.                                                    10
classification - cl.                                                 11
classified - class.                                                  12
classify - class.                                                    13
classroom - clrm                                                     14
clause - cl.                                                         15
clean and jerk (weight lifting) - C&J                                16
Clean League for Environmental Action Now - C.L.E.A.N.               17
Clean Out - C.O.                                                     18
cleaner - clnr                                                       19
cleanout and deck plate - CO&DP                                      20
cleanout door - COD                                                  21
clear - cl.; clr.                                                    22
clear glass - cl gl                                                  23
Clear Tempered Glass - Cl.Te.Gl.                                     24
clear wire glass - cl w gl                                           25
clearance - CL; cl.                                                  26
cleared - cld.                                                       27
clearing - clr.                                                      28
Clearing House - C.H.                                                29
Clement - Clem.                                                      30
Cleopatra - Cleo                                                     31
clerical - cler.                                                     32
clerk - clk.                                                         33
Clerks of Saint Viator - C.S.V.                                      34
Cleveland - Cleve.                                                   35
Clifford - Cliff                                                     36
climate - clim.                                                      37
climatic - clim.                                                     38
climatological - climatol.                                           39
climatology - climatol.                                              40
climb - cl                                                           41
Clinchfield (RR) - CLIN                                              42
clinic - clin.                                                       43
clinical - clin                                                      44
Clinton - Clint                                                      45
clitoris - clit                                                      46
clock - clk.                                                         47
clock driver - CD                                                    48
clock outlet - C                                                     49
clock phase - CP                                                     50
clock pulse - CP                                                     51
clockwise - ckw.                                                     52
close air support - cas                                              53
closed-circuit television - cctv                                     54
close-open - CO                                                      55
closet - clos.                                                       56
```

```
closure - clo.                                                    1
cloth - clo.                                                      2
clothes line hook - CLH                                           3
clothes pole - CP                                                 4
clothing - clo.                                                   5
Cneius - Cn.                                                      6
coal bin - CB                                                     7
coast - C                                                         8
Coast Artillery - C.A.                                            9
Coast Guard - C.G.                                               10
Coast Guard Women's Reserve - SPAR                               11
coat closet - CC                                                 12
coat hook - CH                                                   13
coated - ctd                                                     14
coaxial - coax                                                   15
coaxial cable - COAX                                             16
Cobalt - Co                                                      17
cocaine - c; coc                                                 18
cochlear (a spoon, a spoonful) - coch.                           19
cochlear amplum (a tablespoonful) - coch. amp.                   20
cochlear magnum (a large spoonful) - coch. mag.                  21
cochlear medium (a dessert spoonful) - coch. med.               22
cochlear parvum (a teaspoonful) - coch. parv.                   23
cockpit - ckpt.                                                  24
code - CDE                                                       25
code directing character - CDC                                   26
Code of Federal Regulations - CFR                                27
Code of Federal  Regulations Supplement - CFR Supp.             28
code practice oscillator - CPO                                   29
codex - cod.                                                     30
coding - COD                                                     31
coeducation - coed.                                              32
coeducational - coed.                                            33
coefficient - coef                                               34
coefficient of impact - e                                        35
coefficient of inductance - L                                    36
cofferdam - coff.                                                37
cognate - cog.; cogn.                                            38
cognate with - c.                                                39
coherence - coh                                                  40
coherent digital phased array system - CODIPHASE                 41
coherent oscillator - coho                                       42
coinsurance clause - coins. cl.                                  43
cold - C                                                         44
cold crawn - cd                                                  45
cold rolled steel - CRS                                          46
cold water - CW                                                  47
cold-drawn steel - cds                                           48
cold-rolled steel - crs; cs                                      49
collaboration - collab.                                          50
collaborator - collab.                                           51
collateral - coll.; collat.                                      52
collateral trust - clt.; coll.tr.                                53
collaterally - collat.                                           54
colleague - coll.                                                55
collect - coll.                                                  56
```

49

```
Collect (Bell Telephone) - C                                         1
collect on delivery - C.O.D.; c.o.d.                                 2
collected - col.; coll.                                              3
collection - coll.                                                   4
collection agency - coll agc                                         5
collection and delivery - C&D; c&d                                   6
collection letter - coll/L                                           7
collections - coll.                                                  8
collective - coll.; collect.                                         9
collectively - collect.                                             10
collector - col.; coll.; collr.                                     11
College - C.                                                        12
college - coll.                                                     13
College English - Col.Eng.                                          14
collegiate - coll.                                                  15
collision clause - coll. cl.                                        16
colloquial - coll.; colloq.                                         17
colloquialism - colloq.                                             18
colloquially - colloq.                                              19
cologarithm - colog                                                 20
Cologne - Coln.                                                     21
Colombia - Col.                                                     22
colon - cln; co.                                                    23
Colonel - Col.                                                      24
colonial - col.                                                     25
colony - col.                                                       26
color - clr.                                                        27
color code - cc                                                     28
Color Index - C.I.                                                  29
colorless - colorl.                                                 30
Colorado - Colo.                                                    31
Colorado (RR) - COLO                                                32
Colorado & Southern (RR) - C&S                                      33
Colorado & Wyoming (RR) - C&W                                       34
colored - c; col.                                                   35
Colored People's Television - CPT                                   36
Colossians - Col.                                                   37
colour index - C.I.                                                 38
colt (horse racing) - c.                                            39
Columbia - Col.                                                     40
Columbia (the Dove) - Col                                           41
Columbia Broadcasting System - CBS                                  42
Columbia, Newberry & Laurens (RR) - CN&L                            43
Columbia University - CU                                            44
Columbia Valley Authority - CVA                                     45
Columbium - Cb                                                      46
Columbus and Greenville (RR) - C&G                                  47
column - clm.                                                       48
column(s) - col.                                                    49
Coma Berenices (Berenice's Hair) - Com                              50
combat - cmbt                                                       51
combat zone - CZ                                                    52
combination - comb.                                                 53
combination claiming and allowance race (horse racing) -            54
    Comb.                                                           55
combination of hydrogen and fluorine - HF                           56
```

```
combined receiving and transmitting unit - CRTU              1
combining - comb.                                            2
combining form - comb. form                                  3
combustion - comb.                                           4
comedy - com.                                                5
comic - com.                                                 6
comma - com.                                                 7
comma splice - cs                                            8
command - comd.                                              9
command and control - C&C                                   10
Command Data Acquisition - CDA                              11
Command Module - CM                                         12
command post - CP                                           13
command post digital display - CPDD                        14
command register - CR                                       15
Command Service Module - CSM                                16
commandant - Comdt.; comdt.                                 17
commander - cdr.; Comdr.; comdr.                            18
Commander in Chief - C.I.C.; CINC; Com. in Chf.             19
Commander in Chief, U.S. - CINCUS                           20
Commander of the Order of the British Empire - C.B.E.       21
commanding - cmdg.; comdg.                                  22
Commanding General - CG.                                    23
commanding officer - CO                                     24
commence - cmnce                                            25
commencement - commt.                                       26
comment - cmt.; comm.                                       27
commentary - comm.                                          28
commentator - comt.                                         29
commerce - com.                                             30
commercial - cml.; coml.                                    31
commercial agent - c.a.                                     32
commercial bill of lading - cb/l                            33
commercial paper - com'l. ppr.                              34
commercial projected window - CPW                           35
Commercial Standard - CS                                    36
commercial traveler - c.t.                                  37
commercial weight - c.w.                                    38
commissary - comsry.; comsy.                                39
commission - com.                                           40
Commission on Civil Rights - CCR                            41
commissioned - comd.                                        42
committee - com.                                            43
Committee - Comm.                                           44
Committee for Environmental Preservation - CEP              45
Committee for Homosexual Freedom - CHF                      46
Committee for Military Action (WWII, Comité d'Action        47
   Militaire) - COMAC                                       48
Committee for the Liberation of Paris (WWII, Comité         49
   Parisien de Libération) - CPL                            50
Committee on Political Education - COPE                      51
Committee to Leave the Environment of American Natural -    52
   CLEAN                                                    53
Commodities Credit Corporation - CCC                        54
commodity - commod.                                         55
Commodity Credit Corporation - CCC                          56
```

```
Commodity Stabilization Service - CSS                              1
commodore - Com.                                                   2
common - com.                                                      3
Common Business Oriented Language - COBOL                          4
common carrier - com. carr.                                        5
Common Era - C.E.                                                  6
common law - C.L.; c.l.                                            7
common mode rejection - CMR                                        8
common pleas - c.p.                                                9
Common Prayer - C.P.                                              10
common version - CV                                               11
Common Version (of the Bible) - Com. Ver.                         12
common water (L, aqua communis) - aq. com.                        13
common-law marriage - c-lm                                        14
commonly - com.                                                   15
commonwealth (L, respublica) - Com.; Comm.; (R.)                  16
commune - com.                                                    17
Commune - Comm.                                                   18
communicable disease - CD                                         19
communicate - CMCT; com.                                          20
communication - com.; comm.                                       21
communication data processor - CDP                                22
communication line adapters - CLA                                 23
communication line adapters for teletype - CLAT                   24
communication line terminal - CLT                                 25
communication multiplexer - CM                                    26
communication section - Com Sec                                   27
communications - C/M; com.; comm.                                 28
communications center - COMMCEN                                   29
communications controller - CTMC                                  30
communications failure detecting and switching equipment -        31
   COMMSWITCH                                                     32
communications mode control - CMC                                 33
communications moon relay - CMR                                   34
communications multiplexer - C/M                                  35
communications pool - COMPOOL                                     36
Communications Research Machines, Inc. - CRM (Inc.)               37
communications satellite - COMSAT                                 38
Communications Satellite Corporation - COMSAT                     39
Communications Zone - Com Z; COMMZ                                40
communications-terminal modules - CTM                             41
Communist Party - CP                                              42
Communist Party of India, Marxist-Leninist - CPIML               43
Community - Com.                                                  44
Community Action Agency - CAA                                     45
Community Action Program - CAP                                    46
Community College - CC                                            47
community development - CD                                        48
Community Learning Center - CLC                                   49
Community Service Society - C.S.S.                                50
commutation - comtn.                                              51
companies - cos.                                                  52
companion - comp.; compn.                                         53
Companion of the Bath - C.B.                                      54
company - Co.                                                     55
Company (F, Compagnie) - Cie.; cie.                               56
```

```
computer pneumatic input panel - CPIP                    1
computer process control - CPC                           2
computer-aided instruction - CAI                         3
computer-directed communications - CODIC                 4
computerized on-line testing - COLT                      5
computer-operated electronics display - COED             6
computer-sensitive language - CSL                        7
computing - C                                            8
concave - cv.                                            9
concentrate - conc.                                     10
concentrated - concd.                                   11
concentration - C; concn.                               12
Concentration Camp (Konzentrations-Lager) - K.Z.        13
concerto - cto.                                         14
Concise Oxford Dictionary - COD                         15
conclusion - con.; concl.; conclu.                      16
concrete - con.; conc.                                  17
Concrete - Con.                                         18
concrete block - conc b                                 19
concrete ceiling - conc c                               20
concrete floor - conc f                                 21
Concrete-Painted - Con./Pt.                             22
concurrent - cncr.                                      23
concurrent concession - CC                              24
condemned - CD                                          25
condemno (I condemn) - C.                               26
condensate - cnds.                                      27
condensation trail - contrail                           28
condense - cond.                                        29
condensed - cond.                                       30
condenser - cond.                                       31
condenser water flow - C                                32
condenser water return - CR                             33
condition - CND                                         34
conduct - cdt.; cond.                                   35
conductance - G, g                                      36
conductance, thermal - C                                37
conductivity - cond.                                    38
conductivity, thermal - k                               39
conductor - c; cond.; condr.                            40
conduit - cnd.; cond.                                   41
cone tips - CT                                          42
confabulation - confab                                  43
confection - conf.                                      44
Confederate - Confed.                                   45
Confederate Army - CA                                   46
Confederate States of America - C.S.A.                  47
Confederation - Confed.                                 48
confer - cf.; conf.                                     49
conference - conf.                                       50
Conference (Bell Telephone) - F                         51
conferred - confd.                                      52
confessor - conf.                                        53
confidential document - CD                              54
confine - cnf.                                          55
confined - conf.                                        56
```

confined to barracks - CB; c.b. 1
confinement - conf. 2
confirmed - cfm 3
conform - con. 4
conformist - con. 5
Confraternity of Christian Doctrine - CCD 6
Congo; Capital: Brazzaville - Con. B. 7
Congo; Capital: Léopoldville - Con. L. 8
congregation - cong. 9
Congregation of Jesus and Mary (Eudists) - C.J.M. 10
Congregation of the Blessed Sacrament - S.S.S. 11
Congregation of the Holy Cross - C.S.C. 12
Congregation of the Mission (Vincentians) - C.M. 13
Congregation of the Resurrection - C.R. 14
Congregational - Cong.; Congl. 15
Congress - C.; Cong. 16
Congress of Industrial Organizations - C.I.O. 17
Congress of Racial Equality - CORE 18
Congressional - Cong. 19
Congressional Record - Cong. Rec. 20
conic section - con. sect. 21
conics - con. 22
conjectural - cj. 23
conjugation - conj. 24
conjunction - conj. 25
conjunctive - conj. 26
conjunx (wife) - con. 27
connect - CNCT; conn. 28
connected - conn. 29
connected with - conn.w. 30
Connecticut - Conn.; Ct. 31
connecting circuit - CC 32
connecting rod - con rod 33
connection - conn. 34
conquest - conq. 35
Conrad - Conr. 36
conscientious objector - C.O. 37
consecrated - cons. 38
consecutive - consec. 39
consecutive days - consec. ds. 40
conservation - conserv. 41
Conservative - C. 42
conservative - conserv. 43
conserve - cons. 44
consigned - cons. 45
consignment - cons. 46
consol - con. 47
consolidated - con.; cons.; consol. 48
consolidated annuities - consols. 49
consonant - cons. 50
conspicuous - conspic 51
constable - const. 52
constant - CONST 53
constant boiling mixture - CBM; C.B.M. 54
constant pressure - CP; C.P. 55
constant speed - cons. sp. 56

constant-speed drives - CSD	1
constant-voltage unit - CVU	2
constitution - const.	3
construction - const.; constr.	4
construction company - Cons Co	5
construction section - Cons Sec	6
constructive total loss - c.t.l.	7
constructive total loss only - c.t.l.o.	8
construe - constr.	9
construed - constr.	10
Consul - Con.	11
consul(s) - cons.	12
consult - cons.	13
consultant - cons.	14
consulting - cons.	15
Consumer and Marketing Services - CMS	16
Consumer Price Index - CPI	17
Consumers Research Advisory Council - CRAC	18
contact - cont; CTC	19
contact analog flight display - CAFD	20
containing - cont.; contg.	21
contamination - contam.	22
contemporaries - contemp.	23
contemporary - contemp.	24
contents - cont.	25
continent - cont.	26
continental - cont.; contl.	27
Continental Airlines - CO	28
Contingency Sample Container - CSC	29
continuation - cont.	30
continuation clause - c.c.	31
continue - cont.	32
continued - cont.; contd.	33
continuous - cont.	34
continuous commercial service - CCS	35
continuous wave - cw.	36
continuous wave frequency modulation - CW-FM; C.W.-F.M.	37
continuous waves - cw	38
continuously variable - CV	39
continuous-reading meter relay - CRMR	40
continuous-wave oscillator - CWO	41
continuous-wave video - CWV	42
contra (against) - con.	43
contract - cont.; contr.	44
contracted - contr.	45
contraction - contr.	46
contractor - contr.; cont'r.	47
contradict - contr.	48
contradiction - contra.	49
contrary - contr.	50
contribute - contrib.	51
contributing - contrib.	52
contribution - contrib.	53
Contributions - Contr.	54
contributor - contrib.	55
contributory value - contrib. val.	56

A Contrived Reduction of Nomenclature Yielding Menmonics -   1
   ACRONYM   2
Control - C   3
control - CONT; contr.   4
control and reporting center - CRC   5
control data terminal - CDT   6
control joint - C.J.   7
control mark - CM   8
control of electromagnetic radiation - conelrad   9
control panel - CP   10
control point - CP   11
control precision - CPO   12
control relay - CR   13
control relay forward - CRF   14
control set - CS   15
control signal - CS   16
control systems engineering - CSE   17
control translator - CONTRAN   18
control unit - CU   19
controlled roof sump - C.R.S.   20
controlled switch - CS   21
controller - contr.   22
controller of accounts - c.a.   23
Convair - C   24
convalescent - conv.   25
convector - conv.   26
convector enclosure - Conv Encl   27
convene - cvn   28
convenience - conv.   29
convention - conv.   30
conversation - conv.   31
conversation factor - CF   32
conversion loss - CL   33
convert - cvt.   34
convert gray to binary - CGB   35
Convert Makers of America - C.M.O.A.   36
converter - CV   37
convertible - conv.; cv.; cvt.   38
convertible debentures - cv. db.   39
convertible preferred - cv. pf.   40
convex - cx.   41
conveyorized automatic tube tester - CATT   42
convict - cnvt.   43
cook - ck.   44
cooler - clr   45
cooperative - coop.   46
Cooperative for American Remittances to Everywhere - CARE   47
Cooperative Fuel Research - CFR; C.F.R.   48
cooperatives - coops.   49
coordinate geometry program - COGO   50
Copenhagen - Cpn   51
Copernican - Cop.   52
copies - cop.   53
Copper - Cu   54
copper covered - Cop Cov   55
Copper Range (RR) - CR   56

```
Coptic - Cop                                                          1
copy - cop.; CPY                                                      2
copyright - c.; copr.                                                 3
copyrighted - copr.                                                   4
cord - cd.                                                            5
cord feet - cd. ft.                                                   6
cord foot - cd. ft.                                                   7
cord-foot - cd.-ft.                                                   8
Cordova Airlines, Inc. - COA                                          9
cords - cd.                                                          10
1 Corinthians - 1 Cor                                                11
2 Corinthians - 2 Cor                                                12
cork - ck                                                            13
cork tile - CT                                                       14
corkboard - Cor.Bd.                                                  15
corn, soya, milk - CSM                                               16
Cornell University - CU                                              17
corner - cor.                                                        18
corner guards - CG                                                   19
Cornish - Corn.                                                      20
corollary - corol.                                                   21
Corona Austrinae (the Southern Crown) - CrA                          22
Corona Borealis (the Northern Crown) - CrB                           23
coronary - coron                                                     24
Coroner - Cor.                                                       25
Corporal - Corp.; Corpl.; Cpl.; cpl.                                 26
Corporation - Corp.; corp.                                           27
corps - c.                                                           28
correct - cor.; OK                                                   29
correctable gate - CORREGATE                                         30
corrected - cor.; corr.                                              31
correction - cor.; corr.                                             32
correlation coefficient - r                                          33
correlative - correl.                                                34
correspond - corr.                                                   35
correspondence - corresp.                                            36
correspondent - corspdt.                                             37
corresponding - cor.; corr.; corresp.                                38
corresponding secretary - Cor. Sec.                                  39
corridor - corr.                                                     40
corrosion - corr.                                                    41
corrugate - corr.                                                    42
corrugated - corr.                                                   43
Corrugated Metal Closure-Painted - Cor.Met.Cl./Pt.                   44
corrupt - cor.                                                       45
Corvus (the Crow) - Crv                                              46
cosecant - csc                                                       47
cosine - cos                                                         48
cosmetic(s) - cosm                                                   49
cosmic - cos                                                         50
cosmography - cosmog.                                                51
cosmopolitan - cosmo                                                 52
Cossack - Cos.                                                       53
cost - c.                                                            54
cost and freight - c.a.f.; c.&f.; cf                                 55
cost, freight, and insurance - c.f.&i.                               56
```

```
cost, insurance and freight - c.i.f.                                    1
cost, insurance, freight - c.i.f.                                       2
cost laid down - c.l.d.                                                 3
cost plus fixed fee - CPFF                                              4
cost plus incentive fee - CPIF                                          5
Costa Rica - C.R.                                                       6
cost-of-living allowance - COLA                                         7
cotangent - cot                                                         8
could - cd.                                                             9
council - C                                                            10
Council of Economic Advisers - CEA                                     11
Council on Religion and the Homosexual - CRH                           12
count (numeric) - CT                                                    13
count - ct.                                                            14
count (nobleman) - Cte                                                 15
count forward - CF                                                     16
count reverse - CR                                                     17
countdown - cd                                                         18
counter - CNT; CT; ctr                                                 19
counter electromotive force - counter e.m.f.                           20
counter flashing - cflg                                                21
counter, n stages - CT(N)                                              22
counterattack - catk                                                   23
counterbore - cbr.                                                     24
counterclockwise - cckw.                                               25
counterfire - cf                                                       26
Counterintelligence Corps - CIC                                        27
counterpoint - cpt.                                                    28
countersignature - ctrsig.                                             29
countersigned - ctrsgd.                                                30
countersink - csk.                                                     31
countersunk - ctsk.                                                    32
countersunk screw - CS                                                 33
countersunk wood screw - cws                                           34
Countess - Ctesse                                                      35
counties - cos.                                                        36
countries - cos.                                                       37
counts per million - c.p.m.                                            38
counts per minute - NPM                                                39
counts per minute per gram - c./m./g.                                  40
counts per second - NPS                                                41
county - cnty.                                                         42
County - Co.; co.                                                      43
county commissioner - C.C.                                             44
coupon - c.; cp.                                                       45
coupons - cps.                                                         46
course - C; cs.                                                        47
court - Ct.                                                            48
court of appeals - C.A.; Ct.App.                                       49
Court of Claims - C.Cls.; Ct.Cls.                                      50
Court of Claims Reports - C.Cls.R.                                     51
Court of Common Pleas - Ct.Com.Pleas                                   52
Court of Customs and Patent Appeals - C.C.P.A.                         53
court order - ct. ord.                                                 54
Courthouse - C.H.                                                      55
cover - cov                                                            56
```

```
cover plate - cov pl                                      1
cover point (lacrosse) - CP                               2
covered - cov                                             3
coxswain - coxen.                                         4
craft - cft                                               5
craftsman - cftmn                                         6
Cranch (U.S. Supreme Court Reports) - Cr.                 7
crane - crn                                               8
cranial - c                                               9
craniology - craniol.                                    10
craniometry - craniom.                                   11
cranium - cran.                                          12
crankcase - crkc                                         13
crankshaft - cshaft                                      14
crate - crt.                                             15
Crater (the Cup) - Crt                                   16
crates - crts.                                           17
crazy - czy                                              18
C-reactive protein - CRP                                 19
created - cr.                                            20
credit - cr.                                             21
Credit Card Call (Bell Telephone) - H                    22
credit card purchase - ccp                               23
credit note - C/N; c/n                                   24
credit union - CU                                        25
credited account - C/A                                   26
creditor - cr.                                           27
creditors - crs.                                         28
credits - crs.                                           29
creek - cr.                                              30
cremation - crem                                         31
crescendo - cres.; cresc.                                32
crescent - cres.                                         33
crew chief - CRCHF                                       34
crewman - crmn                                           35
criminal - crim.                                         36
Criminal Investigation Department - C.I.D.               37
Criminal Police (Kriminal polizei) - KRIPO              38
criminology - criminol.                                  39
crimps per inch (fibers) - c.p.i.                        40
cripple - crip                                           41
criterion - crit.                                        42
critic - crit.                                           43
critical - crit.                                         44
critical path method - CPM                               45
critical ratio - CR                                      46
criticism - crit.                                        47
criticized - crit.                                       48
Croatia - Croat.                                         49
Croatian - Croat.                                        50
crocodile(s) - croc(s)                                   51
cross connection - x conn                                52
cross correlation - CC                                   53
cross out - X out                                        54
cross reference - cr. ref.; X-ref.                       55
cross section - X-sect                                   56
```

60

crosscut - Xcut   1
crossing - cross.   2
cross-question - XQ   3
crossroads - Xrds   4
crown octavo - cr. 8vo   5
cruiser - cruis   6
Crusader - Xdr.   7
Crux (the Cross) - Cru   8
crypto-communication network - CRYPTONET   9
cryptograph - CRYPTO   10
cryptographic - CRYPTO   11
crystal(s) - crys.   12
crystalline - cryst.   13
crystallized - cryst.   14
cube - c   15
cubic - c.; cu.   16
cubic centimeter - cc.; cm.^{3}; cu. cm.   17
cubic centimeter (milliliter) - c.c.   18
cubic decimeter - cu. dm.; dm.^{3} 19
cubic dekameter - cu. dkm.; dkm.^{3} 20
cubic feet of gas per day - cfgd   21
cubic feet of gas per hour - cfgh   22
cubic feet of gas per minute - cfgm   23
cubic feet per minute - CFM; c.f.m.   24
cubic feet per second - CFS; c.f.s.   25
cubic foot - cu. ft.; ft.^{3} 26
cubic hectometer - cu. hm.; hm.^{3} 27
cubic inch - cu. in.; in.^{3} 28
cubic kilometer - cu. km.; km.^{3} 29
cubic meter - cu.m.; m.^{3} 30
cubic micron - cu. mu.; mu^3 31
cubic mile - cu. mi.; mi.^{3} 32
cubic millimeter - cu. mm.; mm.^{3} 33
cubic yard - cu. yd.; yd.^{3} 34
cubical - c   35
culture and personality - C&P   36
culvert - culv   37
Cumberland & Pennsylvania (RR) - C&P   38
cumulated - cum.   39
cumulative - cm.; cum.   40
Cumulative Book Index - CBI   41
cumulative preferred - cm.pf.; cu.pf.; cum.pref.   42
cumulo-nimbus - cu.-nb.   43
cumulus - cu.   44
cuneiform - cun   45
cup - c.   46
cupboard - cup.   47
cuprum - Cu   48
curie - c.   49
Curie's constant - C   50
currency - cur.; curr.; cy.   51
currency bond - c.b.   52
current - cur.; curr.; I   53
current account - c/a; c.c.   54
current assets - ca   55
current mode logic - CML   56

```
current operator - next operator - CO/NO                          1
current rate - c.r.                                               2
current series - c.s.                                             3
current times resistance - IR                                     4
current transformer - CT                                          5
curtain(s) - curt.                                                6
curtain rod - CR                                                  7
cuspid - c.                                                       8
custard - cust                                                    9
custodian - cust.; custod.                                       10
custody - cust                                                   11
custom(s) - cust                                                 12
Custom House - C.H.                                              13
Customer Dialed Person (Bell Telephone ) - L                    14
Customer Dialed Station (Bell Telephone) - D                    15
customer engineer - CE                                          16
custos privati sigilli (keeper of the privy seal) - C.P.S.      17
custos sigilli (keeper of the seal) - C.S.                      18
cut in - CI                                                     19
cut out - CO                                                    20
cutlery - cut.                                                  21
cutoff - co                                                     22
cyanide - cyan; cyn                                             23
cybernetic(s) - cyb                                             24
cybernetic organism - CYBORG                                    25
cycle - c.; cy.; cyc.                                           26
cycles - cy.                                                    27
cycles per minute - c.p.m.                                      28
cycles per second - c./s.; c.p.s.                               29
cycles per second (German) - Hz.                                30
cycles shift - CS                                               31
cycling - cyc.                                                  32
cyclone - cyc.                                                  33
cyclopedia - cyclo.                                             34
cyclopedic - cyclo.                                             35
cyclotron - cyclo.                                              36
Cygnus (the Swan) - Cyg                                         37
cylinder - cyl                                                  38
cylinder lock - cyl l                                           39
cylindrical - cyl                                               40
cymbal(s) - cym                                                 41
Cymric - Cym.                                                   42
Cyprus - Cyp                                                    43
Cyrus - Cy                                                      44
cystic fibrosis - cf                                            45
cytology - cyt.                                                 46
Czechoslovakia - Czech.; Czechosl.                              47
da (give) - d.                                                  48
da capo (music) - D.C.                                          49
dachshund - dachs                                               50
dacron - dacr                                                   51
Dahomey - Dah.                                                  52
daily and weekly till forbidden - d.&w.t.f.                     53
daily transaction reporting - DTR                               54
Dakota - Dak                                                    55
dal segno (music) - D.S.                                        56
```

Dallas - Dall.	1
Dalmatia - Dal	2
Dalmatian - Dal	3
dam - d.	4
damage - dam.; damg.; dmg	5
damaged - dmg.	6
damp proofing - dp	7
damper - dmpr	8
dampproofing - dampg.; DP	9
Daniel - Dan; Dn.	10
Danish - Da; Dan.	11
dark - dk.	12
Dartmouth College - DC	13
data acquisition and control system - DAC	14
data acquisition system - DAS	15
data analysis recording tape - DART	16
data available - DA	17
data channel - DC	18
data collection - DC	19
data communications - DATACOM	20
data conversion receiver - DCR	21
data distribution center - DDC	22
data exchange control - DXC	23
data exchange unit - DEU	24
data input clerk - DIC	25
data link - DL	26
data multiplex subsystem - DMSS	27
data optimizing computer - DOC	28
data processing - DP	29
data processing division - DPD	30
data processing center - DPC	31
data processing equipment - DPE	32
data processing group - DPG	33
data processing subsystem - DPSS	34
data processing system - DPS	35
data quality monitors - DQM	36
data recorder - DR	37
data recovery vehicle - DRV	38
data reduction interpreter - DRI	39
data status word - DSW	40
data storage equipment - DSE	41
data synchronization unit - DSU	42
data time group - DTG	43
data transmission - DT	44
data word buffer - DW	45
datacommunications control unit - DCCU	46
data-handling equipment - DHE	47
data-transmission system - DTS	48
date - d.	49
date of availability - doa	50
date of birth - D/B; d/b; DOB; dob	51
date of death - dod	52
date of enlistment - doe	53
date of marriage - dom	54
date of separation - DOS; dos	55
dated - dtd	56

```
dative - dat.                                                      1
datum - dat.                                                       2
daughter - d.; dau.                                                3
Daughters of Bilitis - DOB                                         4
Daughters of the American Revolution - D.A.R.                      5
Daughters of the Revolution - D.R.                                 6
David - Dav.; Dave                                                 7
day - d.; da.                                                      8
day book - db; d.b.                                                9
day letter - DL; dl                                               10
day of Allied Victory in Europe in WWII (May 8, 1945) -           11
   V-E Day                                                         12
day of Allied Victory over Japan in WWII (Sept. 2, 1945) -        13
   V-J Day                                                         14
day of final Allied Victory in WWII (Dec. 31, 1946) - V-Day       15
daylight saving - d.s.                                            16
daylight saving time - DST; D.S.T.                                17
days - ds.                                                        18
days after acceptance - da                                        19
days after date - d.d.                                            20
days after sight - d.s.                                           21
day's date - d.d.                                                 22
days off - do.                                                    23
Dayton - Day                                                      24
Deacon - Dea.                                                     25
dead and buried - d&b                                             26
dead freight - d.f.                                               27
Dead Letter Office - DLO                                          28
Dead On Arrival - D.O.A.                                          29
dead reckoning - d.r.                                             30
dead reckoning analog indicator - DRAI                            31
dead weight - d.w.                                                32
dead weight capacity - d.w.c.                                     33
dead weight tonnage - d.w.t.                                      34
deadhead - d.h.                                                   35
deadweight tons - d.w.t.                                          36
dealer - dlr.                                                     37
debark - dbk                                                      38
debenture(s) - deb(s)                                             39
debenture rights - db. rts.                                       40
debit - dr.                                                       41
debit note - D/N; d/n; dn                                         42
Deborah - Deb.                                                    43
debtor - Dr.; dr.                                                 44
debutante(s) - deb(s)                                             45
decade counting unit - DCU                                        46
deceased - dec.; decd.                                            47
December - D.; Dec.; 10ber                                        48
decessit sine prole (died without issue) - d.s.p.                49
decibel(s) - db.                                                 50
decibel unit - dbu                                                51
deciduous - decid                                                 52
decigram(s) - dg.                                                 53
deciliter - dl.                                                   54
decimal - DEC; dec                                                55
decimal add - DA                                                  56
```

```
decimal classification - DC                                         1
decimal counting unit - DCU                                         2
decimal divide - DD                                                 3
decimal multiply - DM                                               4
decimal subtract - DS                                               5
decimeter - dec.; dm.                                               6
decimillimeters - dmm.                                              7
Decimus - D.                                                        8
decision(s) - d.                                                    9
decision - dec.                                                    10
decision tables - DETAB                                            11
decision tables, experimental - DETAB-X                            12
decistere - ds.                                                    13
deck - dk.                                                         14
deck house - dk hse                                                15
declaration - dec.                                                 16
declension - dec.; decl.                                           17
declination - d                                                    18
decomposition - decomp                                             19
decoder - dcdr                                                     20
decoding memory drive - DE-ME-DRIVE                                21
decontamination - Decon                                            22
decontamination factor - DF; D.F.                                  23
decorate - dec.                                                    24
decorated - dec.                                                   25
decoration - dec.                                                  26
decrease - dcr.; dec.                                              27
decreased - decd.                                                  28
decreasing - dcr.                                                  29
decree(s) - d.                                                     30
decrement - DECR                                                   31
decrescendo - dec.                                                 32
decretum (a decree) - d.                                           33
dedicated - Ded.; ded.                                             34
dedication - dedic.                                                35
deduct - ddt                                                       36
deep - D.                                                          37
deep-drawn - dd                                                    38
defeated - d.                                                      39
defecate - def                                                     40
defecation - def                                                   41
defect - def                                                       42
defection - def                                                    43
defective - def; defec                                             44
defector - def                                                     45
defendant - def.; dft.                                             46
the defendant being absent (L, absente reo) - abs. re.             47
Defender of the Faith - D.F.                                       48
defense - def.                                                     49
Defense Air Transportation Administration - DATA                   50
Defense Intelligence Agency - DIA                                  51
Defense Mobilization Board - DMB                                   52
defense order - DO                                                 53
defensive - def                                                    54
defer - def                                                        55
deferred - def                                                     56
```

65

deferred cable (telegram) - LC   1
deferred delivery - dd   2
deferred payment account - d.p.a.   3
deficiency - def; defi   4
deficiency report - DR   5
deficient - def   6
deficit (stock) - d   7
define - def.   8
Define Area - DA   9
Define Constant - DC   10
define constant with wordmark - DCW   11
define symbol - DS   12
defined - def.   13
definite - def.   14
definite article - def. art.   15
definition - def.   16
definitions - defs.   17
deflate - defl   18
deflect - def   19
defoliate - def   20
defrost - def   21
defunct - def   22
degenerate - deg   23
degree - d.   24
degree(s) - deg.   25
degree(s) Centigrade - C   26
degree(s) Fahrenheit - F   27
degree of freedom - DOF   28
degrees after top center - ATC; A.T.C.   29
degrees before top dead center - DBTDC; D.B.T.D.C.   30
degrees before top dead center (spark advance) - BTDC;   31
  B.T.D.C.   32
degrees Fahrenheit total temperature - FTT   33
degrees of freedom - DF   34
dekagram - dkg.   35
dekaliter - dkl.   36
dekameter - dkm.   37
dekastere - dks.   38
Delaware - Del.   39
Delaware and Hudson (RR) - D&H   40
Delaware, Lackawanna & Western (RR) - DL&W   41
delay - DEL; DL; dly   42
delay line - DL   43
Delayed Action (bomb) - D.A.   44
delayed action - da   45
delayed delivery - d.d.   46
delegate - del.   47
delegation - deleg.   48
delete - d.; del.   49
deleted - D   50
deliberate - del   51
deliberation - delib   52
delicatessen(s) - deli(s)   53
delineate - del   54
delinquency - DEL; DEL'cy   55
delinquent - delinq   56

```
delinquent account - del. acct.                           1
delirium tremens - d.t.; dt's                             2
deliver - del.                                            3
delivered - dd.; d'd.                                     4
delivery - dely.                                          5
delivery order - d/o                                      6
Delphinus (the Dolphin) - Del                             7
Delta Air Lines - DL                                      8
demand - dem                                              9
demand and supply - d&s                                  10
demand draft - d.d.                                      11
demand loan - dl                                         12
Demilitarized Zone - DMZ                                 13
Democrat - D.; Dem.                                      14
Democrat from Alabama - D.-Ala.                          15
Democrat from Alaska - D.-Alaska                         16
Democrat from Arizona - D.-Ariz.                         17
Democrat from Arkansas - D.-Ark.                         18
Democrat from California - D.-Calif.                     19
Democrat from Colorado - D.-Colo.                        20
Democrat from Connecticut - D.-Conn.                     21
Democrat from Delaware - D.-Del.                         22
Democrat from Florida - D.-Fla.                          23
Democrat from Georgia - D.-Ga.                           24
Democrat from Hawaii - D.-Hawaii                         25
Democrat from Idaho - D.-Idaho                           26
Democrat from Illinois - D.-Ill.                         27
Democrat from Indiana - D.-Ind.                          28
Democrat from Iowa - D.-Iowa                             29
Democrat from Kansas - D.-Kans.                          30
Democrat from Kentucky - D.-Ky.                          31
Democrat from Louisiana - D.-La.                         32
Democrat from Maine - D.-Maine                           33
Democrat from Massachusetts - D.-Mass.                   34
Democrat from Maryland - D.-Md.                          35
Democrat from Michigan - D.-Mich.                        36
Democrat from Minnesota - D.-Minn.                       37
Democrat from Mississippi - D.-Miss.                     38
Democrat from Missouri - D.-Mo.                          39
Democrat from Montana - D.-Mont.                         40
Democrat from Nebraska - D.-Nebr.                        41
Democrat from Nevada - D.-Nev.                           42
Democrat from New Hampshire - D.-N.H.                    43
Democrat from New Jersey - D.-N.J.                       44
Democrat from New Mexico - D.-N.M.                       45
Democrat from New York - D.-N.Y.                         46
Democrat from North Carolina - D.-N.C.                   47
Democrat from North Dakota - D.-N.D.                     48
Democrat from Ohio - D.-Ohio                             49
Democrat from Oklahoma - D.-Okla.                        50
Democrat from Oregon - D.-Oreg.                          51
Democrat from Pennsylvania - D.-Pa.                      52
Democrat from Rhode Island - D.-R.I.                     53
Democrat from South Carolina - D.-S.C.                   54
Democrat from South Dakota - D.-S.D.                     55
Democrat from Tennessee - D.-Tenn.                       56
```

```
Democrat from Texas - D.-Tex                                      1
Democrat from Utah - D.-Utah                                      2
Democrat from Vermont - D.-Vt.                                    3
Democrat from Virginia - D.-Va.                                   4
Democrat from Washington - D.-Wash.                              5
Democrat from West Virginia - D.-W.Va.                           6
Democrat from Wisconsin - D.-Wis.                                7
Democrat from Wyoming - D.-Wyo.                                  8
Democratic - D.; Dem.                                            9
Democratic National Committee - DNC                             10
demodulator - DEM                                               11
demographer - demogr                                            12
demography - demogr                                             13
demolish - dml                                                  14
demolition - demo; dml                                          15
demonology - demon.                                             16
demonstrate - demon.; dmnstr.                                   17
demonstration (model) - demo                                    18
demonstration - demon.; dmnstr.                                 19
demonstrative - demon.                                          20
demonstrative adjective - dem. adj.                             21
demonstrative pronoun - dem. pro.                               22
demonstrator - dmnstr.                                          23
demote - dem                                                    24
demur - dem                                                     25
demurrage - dem                                                 26
Denmark - Da; Den.                                              27
denarius (penny) - d.                                           28
denomination - denom.                                           29
density - D.; d.; den.; dens.                                   30
dental - den.; dent.                                            31
Dental Corps - DC                                               32
dental hygienist - Dent. Hyg.                                   33
dentist - dent.                                                 34
dentistry - dent.                                               35
denture - dent.                                                 36
Denver & Rio Grand Western (RR) - D&RGW                         37
Deo gratias (thanks to God) - D.G.                              38
Deo volente (God willing) - D.V.                                39
deoxycorticosterone acetate - DCA                               40
deoxyribonucleic acid - DNA                                     41
depart - dep                                                    42
Department - Dept.                                              43
department - dept.; dpt.                                        44
Department of Agriculture - DOA                                 45
Department of Defense - DOD                                     46
Department of Health, Education and Welfare - HEW               47
Department of Housing and Urban Development - HUD               48
Department of Population and Environment - DPE                  49
Department of Public Works - DPW; D.P.W.                        50
Department of Sanitation - DS                                   51
Department of Transportation - DOT                              52
departure - dep                                                 53
departure point - dp                                            54
dependency - dep.                                               55
dependent - dep.                                                56
```

deponent - dep.; dpt.   1
depose - dep   2
deposit - dep.; dpst.   3
deposit account - D/A; da   4
deposit certificate - dep. ctf.   5
deposit prediction method - DPM; D.P.M.   6
deposit receipt - d.r.   7
deposited carbon - DC   8
depot - dep.   9
depreciation - depr.   10
depression - depr.   11
Deprived Areas Recreation Team - DART   12
depth - d   13
depth of snow - S   14
deputy - dep.; dept.   15
der - d.   16
derivation - der.; deriv.   17
derivative - der.; deriv.   18
derive - der.   19
derived - der.   20
derived from - der.   21
dematological - dermatol.   22
dermatologist - dermatol.   23
dermatology - dermat.; dermatol.   24
derogatory - derog.   25
descendant - desc.   26
Descent Orbit Insertion - DIO   27
Descent Propulsion System - DPS   28
described as follows - daf   29
describing function - DF   30
descriptive - descr.   31
desert - des   32
deserted - d.   33
deserter - d.   34
desiderate - desid   35
desideratum - desid   36
design - des.   37
design specification(s) - d.spec.(s.)   38
designate - des   39
designated ground zero - dgz   40
designation - des   41
designed - des.   42
designer - desig.   43
desire - des.   44
desired - desid.   45
despatch - desp.   46
dessert - des   47
a dessert spoonful (L, cochlear medium) - coch. med.   48
destination - destn.; dstn.   49
destructive readout - DRO   50
detach - det.   51
detached - det.   52
detachment - det.   53
detail - det.   54
detain - dtn   55
detection - det.   56

```
detector - det.                                                      1
detention - detn                                                     2
detonator - det                                                      3
Detroit - Det.                                                       4
Detroit Amateur Baseball Federation - DABF                           5
Detroit & Mackinac (RR) - D&M                                        6
Detroit, Caro & Sandusky (RR) - DC&S                                 7
Detroit Police Officers' Association - DPOA                          8
Detroit Public Library - DPL                                         9
Detroit Society for the Advancement of Culture and Education        10
     DSACE                                                          11
Detroit Stock Exchange - DSE; De                                    12
Detroit, Toledo & Ironton (RR) - DT&I                               13
Deus (God) - D.                                                     14
deuterium - D                                                       15
Deutero-Isaiah - Dt-Is                                              16
Deuteronomy - Dt                                                    17
Deutero-Zechariah - Dt-Zech                                         18
Deutsch Mark - DM                                                   19
Deutsche - Deut.                                                    20
developed country - DC                                              21
developed horsepower - dhp                                          22
developed length - dev. lgth.                                       23
development - devel.                                                24
Development Loan Fund - DLF                                         25
deviation - dev.                                                    26
deviation clause - d/c; d.c.                                        27
device - dv                                                         28
Device for Automatic Desensitization - DAD                          29
device selector - DS                                                30
device-switching unit - DSU                                         31
Devonshire - Dev.                                                   32
Dewey Decimal Classification - DDC                                  33
dewpoint - dp                                                       34
dew-point temperature - TdTd                                        35
dexedrine - dexe; Dexies                                            36
dexter (right) - d.                                                 37
dextro - D.; d.                                                     38
diagnose - diag                                                     39
diagnosis - diag                                                    40
diagonal - DGNL; diag                                               41
diagram - diag.                                                     42
diagram(s) - diagr.(s.)                                             43
dial pulsing - DP                                                   44
dial system - DS                                                    45
dialect - d.; dial.                                                 46
dialectal - d.; dial.                                               47
dialectic - dial.                                                   48
dialectical - dial.                                                 49
diameter - D.; d.; dia.; diam.                                      50
diameter at breast height - d.b.h.                                  51
diamond - dmd                                                       52
diamond pyramid hardness - DPH; D.P.H.                              53
diaphragm - diaph                                                   54
dichlorodiphenyl-trichloroethane - D.D.T.                           55
dictaphone - dicta.                                                 56
```

```
dictation - dict.                                                        1
dictator - dict.                                                         2
diction - d.; dict.                                                      3
dictionary - dict.                                                       4
Dictionary of American Biography - DAB                                   5
Dictionary of American Slang - Dict Amer Slang                           6
Dictionary of National Biography - DNB                                   7
did not finish (yacht racing) - DNF                                      8
died (L, obiit) - d.; (ob.)                                              9
died without issue (L, decessit sine prole) - d.s.p.                    10
died without issue (L, obiit sine prole) - ob.s.p.                      11
dielectric constant - DC; D-C; D.-C.; D.C.; K                           12
dielectric loading factor - DL                                          13
diesel electric - dsl elec                                              14
dietetic(s) - diet.                                                     15
difference - diff.                                                      16
difference between air temperature and sea temperature -               17
    $T_sT_s$                                                            18
different - diff.                                                       19
differential - diff.                                                    20
differential equation solver - DES                                     21
differential generator - DG                                            22
differentiation - d                                                    23
differs - diff.                                                        24
difficult - difclt.                                                    25
difficulty - difclty.                                                  26
diffraction - diffr                                                    27
diffuser - dfsr                                                        28
diffusion - diffu                                                      29
digest - dig.                                                          30
digestion - dig.                                                       31
digit - D                                                              32
digit present - DP                                                     33
digit/record mark - DIGRM                                              34
digit storage relay - DSR                                              35
digital - D                                                            36
digital arithmetic center - DAC                                        37
digital attenuator system - DAS                                        38
digital communication system - DIGICOM                                 39
digital comparator - DC                                                40
digital counting unit - DCU                                            41
digital data acquisition system - DDAS                                 42
digital data conversion equipment - DDCE                               43
digital data converter - DDC                                           44
digital data transceiver - DDT                                         45
digital data transmitter - DDT                                         46
digital differential analyzer - DDA                                    47
digital display - DD                                                   48
digital display generator - DDG                                        49
digital expansion system - DES                                         50
digital experimental airborne navigator - DEXAN                        51
digital input - DI                                                     52
digital input/output buffer - DIOB                                     53
digital message entry device - DMED                                    54
digital microcircuit - DMC                                             55
digital multimeter - DMM                                               56
```

digital output - DO   1
digital output/input translator - DO/IT   2
digital pattern generator - DPG   3
digital radiometers - DRM   4
digital resolver - DR   5
digital stepping recorder - DSR   6
digital technique - DT   7
digital telemetering register - DTR   8
digital voltmeter - DVM   9
digital volt-ohmmeter - DVOM   10
digital-to-analog converter - DAC   11
dilation and curettage - d&c   12
dilute - dil.   13
dilution units per milligram - du./mg.   14
dime - D.; d.   15
dimension - dim.; dmn.   16
dimensional - dmn.   17
Dimethyltryptamine - DMT   18
diminuendo - dim.   19
diminutive - dim.; dimin.   20
dinar - d.   21
diner per filament - d.p.f.   22
Diners Club - DC   23
dinette - Dt.   24
dining alcove - DA   25
dining room - DR   26
diocesan - dioc.   27
diocese - dioc.   28
diode - D; dio   29
diode function generator - DFG   30
diode gate - DG   31
diode logic - DL   32
diode recovery tester - DRT   33
diopter - d; diop   34
dioptrics - diop   35
diphtheria - dip.   36
diphthong - dipth   37
diploma - dip.; dipl.; dpl.   38
diplomacy - dipl.   39
diplomat - dip.; dipl.   40
diplomatic - dipl.   41
dipsomania - dipso   42
dipsomaniac - dipso   43
Diptheria, Pertussis, Tetanus - D.P.T.   44
direct action - d.a.   45
direct conversion reactor - DCR   46
direct current - DC; D-C; D.-C.; D.C.; d.c.   47
direct current working voltage - DCWV   48
direct digital control - DDC   49
direct distance dialing - DDD   50
direct energy conversion - DEC   51
direct flow - D-F   52
direct memory address - DMA   53
direct operating cost - DOC   54
direct or reverse - D/R   55
direct question - dq   56

direct readout miss-distance indicator - DROMDI   1
direct support - ds   2
direct-coupled transistor logic - DCTL   3
direct-coupled unipolar transistor logic - DCUTL   4
direction and speed of movement of ship - $D_S V_S$ 5
direction center - DC   6
direction finder - DF; D.F.; df   7
direction of movement of the waves - $d_W d_W$ 8
direction of surface wind - dd   9
directional coupler - DC   10
Director - Dir.   11
directory - direct.   12
directory tape processor - DTP   13
direct-viewing storage tube - DVST   14
disability - disabl   15
Disabled American Veterans - DAV   16
disapprove - disap   17
disband - dsbn   18
disbursements - disbs.   19
disc jockey - dj   20
Discaled Carmelites - O.C.D.   21
discharge - dis.; disch.   22
discharged - disch.   23
Disciples of Christ - DC   24
disciplinary - dis.   25
discipline - dis.   26
discolored - discol.   27
disconnect - disc.   28
discontinue - disc.   29
discontinued - discontd.   30
discount - dis.; disc.; disct.   31
discover - disc.   32
discovered - disc.   33
discoverer - disc.   34
discrete address - DA   35
discrete frequency generator - DFG   36
diseases - dis.   37
disembark - disemb   38
dishonorable - dishon.   39
dishonorably - dishon.   40
dishwasher - DW   41
disinfectant - disin   42
disintegrations per minute - d.p.m.   43
disjunctively linear - DL   44
disk jockey - dj   45
dismiss - dism.   46
dismissal - dism.   47
dismissed - dismd.   48
disordered action of the heart - D.A.H.   49
dispatch - dspch   50
dispatcher - dispr; dspch   51
dispensary - disp.   52
dispensatories - dispen.   53
displaced person - DP; dp   54
displacement - displ   55
display - D   56

```
Display and Keyboard - DSKY                                      1
disposal - dspo                                                  2
dispose - dspo                                                   3
disposition - disp                                               4
dissection - dissec                                              5
disseminate - dissem                                             6
dissent - diss.                                                  7
dissertation - diss.                                             8
dissipation - diss.                                              9
dissipation factor - DF                                         10
dissolve or dilute (L, dilue) - dil.                            11
dissolved - dissd.                                              12
dissyllable - dissyl                                            13
distance - dist.                                                14
distance (radio) - DX; D.X.; dx                                 15
distant - dist.                                                 16
distant (radio) - DX; D.X.                                      17
distant early warning line - DEW line                           18
distant station reception - DX                                  19
distillation - distil                                           20
distilled - distil                                              21
distilled water (L, aqua destillata) - (aq. dest.); dw          22
distilling - distil                                             23
distinguish - dist.; distng.                                    24
distinguished - dist.                                           25
Distinguished Service Cross - D.S.C.                            26
Distinguished Service Medal - D.S.M.                            27
Distinguished Service Order - D.S.O.                            28
distinguished visitor - DV                                      29
distinguishing - disting.                                       30
distribute - distr.                                             31
distributed - dist.; distr.                                     32
distributed lab - DL                                            33
distribution - distr.                                           34
distribution (statistics) - t                                   35
distribution point - dp                                         36
distributor - distr.                                            37
district - dis.; disc.; disct.; dist.                           38
District Attorney - DA; D.A.                                    39
District Court - Dist. Ct.                                      40
district judge - D.J.                                           41
District Manager - Dist. Mgr.                                   42
District of Columbia - D.C.                                     43
District of Columbia Appeal Cases - App. D.C.                   44
Distrito Federal - D.F.                                         45
ditto - do.                                                     46
dive - dv                                                       47
divergence - div.                                               48
diverse - div.                                                  49
diversion - div.                                                50
divide - div.                                                   51
divided - div.                                                  52
divident - d.; div.                                             53
dividends - divs                                                54
divine - div.                                                   55
Divinity - Div.                                                 56
```

74

```
division - div.                                                   1
divisor - div.                                                    2
divorce - div.                                                    3
divorced - d; div.                                                4
do not repeat - n.r.; non. rep.                                   5
dock - dk                                                         6
dock warrant - D.W.                                               7
docket - dkt                                                      8
dockyard - dkyd                                                   9
doctor - doc                                                      10
Doctor - Doct.; Dr.; M.D.                                         11
Doctor of Both Laws (Civil & Canon) - J.U.L.                      12
Doctor of Both Civil and Canon Laws - J.U.D.                      13
Doctor of Both Civil and Canon Law (L, Utriusque Juris            14
    Doctor) - U.J.D.                                              15
Doctor of Canon Law - D.C.L.; J.C.D.                              16
Doctor of Chiropractic - D.C.                                     17
Doctor of Civil Law (L, Juris Civilis Doctor) - D.C.L.;           18
    (J.C.D.)                                                      19
Doctor of Dental Medicine - D.M.D.                                20
Doctor of Dental Surgery - D.D.S.                                 21
Doctor of Divinity - D.D.                                         22
Doctor of Education - Ed.D.                                       23
Doctor of Engineering - Eng.D.                                    24
Doctor of Fine Arts - A.F.D.; D.F.A.                              25
Doctor of Humanities - L.H.D.                                     26
Doctor of Juridical Science - S.J.D.                              27
Doctor of Jurisprudence (L, Juris Doctor) - J.D.                  28
Doctor of Law (L, Juris Doctor) - J.D.; Jur.D.                    29
Doctor of Laws (L, Jurum Doctor) - J.D.                           30
Doctor of Laws (L, Legum Doctor) - LL.D.                          31
Doctor of Letters - D.Litt.; Litt.D.                              32
Doctor of Library Science - D.L.S.                                33
Doctor of Literature - D.Lit.; Lit.D.; Litt.D.                    34
Doctor of Medicine - M.D.                                         35
Doctor of Music (L, Musicae Doctor) - D.Mus.; Mus.D.;             36
    Mus.Doc.; Mus.Dr.                                             37
Doctor of Osteopathy - D.O.                                       38
Doctor of Pedagogy - Pd.D.                                        39
Doctor of Pharmacy - Pharm.D.                                     40
Doctor of Philosophy (L, Philosophiae Doctor) - Ph.D.            41
Doctor of Podiatry - Pod.D.                                       42
Doctor of Political Science (L, Rerum Politicarum Doctor) -       43
    R.P.D.                                                        44
Doctor of Public Health - D.P.H.                                  45
Doctor of Public Hygiene - D.P.Hy.                                46
Doctor of Sacred Scripture - S.S.D.                               47
Doctor of Sacred Theology (L, Sacrae Theologiae Doctor) -         48
    S.T.D.                                                        49
Doctor of Science - D.S.; D.Sc.; Sc.D.                            50
Doctor of the Humanities - L.H.D.                                 51
Doctor of the More Humane Letters (L, Litterarum Humaniorum       52
    Doctor) - L.H.D.                                              53
Doctor of Theology (L, Theologiae Doctor) - D.Th.; Th.D.          54
Doctor of Veterinary Medicine - D.V.M.; V.M.D.                    55
Doctor of Veterinary Medicine and Surgery - D.V.M.S.             56
```

```
Doctors - Drs.                                          1
document(s) - doc.                                      2
document signed - D.S.; d.s.                            3
documents attached - da                                 4
documents upon acceptance - D/A                         5
documents upon payment - D/P                            6
Dodge Revolutionary Union Movement - DRUM               7
doing business as - d.b.a.                              8
dollar - D; d.; dol.                                    9
dollars - dols.                                        10
dollars per share - dls/shr                            11
dollar trade-off - DTO                                 12
dolly - dly                                            13
Dolophine - Dollies                                    14
domain - dom.                                          15
domestic - dom.                                        16
domestic economy - dom.econ.                           17
domestic exchange - dom.ex.                            18
dominant wavelength - DWL; D.W.L.                      19
Dominican Republic - Dom.Rep.                          20
Dominicana de Aviacion - CDA                           21
dominion - dom.                                        22
Dominion Atlantic (Mar. Prov.) (RR) - DA               23
Dominion of Canada - Dom Can                           24
Dominus (Lord) - D.                                    25
Dominus noster (our Lord) - D.N.                       26
Donald - Don                                           27
door - d.; dr.                                         28
door opening - D.O.                                    29
Doppler velocity and position - DOVAP                  30
Dorado (the Goldfish) - Del                            31
Doric - Dor.                                           32
dormitories - dorms                                    33
dormitory - dorm                                       34
Dorothea - Dora                                        35
Dorothy - Dor                                          36
dorsal - d                                             37
dosage - dos                                           38
a dose (L, dosis) - D.; d.                             39
Douay Version (of the Bible) - D.V.                    40
double - d.; dbl.; dub.                                41
double acting - DA; dbl.act.                           42
double column - d.c.                                   43
double concave - dcc                                   44
double convex - dcx                                    45
double deck - d.d.                                     46
double diffused - DD                                   47
double entry - d.e.                                    48
double faults (tennis) - DF                            49
double glass - DG                                      50
double hung window - DHW                               51
double plays (baseball) - DP                           52
double pole - dp                                       53
double time - d.t.                                     54
double-barreled - double-B                             55
double-base diode - DBD                                56
```

```
double-breasted - db                                    1
doublecross - double-X                                  2
doubled - dbl.                                          3
double-groove - DG                                      4
double-lens reflex - dlr                                5
double-pole, double-throw - DPDT                        6
double-pole, single-throw - DPST                        7
Douglas - D                                             8
Dover - Dov                                             9
dovetail - dvtl                                        10
Dow Jones - DJ                                         11
Dowager - Dow.                                         12
dowel - dow; dwl                                       13
Dow-Jones - D-J                                        14
down - dn.                                             15
downspout - DS                                         16
dozen(s) - doz.                                        17
Draco (the Dragon) - Dra                               18
draft - Dft.; dft.                                     19
a draft (L, haustus) - haust.                          20
draftsman - dftmn; dftsmn.                             21
drain - dr.                                            22
drain board - DB                                       23
drainage - drain.                                      24
dram(s) - dr.                                          25
dram, apothecaries' - dr.ap.                           26
dram, avoirdupois - dr.av.                             27
dram, fluid - fl.dr.                                   28
drawback - dbk.                                        29
drawer - dr.                                           30
drawers - drs.                                         31
drawing - dwg.                                         32
drawn - dr.; drn.                                      33
drawn over mandrel - dom                               34
dredging - dred.                                       35
dressed (lumber) - DRS                                 36
dressed & matched - D&M                                37
dressing table - DR T                                  38
dressmaker - drsmkr.                                   39
drill - dr                                             40
drinking fountain - DF                                 41
drinking water fountain - D.W.F.                       42
drip-proof - dp                                        43
drive - dr                                             44
driver - dvr                                           45
driver's license - dl                                  46
driving (horse racing) - d.                            47
driving power - DP                                     48
drop - gt.                                             49
drop by drop (Latin) - guttatim                        50
drop cord (outlet) - D                                 51
drop forge - df                                        52
drop point - dp                                        53
dropout - d-o                                          54
drops (L, guttae) - gtt.                               55
drum - D; dr.                                          56
```

77

drum demand - DD   1
drum information display - DID   2
drunk and disorderly - D.&D.   3
dry basis - DB; D.B.   4
dry well - dw   5
drydock - dd   6
dryer - D   7
Du Bois Clubs of America - DBCA   8
dubious - dub.   9
Dublin   Dub.   10
duct section, exhaust - E   11
duct section, fresh air - FA   12
duct section, recirculation - R   13
duct section, supply - S   14
due date - dd   15
Duke - Du.   16
Duke University - DU   17
Duluth - Dul   18
Duluth, Missabe & Iron Range (RR) - DM&IR   19
Duluth, South Shore & Atlantic (RR) - DSS&A   20
Duluth, Winnipeg & Pacific (RR) - DW&P   21
dumbwaiter - DW   22
dump - dp.   23
dump truck - dp. trk.   24
dun - dn.   25
Dun & Bradstreet - D&B   26
Dunkirk - Dnk   27
duodecimo - 12 mo, 12° 28
duplex - dpl; dx   29
duplicate - dup.   30
duplicated - dup.   31
duplicating - dupl.   32
duplication - dup.   33
duration - D.; dur.   34
dust jacket - dj   35
Dutch - D.; Du.   36
Dutch Reformed - D.R.   37
dwelling - dwel.; dwg.   38
Dwight David Eisenhower - DDE   39
Dylan Thomas - DT   40
dynamic(s) - dyn.; dynam.   41
dynamic load characteristic - DL   42
dynamic programming - DP   43
dynamite - dyna; dynmt   44
dynamo - dynam   45
dyne - d.   46
dysentary - dysen   47
dysprosium - Ds; Dy   48
each - ea.   49
each face - EF   50
Earl - E.   51
earliest arrival time - EAT   52
earliest possible date - epd   53
early - e.   54
Early Apollo Scientific Experiments Payload - EASEP   55
Early English Text Society - EETS   56

```
Early Modern Dutch - Early Mod. D.                                     1
Early Modern English - Early Mod. Eng.                                 2
earned points (tennis) - EP                                            3
earned run average (baseball) - ERA                                    4
earned runs (baseball) - ER                                            5
earth - E.; e.                                                         6
Earth Orbit Rendezvous - EOR                                           7
earth satellite vehicle - ESV                                          8
eased up (horse racing) - u.                                           9
easement - easemt                                                     10
easily (horse racing) - e.                                            11
east - E                                                              12
east by north - EbN                                                   13
east by south - EbS                                                   14
East Frisian - E. Fris.                                               15
East Indian - E.Ind.                                                  16
East Tennessee & Western North Carolina (RR) - ET&WNC                 17
eastbound - EB                                                        18
Eastern Airlines - EA                                                 19
eastern daylight time - EDT; e.d.t.                                   20
eastern equine encephalitis - EEE                                     21
Eastern Provincial Airways - PV                                       22
eastern standard time - EST; e.s.t.                                   23
eastern time - ET; e.t.                                               24
east-northeast - ENE                                                  25
east-southeast - ESE                                                  26
easy - e-z                                                            27
easy processing channel - EPC                                         28
Ebenezer - Eb.                                                        29
ebullition - ebul                                                     30
eccentric - ecc                                                       31
eccentric(s) - eccen                                                  32
Eccentric Orbiting Geophysical Observatory Satellite - EGO            33
eccentricity - E                                                      34
Ecclesiastes (Qoheleth) - Eccl                                        35
ecclesiastic - eccles.                                                36
ecclesiastical - eccles.                                              37
Ecclesiasticus - Ecclus.                                              38
echelon - ech.                                                        39
eclectic - eclec.                                                     40
eclipse - ecl                                                         41
ecological - ecol.                                                    42
Ecological Society of America - ESA                                   43
ecology - eco.; ecol.                                                 44
economic(s) - ec                                                      45
economic - econ                                                       46
Economic Administrative Head Office of the S.S.                       47
    (Wirtschaftsverwaltungs-hauptamt) - W.V.H.A.                      48
Economic and Social Council - Ecosoc                                  49
Economic Cooperation Administration - ECA; E.C.A.                     50
economic order quantity - EOQ                                         51
economic status - ES                                                  52
economical - econ.                                                    53
Economics - Econ.                                                     54
economics - econ.                                                     55
economist - econ.                                                     56
```

```
eighteen - XVIII                                                      1
eighteen-one balkline (billiards) - 18.1                              2
eighteen-two balkline (billiards) - 18.2                              3
eighty - LXXX                                                         4
ejector - eject.                                                      5
El Salvador - El Sal; Sal.                                            6
elapsed time - ETIM                                                   7
elapsed-time indicator - eti                                          8
elasticity - E                                                        9
elbow - ell                                                          10
eldest - e.; eld.                                                    11
elect - el.                                                          12
elected - el.                                                        13
election - el.                                                       14
Election Vote Analysis - E.V.A.                                      15
Electric - Elec.                                                     16
electric - elec.; elect.                                             17
electric horsepower - ehp                                            18
electric light - el lt                                               19
electric panel - EP                                                  20
electric storage battery - esb                                       21
electric water cooler - E.W.C.                                       22
electrical - elec.; elect.                                           23
electrical continuous cloth - Ecc; Ec.c.                             24
electrical differential - ED                                         25
electrical discharge machinery - EDM; E.D.M.                         26
Electrical Engineer - E.E.                                           27
electrical kilowatts - EKW                                           28
electrical panel - E.P.                                              29
electrical power unit - EPU                                          30
Electrical Stimulation of the Brain - ESB                            31
electrician - elec.; electn.                                         32
electricity - elec.; elect.                                          33
electrocardiocorder - ECC                                            34
electrocardiogram - ECG                                              35
electrocardiogram simulator - EKS                                    36
electrochemical - electrochem.                                       37
electrochemical diffused-collector transistor - ECDC                 38
electrochemist - electrochem.                                        39
electrochemistry - electrochem.                                      40
electroencephalogram - EEG                                           41
electroencephalograph - EEG                                          42
electrokardiogram - EKG, ekg                                         43
electrolysis - electrol                                              44
electromagnetic - EM                                                 45
electromagnetic amplifying lens - EAL                                46
electromagnetic interference - emi                                   47
electromagnetic storage - ES                                         48
electromagnetic unit - emu; e.m.u.                                   49
electromagnetic units - E.M.U.; e.m.u.                               50
electromechanical - EM                                               51
electromechanical power - EMP                                        52
electrometer - ELT                                                   53
electromicroscopic - EM                                              54
electromotive difference of potential - emdp                         55
electromotive force - E.M.F.; e.m.f., emf                            56
```

81

```
electron - e                                                      1
electron beam parametric amplifier - EBPA                         2
electron diffraction instrument - EDI                             3
electron paramagnetic resonance - EPR; E.P.R.                     4
electron tube - etu                                               5
electron volt - eV                                                6
electron volt(s) - ev.; e.v.                                      7
electron-coupled oscillator - ECO                                 8
electrone-phalograph - EEG                                        9
electronic accounting machine - EAM                              10
electronic automatic exchange - EAX                              11
electronic conductivity - EC                                     12
electronic contact operate - ECO                                 13
electronic countermeasures - ECCM                                14
electronic countermeasures equipment - ECME                      15
electronic data processing - EDP                                 16
electronic data-processing center - EDPC                         17
electronic data-processing equipment - EDPE                      18
electronic data-processing machine - EDPM                        19
electronic data-processing system - EDPS                         20
electronic display unit - EDU                                    21
electronic ground automatic destruct sequencer - EGADS           22
electronic management system - EMS                               23
electronic medical system - EMS                                  24
electronic private branch exchange - EPBX                        25
electronic program control - EPC                                 26
electronic reading automation - ERA                              27
electronic remote switching - ERX                                28
electronic security - ELSEC                                      29
electronic selective switching unit - ESSU                       30
Electronic Service Association - ESA                             31
electronic sweep generator - ESG                                 32
electronic switching system - ESS                                33
Electronic Telegraph System - ETS                                34
electro-optical system - EOS                                     35
electrophysical - electrophys.                                   36
electrophysicist - electrophys.                                  37
electrophysics - electrophys.                                    38
electroplate - ep                                                39
electrosensitive programming - ESP                               40
electrostatic - es                                               41
electrostatic flux density - D                                   42
electrostatic unit - e.s.u.                                      43
element - ELEM; elm.                                             44
element(s) - elem.                                               45
elemental - elem.                                                46
elementary - elem.                                               47
elements - elem.                                                 48
elevate - elev.                                                  49
elevated - elev.                                                 50
elevated railroad - El; L                                        51
elevation (grade level only) - el.                               52
elevation - elev.                                                53
elevation facade - elev.                                         54
elevator - elev.                                                 55
eleven - XI                                                      56
```

```
Elgin, Joliet & Eastern (RR) - EJ&E          1
Elias - Eli.                                 2
eligible - elig                             3
Elijah - Elij.                              4
eliminate - elim.                           5
elimination - elim.                         6
Elisabeth - Elis.                           7
elixir - elix                               8
Elizabeth - Eliz.                           9
ell - L                                     10
elliptic - ellip.                           11
elliptical - ellip.; ellipt.                12
elocution - elo                             13
elongate - elong.                           14
elongated punch - EP                        15
elongation - elong.                         16
eloquence - elo                             17
Elvira - El                                 18
em - M                                      19
emanation - Em.; eman.                      20
Emanuel - Em.                               21
embankment - emb.                           22
embargo - emb.                              23
embark - emb.                               24
embarkation - emb.; embkn.                  25
embassy - emb.                              26
embossed - emb.                             27
embroidery - emb.                           28
embryo - emb.                               29
embryology - emb.; embryol.                 30
emergency - emer.; emerg.                   31
emergency capability - ec                   32
emergency request - ER                      33
emergency rescue - ER                       34
Emeritus - Emer                             35
emigrant - emig                             36
emigration - emig                           37
Emily - Em.                                 38
eminence - em.                              39
emission - emis                             40
emission control - em con                   41
emitter - E                                 42
emitter-coupled logic operator - ECLO       43
emitter-coupled transistor logic - ECTL     44
Emma - Em.                                  45
Emmanuel - Em.                              46
Emperor (L, Imperator) - Emp.; (Imp.)       47
emphasis - emp.; emph.                      48
emphatic - emph.                            49
empire - emp.                               50
employ - empl.                              51
employed - empd.                            52
employee - empl.                            53
employer - empl.                            54
employment - empl.                          55
employment agency - emp. agcy.              56
```

```
Empress (L, Imperatrix) - Emp.; (Imp.)                        1
empties - mt's                                                 2
empty - mt                                                     3
emulsifier - e                                                 4
emulsion - e; emul.                                            5
en - N                                                         6
en route - enrt                                                7
enamel - E; enam                                               8
enclose - encl.                                                9
enclosed - enc.; encl.; encld.                                10
enclosure - enc.; encl.                                       11
encyclopedia - ency.; encyc.                                  12
Encyclopedia Americana - Ency. Amer.                          13
Encyclopedia Britannica - Ency. Brit.                         14
end (football) - E.                                           15
end interruption sequence - EIS                               16
end of file - EOF                                             17
end of job - EOJ                                              18
end of life - EOL                                             19
end of message - EOM                                          20
end of month - e.o.m.                                         21
end of program - EP                                           22
end of tape - EOT                                             23
end of transmission - eot                                     24
end point - EP; E.P.                                          25
end to end - E to E                                           26
endocrine - endo                                              27
endocrinology - endo                                          28
end-of-reel - EOR                                             29
endorse - end.                                                30
endorsed - end.                                               31
endorsement - end.                                            32
endowment - endow.                                            33
endpaper - ep                                                 34
ends annealed - ea                                            35
end-to-end - e-to-e                                           36
enemy dead - ed                                               37
enemy-occupied territory - eot                                38
energize - ener                                               39
energy - ener                                                 40
engine - eng                                                  41
engine room - eng rm                                          42
engine test vehicle - etv                                     43
engineer - E.; eng.; engr.                                    44
Engineer of Mines - E.M.                                      45
engineering - eng.                                            46
Engineering - Engineer.                                       47
engineering change notice - ECN                               48
engineering change proposed - ECP                             49
engineering changes - EC                                      50
engineer-in-training - EIT                                    51
engineers - engrs.                                            52
England - Eng.                                                53
English - Eng.                                                54
English Revised Version (of the Bible) - E.R.V.              55
engrave - engr.                                               56
```

```
engraved - eng.; engr.                                              1
engraver - eng.; engr.; engrv.                                      2
engraving - eng.; engrv.                                            3
engraving(s) - engr.                                                4
enlarge - enl.                                                      5
enlarged - enl.; enlgd.                                             6
enlist - enl.                                                       7
enlisted - enl.                                                     8
ensign - Ens.                                                       9
entered - entd.                                                    10
Enterprise (Bell Telephone) - E                                    11
entitle - entl                                                     12
entomological - entom.                                             13
entomology - entom.; entomol.                                      14
entrance - e.; ent; entr                                           15
envelope - env                                                     16
envelope delay distortion - EDD                                    17
environ - env                                                      18
environment - envir.                                               19
Environmental Action for Survival - ENACT                          20
Environmental Protection Agency - EPA                              21
Environmental Quality Council - EQC                                22
Environmental Science Services Administration - ESSA               23
envoy - env                                                        24
ephemeral - ephmer                                                 25
Ephemeris Time - E.T.                                              26
Ephesians - Eph                                                    27
epidemic - epid                                                    28
epilogue - epil.                                                   29
Epiphany - Epiph                                                   30
Episcopal - Episc.                                                 31
Episcopus (bishop) - Ep.                                           32
epitaph - epit.                                                    33
epitome - epit.                                                    34
equal - eq.                                                        35
Equal Employment Opportunities Commission - EEOC                   36
equal parts (L, partes aequales) - p.a.e.                          37
equal parts of each - āā                                           38
equal zero - E/Z                                                   39
Equaleus (the Foal) - Equ                                          40
equalize - eq.                                                     41
equalizer - EQ                                                     42
equate - EQU                                                       43
equation - eq.                                                     44
Equator - Eq                                                       45
equator - equat                                                    46
equatorial - equat                                                 47
equinox - equin                                                    48
equip - eqp                                                        49
equipment - EQP; eqpt; equip.                                      50
equipment component list - ECL                                     51
equity - eq.                                                       52
equivalent - eq.; equiv.                                           53
equivalent air speed - eas                                         54
equivalent background input - EBI                                  55
equivalent direct radiation - EDR                                  56
```

```
equivalent focal length - EFL; E.F.L.                          1
equivalent full power hours - EFPH                             2
Erasmus - Eras                                                 3
Erbium - Er                                                    4
erection - erect.                                              5
erg - e.                                                       6
Ergebnisse - Ergebn.                                           7
Eric - Er.                                                     8
Eridanus (the River Eridanus) - Eri                            9
ermine - erm                                                  10
Ernest - Ern.                                                 11
erroneous - err.; erron.                                      12
erroneously - erron.                                          13
error(s) - e; err.                                            14
error (scoring) - -                                           15
error correcting - EC                                         16
errors (baseball) - e.                                        17
errors (tennis) - E.                                          18
errors and omissions excepted - E.&O.E.; e.&o.e.              19
errors excepted - e.e.                                        20
erthyrocyte sedimentation rate - ESR                          21
Escanaba & Lake Superior (RR) - E&LS                          22
escape - esc                                                  23
eschatological - eschat.                                      24
eschatology - eschat.                                         25
escort - esc                                                  26
escrow - esc; escr                                            27
escutheon - esc                                               28
Eskimo - Esk.                                                 29
especial - esp.                                               30
especially - esp.; espec.                                     31
Esperanto - Esp.                                              32
espionage - espg                                              33
Esquimalt & Nanaimo (B.C.) (RR) - E&N                         34
Esquire - Esq.                                                35
essence(s) - ess.                                             36
essence (L, essentia) - ess.                                  37
essential - esn.; esntl.                                      38
essential elements of information - EEI                       39
Essex - Ess.                                                  40
establish - est.; estab.                                      41
established - est.; estab..                                   42
establishment - estab.                                        43
estate - est.                                                 44
Esther - Est.; Esth.                                          45
esthetics - esth                                              46
Esthonia - Esth                                               47
estimate - est.                                               48
estimated - est.                                              49
estimated position - ep                                       50
estimated shipping date - esd                                 51
estimated time of arrival - e.t.a.                            52
estimated time of return - e.t.r.                             53
estimated weight - est. wt.                                   54
estimation - estn                                             55
estuary - est.                                                56
```

```
et alibi (and elsewhere) - et al.                          1
et alii or aliae (and others) - et al.                     2
et cetera - &c.                                            3
et ceteri, ceterae, or cetera (and others, and so forth) - 4
   etc.                                                    5
et sequentia (and the following) - et seq.; seq.           6
et uxor (and wife) - et ux.                                7
etched plate - EP                                          8
etching - etch.                                            9
etching by transmitted light - ETL                        10
Ethel - Eth.                                               11
ether - eth                                                12
ethical - eth                                              13
Ethiopia - Eth.                                            14
Ethiopian - Eth.                                           15
Ethiopic - Eth.                                            16
ethnographical - ethnog.                                   17
ethnography - ethnog.                                      18
ethnological - ethnol.                                     19
ethnology - ethnol.                                        20
Etruscan - Etr                                             21
etymological - etym.                                       22
etymologically - etym.                                     23
etymology - etym.                                          24
Euclid - Eucl                                              25
Eudora - Dora                                              26
Eugene - Eug.                                              27
eugenics - eugen                                           28
Eunice - Euni                                              29
euphemism - euphem.                                        30
euphemistic - euphem.                                      31
euphonic - euphon                                          32
Europe - Eur.                                              33
European - Eur.                                            34
European Atomic Energy Community - Euratom                 35
European Defense Community - EDC                           36
European Launcher Development Organization - ELDO          37
European Recovery Program - ERP; E.R.P.                    38
European Southern Observatory - E.S.O.                     39
European Space Research Organization - ESPO                40
Europium - Eu                                              41
Eusebius - Eus.                                            42
Eustace - Eu.; Eust.                                       43
eutectic - eutec                                           44
evacuate - evac.                                           45
evacuation - evac.                                         46
evacuation unit - EU                                       47
evaluate - eval                                            48
evaluation - eval                                          49
Evangelical - Evan.                                        50
evangelical - evang.                                       51
Evangelical Lutheran - E Luth                              52
Evangelical Reformed - ER                                  53
Evangelical United Brethren - EUB                          54
Evangelist - Evan.                                         55
evangelist - evang.                                        56
```

```
evaporate - evap.                                        1
evaporated - evapd.                                      2
evaporation - evap.                                      3
Evelyn - Evel.                                           4
evening - eve.; P.M.; p.m.                               5
Everett - Ev.                                            6
every hour - o.h.; q.h.                                  7
every morning - o.m.                                     8
every night - o.n.                                       9
every other day - e.o.d.                                10
every second hour - q.2h.                               11
every third hour - q.3h.                                12
every three hours (medical) - q.3h                      13
everywhere (L, passim) - pass.                          14
evident - evid.                                         15
evolution - evol                                        16
ex - x                                                  17
ex coupon - ex cp.; x-cp.                               18
ex dividend - ex div.; x-div.                           19
ex interest - ex int.; x-int.                           20
ex officio (by authority of the office) - ex off.       21
ex rights - ex rts.; X-rts.                             22
exactness - e                                           23
exaggerate - exag                                       24
examination - ex.                                       25
examination(s) - exam(s)                                26
examine - exam.                                         27
examined - ex.; exam.                                   28
examinee - exam.                                        29
examiner - exmr.                                        30
example - ex.                                           31
examples - exx.                                         32
excavate - exc.                                         33
excavated - excav.                                      34
excellence - exc.                                       35
Excellency - Exc.                                       36
Excellent - E                                           37
excellent - exc.; xlnt                                  38
excellent (grading) - A                                 39
Excelsior - Ex                                          40
except - ex.; exc.; xcpt                                41
except otherwise herein provided - eohp                 42
excepted - exc.                                         43
exception - ex.; exc.                                   44
exceptions noted - en                                   45
excess profits tax - EPT                                46
exchange - ex.; exch.; X; xch                           47
exchange bill of lading - Ex B/L                        48
exchangeable - exch.                                    49
exchanged - exch.                                       50
Exchequer - Ex; Excheq                                  51
exchequer - exch.                                       52
excite - exc.                                           53
exciter - exc                                           54
exclamation - exclam.                                   55
exclamatory - exclam.                                   56
```

```
exclude - excl.                                             1
excluding - excl.                                           2
exclusive - excl.                                           3
excursion - ex.; exc.                                       4
excuse - exc.                                               5
excused from duty - efd                                     6
execute input/output - XIO                                  7
executed - ex.                                              8
executive - ex.; exec.                                      9
executive clerk - exec. clk.                               10
Executive Committee - Exec. Com.                           11
executive document - Ex. Doc.                              12
executive management responsibility - EMR                  13
executive order - EO                                       14
executor - exec.; exor.; exr.                              15
executrix - exrx.                                          16
exempli gratia (for example) - e.g.                        17
exercise - exer                                            18
Exeter - Ex                                                19
exhaust - exh.; xhst                                       20
exhaust duct section - E                                   21
exhibit - exhib.                                           22
exhibition - exhbn.                                        23
exhibits - xbts                                            24
existence doubtful - ED                                    25
existing - exist.                                          26
exit light outlet - X                                      27
Exodus - Ex.                                               28
exotic - exot                                              29
Expanded Direct Distance Dialing - EDDD                    30
expanded metal - em                                        31
expansion - exp.; expn.                                    32
expansion bolt - exp bt                                    33
expansion joint - exp jt                                   34
expedite - exped; xpd                                      35
expedition - expdn.; exped.                                36
expenditure - expnd                                        37
expense - exp.                                             38
expenses - exp.; exs.                                      39
experiment - exper.                                        40
experimental - exper.; X                                   41
experimental data-handling equipment - EDHE                42
experimental memory-address register - EMAR                43
Experimentale - Exper.                                     44
expiration - exp.; expn.; expr.                            45
expire - exp; expr                                         46
expired - exp; exprd                                       47
explain - expl.                                            48
explained - expl.                                          49
explanatory - expl.                                        50
exploration - explor                                       51
explosive(s) - explos.                                     52
explosive - xpl                                            53
exponent - exp                                             54
export - exp.                                              55
exportation - exp.                                         56
```

exporter - exp. 1
exposé - expo 2
Exposed Construction Painted - Exp.Cons./Pt. 3
exposition - expn.; expo 4
express - exp.; X 5
express paid - xp 6
Expressway - Xway; Xwy. 7
expurgate - exp.; expur 8
expurgated - exp.; expur 9
extemporaneous - extemp 10
extend - ext. 11
extended area service - EAS 12
extended coverage - ec 13
extended play - EP 14
extension - ext; exten; EXTSN 15
Extension Media Center - EMC 16
exterior - ext. 17
external - ext; extern 18
external device - ED; EXD 19
external environment - EE 20
external-device control word - EDCW 21
externally - extern 22
externally specified indexing - ESI 23
extinct - ext. 24
extinguisher - extg. 25
extinguisher, fire - F ext 26
extra - ext.; x 27
extra duty - e.d. 28
extra fancy - ex. fcy. 29
extra fine - ef; xf 30
extra heavy - e.h.; XH; x hvy 31
extra high voltage - ehv 32
extra large - xl 33
extra long - xl 34
extra strength - e.s. 35
extra strong - xs 36
extracellular fluid - E.C.F. 37
extract - ext. 38
extract - extr. 39
extraction - extn. 40
extradition - extrad 41
Extrados - Ex 42
extra-high tension - eht 43
extra-high voltage - ehv 44
extra-low voltage - elv 45
extraordinary - extr. 46
Extraordinary action of classification (Ger, Ausserordent- 47
    liche Befriedigungs Aktion) - ACTION A-B 48
extrasensory perception - ESP 49
Extra-Vehicular Activity (Moonwalk) - EVA 50
extreme - extrm 51
extreme high water - ehw 52
extreme high-frequency - ehf 53
extreme low water - elw 54
extreme pressure - EP 55
Extreme Right French Political Organization (Comité Secret 56

```
d'Action Revolutionnaire) - C.S.A.R.                          1
extreme temperatures - T_eT_e                                 2
extremely high frequency - EHF                                3
extremity - extrem.                                           4
extrude - extr.                                               5
extruded - ext'd; extr.                                       6
extrusion - extr.                                             7
eye - E                                                       8
eye and ear - e&e; ee                                         9
eye, ear, nose, and throat - E.E.N.T.                        10
Ezekiel - Ez.; Ezek.                                         11
Ezra - Ez.; Ezr.                                             12
fabric - fab                                                 13
fabricate - fab                                              14
fabrication - fabr                                           15
facade - fac                                                 16
Face Brick - Fa.Br.                                          17
face plate - F.Pl.                                           18
face to face - F to F                                        19
facetious - facet.                                           20
facetiously - facet.                                         21
facial - fac                                                 22
facility - fac; facil                                        23
facing - fcg                                                 24
facing tile - F.T.                                           25
facsimile - fac.; facsim.; fax                               26
facsimiles - facs.                                           27
factor - fac.                                                28
factor of safety - fs                                        29
factory - fac.; fcty.                                        30
factory finish - fact. fin.                                  31
factory finished - ff                                        32
facts - fax                                                  33
factum similis (facsimile, an exact copy) - fac.             34
faculty - fac                                                35
Fahrenheit - F.                                              36
Fahrenheit (thermometer) - Fahr.                             37
failure (grading) - E                                        38
failure analysis report - FAR                                39
failure cause data report - FCDR                             40
failure, unsatisfactory - FUR                                41
faint - ft.                                                  42
fair (grading) - C                                           43
fair average quality - f.a.q.                                44
Fair Employment Practices Committee - FEPC                   45
Fair Labor Standards Act - FLSA                              46
Fairchild - F                                                47
faithfully - ffly                                            48
Falkland Islands - F.I.; Falk.Is.                            49
familiar - fam.                                              50
family - fam.                                                51
fan (outlet) - F                                             52
fanatic - fan.                                               53
fancy - fcy                                                  54
fantasia - fan.                                              55
fantasy - fan.                                                56
```

farad(s) - F,f   1
Faraday - F   2
farm - fm   3
Farm Credit Administration - FCA   4
farmer - fm   5
Farmers Home Administration - FHA   6
farthing - f.   7
farthing (L, quandrans) - qr.   8
farthings (L, quadrantes) - qrs.   9
fascicle - fasc.   10
fascicule - fasc.   11
fasciculus (a bundle) - fasc.   12
fast - f   13
fast (horse racing, condition of track) - fst.   14
fast burst reactor - FBR   15
fastener - fastnr   16
fat - F   17
fatal dose (drugs) - D.D.   18
father - f   19
Father - Fr.   20
father (L, pater) - P.; p.   21
Father (F, Pere) - P.   22
Fathers of the Sacred Hearts of Jesus and Mary (Picpus   23
    Fathers) - S.S.C.C.   24
fathom - f.; fath.; fm.   25
fathom(s) - fth.; fthm.   26
fathometer - fm   27
fathoms - fms.   28
favor - fav   29
favorable - fav   30
favorite - fav   31
feast - F.   32
feather - feath   33
February - F.; Feb.   34
fecit - fec.   35
Federal - Fed   36
Federal Aviation Agency - FAA   37
Federal Bureau of Investigation - FBI   38
Federal Communications Commission - FCC   39
Federal Deposit Insurance Corporation - FDIC   40
Federal Excise Tax - FET   41
Federal Home Loan Bank Board - FHLBB   42
Federal Housing Administration - FHA   43
Federal Income Tax - FIT   44
Federal Insurance Contributions Act - FICA   45
Federal Maritime Board - FMB   46
Federal Maritime Commission - FMC   47
Federal Mediation and Conciliation Service - FMCS   48
Federal National Mortgage Association - FNMA   49
Federal Power Commission - FPC   50
Federal Radio Commission - FRC   51
Federal Register - F.R.   52
Federal Reserve Bank - FRB; Fed.Res.Bk.   53
Federal Reserve Board - Fed.Res.Bd.   54
Federal Reserve System - FRS   55
Federal Security Agency - FSA   56

Federal Specifications - FS 1
Federal Supplement - F.Supp. 2
Federal Trade Commission - FTC 3
Federal Water Pollution Control Administration - FWPCA 4
Federally Employed Women - FEW 5
federated - fed. 6
Federation - Fed. 7
federation - fed. 8
feed water - FW 9
feedback - F 10
feedback mechanism - FM 11
feedback shift register - FSR 12
feeder - fdr 13
feet - ft. 14
feet board measure- fbm; f.b.m.; ft.b.m. 15
feet per hour - ft/hr 16
feet per minute - f.p.m. 17
feet per second - f.p.s.; f.s. 18
feet surface measure - FTSM 19
Felicita - Fel 20
Felix - Fel 21
Fellow - F. 22
fellow (L, socius or sodalis) - S. 23
Fellow American Institute of Architects - F.A.I.A. 24
Fellow of the American Academy (of Arts and Sciences) 25
 (L, Academiae Americanae Socius) - A.A.S. 26
Fellow of the American College of Physicians - F.A.C.P. 27
Fellow of the American College of Surgeons - F.A.C.S. 28
Fellow of the American Geographical Society - F.A.G.S. 29
Fellow of the American Institute of Architects - F.A.I.A. 30
Fellow of the American Philosophical Society (L, Societatis 31
 Philosophiae Americanae Socius) - S.P.A.S. 32
Fellow of the British Academy - F.B.A. 33
Fellow of the Chartered Institute of Secretaries - F.C.I.S. 34
Fellow of the Chemical Society - F.C.S. 35
Fellow of the Historical Society (L, Historiae Societatis 36
 Socius) - H.S.S. 37
Fellow of the Historical Society (L, Societatis Historiae 38
 Socius) - S.H.S. 39
Fellow of the Institute of Chartered Accountants - F.C.A. 40
Fellow of the Institute of Chemistry - F.I.C. 41
Fellow of the Royal Geographical Society - F.R.G.S. 42
Fellow of the Royal Society (L, Fraternitatis Regiae Socius) 43
 F.R.S. 44
Fellow of the Royal Society (L, Regiae Societatis Sodalis) - 45
 R.S.S. 46
Fellow of the Royal Society (L, Societatis Regiae Socius or 47
 Sodalis) - S.R.S. 48
Fellow of the Royal Society of Antiquaries (L, Antiquariorum 49
 Regiae Societatis Socius) - A.R.S.S. 50
Fellow of the Society of Antiquaries (L, Societatis 51
 Antiquariorum Socius) - S.A.S. 52
Fellow of the Society of Actuaries - F.S.A. 53
Fellow of the Society of Antiquaries - F.S.A. 54
Fellow Royal Institute of British Architects - F.R.I.B.A. 55
Fellowship of Reconciliation - FOR 56

```
female - F.; f.; fem.                               1
feminine - f.; fem.                                 2
Feminine Deodorant Spray - FDS                      3
fencing - fenc.                                     4
Ferdinand - Fd.; Ferd.                              5
fermentology - fermentol                            6
Fernwood, Columbia & Gulf (RR) - FC&G               7
fertility - fert                                    8
fertilization - fert                                9
fertilizer - fert                                  10
festival(s) - fes                                  11
festival - fest                                    12
festive - fest                                     13
festivities - fest                                 14
festivity - fest                                   15
feudal - feud.                                     16
feudalism - feud.                                  17
fever of unknown origin - f.u.o.                   18
fever, undetermined origin - FUO                   19
fiat (let it be made) - f.                         20
fiber - fbr                                        21
Fiber Acoustic Tile - F.Ac.T                       22
fiber optic photo transfer - FOPT                  23
fibula - fib.                                      24
fiction - fic.; fict.                              25
fictitious - fict.                                 26
Fidei Defensor - F.D.                              27
fidelity - fid.                                    28
fiduciary - fid                                    29
field - F.; fd.; fld.                              30
field engineers - FE                               31
field goals (basketball) - FG                      32
field goals (football) - FG                        33
field intensity - FI                               34
Field Officer - F.O.                               35
field service representative - FSR                 36
field-effect transistor - FET                      37
fielder's choice (baseball) - FC                   38
fifteen - XV                                        39
fifty - L                                          40
fifty thousand - L                                 41
fighter - ftr                                      42
figurative - fig.                                  43
figuratively - fig.                                44
figure(s) - fig.                                   45
figure three (figure skating) - 3                  46
figures - figs.                                    47
Fiji Islands - FI                                  48
filament - f; fil.                                 49
file cabinet - fc                                  50
filial generation - F                              51
filius (son) - F.                                  52
fillet - fil.                                      53
filling - fill.                                    54
fillister - fil.                                    55
fillister head - fil.h.                            56
```

94

```
first lieutenant - 1st Lt.                                        1
first rate - A-1                                                  2
first sergeant - 1st Sgt.                                         3
First US Army - FUSA                                              4
Firth of Forth - F of F                                           5
fiscal year - FY                                                  6
Fissured Mineral Acoustical Board - F.M.Ac.B.                     7
Fissured Mineral Acoustical Tile  - F.M.Ac.T.                     8
fitter - ftr.                                                     9
fitting - ftg.                                                   10
five - V                                                         11
five hundred - D_                                                12
five thousand - V̄                                               13
five-three-two-one defense (football) - 5-3-2-1                  14
fixed - F; fxd                                                   15
fixed focus - f.f.                                               16
fixed interval - FI                                              17
fixed price - fp                                                 18
fixture - fix.                                                   19
Fjord - Fd                                                       20
flag - FLG                                                       21
flagstone - flgstn                                               22
flame proof - FP                                                 23
flameproof - fl. prf.                                            24
flange - flg.                                                    25
flanged - flgd.                                                  26
flash - fl                                                       27
flashing - flash .                                               28
flashpoint - fl. pt.                                             29
flat - f                                                         30
flat finish - F                                                  31
flat grain - F G                                                 32
flat head - F H                                                  33
flat headed screw - FHS                                          34
flat headed wood screw - FHWS                                    35
flathead - fh; fl.hd.                                            36
flat-headed wood screw - fhws                                    37
flavor - flav                                                    38
fleet - flt                                                      39
fleet post office - FPO                                          40
Flemish - Fl.; Flem.                                             41
flexible - flex.; flx.                                           42
flight - flt.                                                    43
flight commander - Flt. Cmdr.                                    44
Flight Control System - F/CS                                     45
flight deck - fd                                                 46
flight level - fl                                                47
Flight Lieutenant - Flt. Lt.                                     48
flight plan - flt. pln.                                          49
flight programmer - flt/pg                                       50
flip-flop - F-F                                                  51
float - flt.                                                     52
floater - fltr.                                                  53
floating - fltg.                                                 54
floating input-floating output - FIFO                            55
floating point means and variance - FMEVA                        56
```

```
floating point root isolation - FRTISO                    1
floating sign - FS                                         2
floating-point binary - FLBIN                              3
floating-point decimal - FLDEC                             4
floor - fl.; flr.                                          5
floor cabinet - FL CAB                                     6
floor drain - F.D.                                         7
flooring - flg.                                            8
Florence - Flo.                                            9
flores (flowers) - fl.                                    10
floriculture - flor                                       11
Florida - Fla.                                            12
Florida East Coast (RR) - FEC                             13
florin - F; fl.                                           14
Florists' Transworld Delivery - FTD                       15
floruit (flourished) - fl.                                16
flotation - flot                                          17
flotilla - flot                                           18
flotsam - flot                                            19
flour - fl.                                               20
flourished (L, floruit) - fl.; flor.                      21
flow indicator - FI                                       22
flow meter - fl/mtr                                       23
flow rate - fl/rt                                         24
flower - fl.                                              25
flowers - flrs.                                           26
fluctuate - fluc                                          27
fluctuating - fluc                                        28
fluctuation - fluc                                        29
fluid (ounce) - f.                                        30
fluid (L, fluidus) - fl.                                  31
fluid ounce(s) - fl. oz.                                  32
fluorescence - fluor.                                     33
fluorescent - fluor.; fluores.                            34
fluorescent indicator analysis - FIA; F.I.A.              35
fluoridation - fluor                                      36
fluoride - fluor                                          37
fluorine - F; Fl; fluor                                   38
fluoroscope - fluor                                       39
flush - fl                                                40
flush metal saddle - FMS                                  41
flush metal threshold - FMT                               42
flush threshold - FT                                      43
Flushing - Fls                                            44
flute - fl.                                               45
focal - foc                                               46
focal distance - F.D.                                     47
focal distance - fd                                       48
focus - foc                                               49
focusing - foc                                            50
fodder - fod                                              51
fog - f                                                   52
fog bell - fb                                             53
folded - fold.                                            54
folio - f.; f°; fo.; fol.                                 55
folio recto (right-handed page) - f.r.                    56
```

```
folio verso (on the back of the leaf) - f.v.            1
folios - ff.                                            2
follow copy - f.c.                                      3
follow up - fu.; f.up                                   4
followed - fol.                                         5
following - f.; ff.; fol.; foll.                        6
the following (L, sequens, sequentes, sequentia) - seq. 7
the following (one) - sq.                               8
the following (ones) (L, sequentia) - seqq.; sq.; sqq.  9
following items not available - fina                    10
following pages - ff.                                   11
Food and Agricultural Organization (U.N.) - FAO         12
Food and Drug Administration - FDA                      13
foolscap - fcap; fcp.                                   14
foot - ft.                                              15
foot, feet (symbol) - '                                 16
foot bath - FB                                          17
foot per second - fps                                   18
foot pound - ft. lb.                                    19
foot second - fs                                        20
footbridge - ftbrg                                      21
foot-candle - ft.-c.                                    22
footing - ftg                                           23
foot-lambert - ft.-l.                                   24
footnote - fn                                           25
footnote(s) - ftnt.                                     26
foot-pound - F.P.; f.p.                                 27
foot-pound(s) - ft.-lb.                                 28
foot-pound-second system - f.p.s. system                29
for (L, pro) - p.                                       30
for example (L, exempli gratia) - e.g.                  31
for example (L, verbi gratia) - v.g.                    32
for instance - fi                                       33
for (or on) our part (L, nobis) - nob.                  34
for the beginning (L, pro tempore) - pro tem.           35
for the time (L, pro tempore) - pro tem.                36
force - f                                               37
forced landing - fd ldg                                 38
forceout (baseball) - XX                                39
Forces Françaises de l'Intérieur (WWII) - FFI           40
Fordham University - F.U.                                41
fore and aft - f.&a.                                    42
forecast - fcst                                         43
forecastle - f; fcsle                                   44
forehatch - fh                                          45
foreign - fgn; for.                                     46
Foreign Agricultural Service - FAS                      47
foreign duty pay - fdp                                  48
foreign exchange - F.X.; f.x.                           49
foreign minister - For. Min.                            50
Foreign Office - F.O.                                   51
foreigner - for.                                        52
foreman - fman; formn.                                  53
forenoon - A.M.; a.m.                                   54
forensic - for.                                         55
foresight - fs                                          56
```

```
forest - for                                                    1
Forest Service - FS                                             2
forester - for.                                                 3
forestry - for.                                                 4
forever yours - fey                                             5
forewoman - forwn                                               6
forfeit - forf.                                                 7
forfeiture - forf.                                              8
forge - forg.                                                   9
forged - forg.                                                 10
forgery - forg.                                                11
forging - forg.                                                12
Forgotten Boys of Iceland - FBI                                13
fork - fk                                                      14
form - fm                                                      15
form die - fmdi                                                16
formaldehyde - formal.                                         17
formation - fmn.; formn.; frmn.                                18
formed - f.                                                    19
formed from - f.                                               20
formed of - f.                                                 21
former - fmr; frmr                                             22
formerly - fmrly                                               23
formerly known as - fmly.k.a.                                  24
Formosa - For.                                                 25
formula translator - FORTRAN                                   26
Fornax (the Furnace) - For                                     27
fort - ft.                                                     28
Fort Worth & Denver City (RR) - FW&DC                          29
forte (strong) - f.                                            30
fortification - fort.; ft.                                     31
fortified - fort.                                              32
fortissimo (very loud) - ff; ff.                               33
forty - XL                                                     34
forty-eightmo - 48mo; 48º                                      35
forward - fwd.                                                 36
Forward (figure skating direction) - F                         37
forward propagation ionospheric scatter - FPIS                 38
forwarded - fwdd.                                              39
fossil - fos                                                   40
found - fnd.                                                   41
foundation - fdn.; fnd.; fndn.                                 42
founded - fndd.                                                43
founder - fndr.                                                44
founding - fndg.                                               45
foundry - fdry.                                                46
fountain - fount                                               47
four - IV                                                      48
four hundred - CD                                              49
four hundred and forty yard race (quarter of a mile) - 440     50
four thousand - MV̄                                             51
four times a day (L, quater (in) die) - q.d.; q.i.d.           52
fourteen - XIV                                                 53
fourteen-one continuous (billiards) - 14.1                     54
fourteen two balkline (billiards) - 14.2                       55
four-wheel drive - fwd                                         56
```

```
four-year-old horse - 4YO                                          1
fraction of celestial dome covered by cloud (in eighths) - N       2
fractional - frl.                                                  3
fractional horsepower - fhp                                        4
fragile - frag                                                     5
fragment(s) - fr.                                                  6
fragment - frag.                                                   7
frame - fr.                                                        8
framed - fd.                                                       9
frames per second - fps                                           10
framework - frwk                                                  11
framing - frg.; frm.                                              12
franc - f; f.; fr.                                                13
France - Fr.                                                      14
Franciscan - Fran                                                 15
Franciscan Fathers - O.F.M.                                       16
Franciscan Fathers of the Atonement - S.A.                        17
Franciscan Tertiaries - T.O.S.F.                                  18
Franconian - Frank.                                               19
francs - frs.                                                     20
Francs-Tireurs et Partisans (WWII) - FTP                          21
Frank - Fk.                                                       22
Frankfort & Cincinnati (RR) - F&C                                 23
Frankfurter Allgemeine Zeitung (West German newspaper) - FAZ      24
Frankish - Frank.                                                 25
Franklin - Fkn.                                                   26
Franklin Delano Roosevelt - FDR                                   27
frater - Fr.                                                      28
Fraternal Order of Eagles - F.O.E.                                29
Fraternitatis Regiae Socius (Fellow of the Royal Society)         30
    F.R.S.                                                        31
fraternity - Frat.; frat.                                         32
fraudulent - fraud                                                33
Frederic - Fred                                                   34
Frederick - Fred                                                  35
free alongside ship - F.A.S.; f.a.s.                              36
Free and Accepted Masons - F.A.M.                                 37
free and clear - f/c                                              38
free at quay - faq                                                39
free delivery - f.d.                                              40
Free Democratic Party - FDP                                       41
free from alongside (ship) - F.F.A.; f.f.a.                       42
free from infection - f.f.i.                                      43
free in truck - f.i.t.                                            44
free in wagon - f.i.w.                                            45
Free Methodist - FMeth.                                           46
free of all average - f.a.a.                                      47
free of capture and seizure - fc&s                                48
free of charge - F.O.C.; f.o.c.                                   49
free of damage - F.O.D.; f.o.d.                                   50
free of general average - f.g.a.                                  51
free on board - F.O.B.; f.o.b.                                    52
free on quay - f.o.q.                                             53
free on rail - f.o.r.                                             54
free on rails - F.O.R.; f.o.r.                                    55
free on road - f.o.r.                                             56
```

```
free on steamer - f.o.s.                                          1
free on truck - f.o.t.                                            2
free piston vessel - FPV                                          3
Free throws (basketball) - F; FT                                  4
freeboard - fbd                                                   5
freehold - fhld                                                   6
Freeway - Frwy                                                    7
freezing point - f.p.                                             8
freight - fgt.; frt.                                              9
freight agent - F.A.                                             10
freight and demurrage - f&d                                      11
freight bill - f.b.                                              12
freight, insurance, carriage - f.i.c.                            13
freight prepaid - frt. ppd.                                      14
freight release - F/R; f/r                                       15
French - F.; Fr.                                                 16
French American - Fr.Am.                                         17
French Canadian - Fr. Can.                                       18
French francs - FF                                               19
French Guiana - Fr. Gu.                                          20
French North Africa (Fr, Afrique Francaise du Nord) - AFN        21
French Somaliland - Fr. Som.                                     22
frequency - F; f; fqcy; freq.                                    23
frequency control and analysis - FC&A                            24
frequency division multiplexing - fdm                            25
frequency interference control - fic                             26
frequency modulation - FM; F-M; F.-M.; F.M.                      27
frequency modulation with feedback - FMFB                        28
frequency of every allowable term - FEAT                         29
frequency time control - FTC                                     30
frequency-division multiply - fdm                                31
frequency-measuring equipment - FME                              32
frequency-shift keying - FSK                                     33
frequent - fr.; freq.                                            34
frequentative - freq.                                            35
frequently - freq.                                               36
fresh air duct section - FA                                      37
fresh air intake - FAI                                           38
fresh water - f.w.                                               39
freshman - fresh.; frosh.                                        40
freshmen - fresh.; frosh.                                        41
Friar - Fr.                                                      42
Friars Minor Conventual or Black Franciscans - O.F.M.Conv.       43
friction - fric                                                  44
friction horsepower - FHP; F.H.P.                                45
frictional - fric                                                46
Friday - F.; Fr.; Fri.                                           47
friend - frd                                                     48
friendly - frd                                                   49
Friends - Fr                                                     50
Friends of the Earth - FOE                                       51
Frisian - Fris.                                                  52
frog - fg                                                        53
from - fm.; fr.                                                  54
from the beginning (L, ab initio) - ab init.; ab initio;         55
    ab ovo                                                       56
```

```
galley - gal.                                        1
Gallium - Ga                                         2
gallon(s) - gal.                                     3
gallon (L, congius) - cong.                          4
gallon capacity - gal cap                            5
gallons - gall.; gals.                               6
gallons per acre per day - GPAD; gpad                7
gallons per day - GPD; gpd                           8
gallons per hour - GPH; gph                          9
gallons per minute - GPM; gpm                       10
gallons per second - GPS; gps                       11
Gallo-Romance - Gallo-Rom.                          12
galvanic - galv.                                    13
galvanism - galv.                                   14
galvanized - galv.                                  15
galvanized steel - galv S; gs                       16
galvannealed - galvnd                               17
galvanometer - galvo                                18
Galveston - Galv                                    19
Galway - Galw                                       20
Gambia - Gam.                                       21
game theory - GT                                    22
games behind (baseball) - GB                        23
games played - G                                    24
games room - GR                                     25
games won (tennis) - G                              26
gamma globulin - gg                                 27
gamut - gam.                                        28
ganglia - gang.                                     29
ganglion - gang.                                    30
gap filler - gf                                     31
garage - gar.                                       32
garbage - garb.                                     33
garbage in, garbage out - gigo                      34
garden - gard; gdn.                                 35
gardener - gard                                     36
gardening - gard                                    37
gardens - gdns.                                     38
garrison - gar.                                     39
gas constant - R                                    40
gas range - G                                       41
gas turbine ship - GTS                              42
gasket - gskt                                       43
Gaston - Gast                                       44
gastric - gast                                      45
gastro-intestinal - G.I.                            46
gastronomy - gastro                                 47
gate - gt                                           48
gate driver - GD                                    49
gate valve - GT                                     50
gauge - g.; ga.                                     51
gauge atmosphere - g.a.                             52
Gaulish - Gaul.                                      53
gauss-oersteds - g.o.                               54
Gay Liberation League - GLL                         55
Gay-Pay-Do - G.P.U.                                 56
```

```
Gazette - Gaz.                                              1
gazette - gaz.                                             2
gazetteer - gaz.                                           3
Gazzetta - Gazz.                                           4
gear - gr                                                  5
gelatine - gel                                             6
gelatinous - gel                                           7
Gelding - g.                                               8
Gemeineschaft und Geselischaft - G&G                       9
Gemini (the Twins) - Gem                                  10
gender - g.; gen.                                         11
genealogical - geneal.                                    12
genealogy - gen.; geneal.                                 13
genera - gen                                              14
General - Gen.; Genl.                                     15
general - gen.                                            16
General Accounting Office - GAO                           17
General Agent - G.A.                                      18
General Agreement on Tariffs and Trades - GATT            19
General Assembly - G.A.                                   20
General Audience (all ages admitted)(movie code) - G      21
general average - G/A; g.a.; gen av                       22
general contract - gen cont                               23
general court-martial - G.C.M.; g.c.m.                    24
General Education Development Examination - GED            25
General Educational Development Test - GED                26
General Electric - GE                                     27
General Electric Company - G.E.                           28
General Headquarters - GHQ                                29
General Hospital - Gen. Hosp.                             30
general intelligence - g                                  31
general issue - GI                                        32
general manager - G.M.                                    33
general, medical, and surgical - G.M.&S.                  34
General Motors - GM                                       35
General Motors Corporation - GMC                          36
general operational requirement - GOR                     37
general order - G.O.                                      38
General Post Office - G.P.O.                              39
General Practitioner - G.P.                               40
general public - gen pub                                  41
general quarters - GQ                                     42
General Secretary - G.S.                                  43
General Services Administration - GSA                     44
General Staff - G.S.                                      45
general store - GS                                        46
generally - gen.; genl.                                   47
general-purpose computer - GPC                            48
general-purpose digital computer - GPDC                   49
generation - gen.                                         50
generation of filial offspring - F                        51
generator - gen                                           52
generic - gen.                                            53
Genesis - Gn                                              54
genetic(s) - gen                                          55
geneticist - genet                                        56
```

```
genetics - genet                                                    1
Geneva - Gen.                                                       2
genital - gen                                                       3
genitive - g.; gen.; genit.                                         4
Genoa - Gen                                                         5
gentian - gen                                                       6
gentleman - Gent.; gent.                                            7
gentlemen - Gent.; gent.                                            8
Gentlemen (Fr, Messieurs) - Messrs.; MM.                            9
genus - gen.                                                       10
geodesic - geod                                                    11
geodesist - geod                                                   12
geodesy - geod                                                     13
geodetic - geod                                                    14
geodynamic(s) - geod.                                              15
Geoffrey - Geof.                                                   16
geographer - geog.                                                 17
geographic - geog.                                                 18
geographical - geog.                                               19
Geographical - Geogr.                                              20
geography - geog.                                                  21
geologic - geol.                                                   22
geological - geol.                                                 23
Geological Survey - Geol Surv; G.S.                                24
Geologische - Geol.                                                25
geologist - geol.                                                  26
geology - geol.                                                    27
geometry - geom                                                    28
geophysics - geoph                                                 29
geopolitical - geopol                                              30
geopolitics - geopol                                               31
George - Geo.                                                      32
George Bernard Shaw - GBS                                          33
George Washington University - G.W.U.                              34
Georgia - Ga.                                                      35
Georgia (RR) - GA                                                  36
Georgia & Florida (RR) - G&F                                       37
Georgia, Ashburn, Sylvester & Camilla (RR) - GAS&C                 38
Georgia Northern (Ga) (RR) - GN                                    39
Georgian - Geor                                                    40
Georgius Rex - G.R.                                                41
geriatrics - geriat.                                               42
German - G.                                                        43
German Democratic Republic (East Germany) - GDR                    44
German Documents - G.D.                                            45
German High Command (Oberkommando der Wehrmacht) - O.K.W.          46
German News Bureau (Deutsches Nachrichten Buro) - D.N.B.           47
German Workers' Party (Deutsche Arbeiter Partei) - D.A.P.          48
Germanic - Gmc.                                                    49
Germanium - Ge                                                     50
Germany - Ger.                                                     51
Gertrude - Gert                                                    52
gerund - ger.                                                      53
gerundive - ger.                                                   54
Gesellschaft - Gesellsch.                                          55
Get Oil Out (of Santa Barbara) - GOO                               56
```

```
Ghana - Gh                                                        1
Gibraltar - Gib.                                                  2
giga - G                                                          3
giga electron volt - g.e.v.                                       4
gigacycle(s) - gc                                                 5
gigacycles per second - gc./s.                                    6
gilbert - g                                                       7
Gilbert - Gil; Gilb.                                              8
gill(s) - gi.; gl.                                                9
gilt - glt.                                                      10
gilt bevelled edge - gbe                                         11
gilt edge(s) - g.e.                                              12
gilt top edge - g.t.e.                                           13
girder - gir.                                                    14
Girl Scouts of America - GSA                                     15
Girls Against Midi Skirts - G.A.M.S.                             16
give (L, da) - d.                                                17
give of such a dose - d.t.d.                                     18
give the following directions - S. or Sig.                       19
glacial - glac                                                   20
gladiolas - glads                                                21
Glasgow - Glas                                                   22
glass - gl.                                                      23
Glass Fiber Board - Gl.F.Bd.                                     24
Glass Mosaics - Gl.Mos.                                          25
glaze - gl.                                                      26
glazed - gl.                                                     27
glider - gli.                                                    28
Global Atmospheric Research Program - GARP                       29
Global Observational System - GOS                                30
Global Surveillance Station - GSS                                31
Global Telecommunications System - GTS                           32
globule - glob                                                   33
glockenspiel - glock                                             34
Gloria Patri - G.P.                                              35
glory - gl.                                                      36
gloss - gl.                                                      37
glossary - gloss.                                                38
Gloucestershire - Glos.                                          39
glucinum - Gl                                                    40
glycerine - gly                                                  41
go ahead - ga                                                    42
goalkeeper - G                                                   43
goals against (in ice hockey standing) - A                       44
goals for (in ice hockey standing) - F                           45
goals scored - G                                                 46
God (L, Deus) - D.                                               47
God willing (L, Deo volente) - D.V.                              48
going back to - g.                                               49
Gold - Au                                                        50
gold - g                                                         51
gold bonds - g.b.; gd. bds.                                      52
Golf Association of Michigan - GAM                               53
gondola - gond                                                   54
Gone With the Wind - GWTW                                        55
good - g; gd.; XX                                                56
```

105

```
good (grading) - B                                            1
good (horse racing, condition of the track) - gd.            2
good evening - ge                                             3
good morning - gm                                             4
good night - gn                                               5
good old days - g.o.d.                                        6
good till cancelled - GTC; g.t.c.                             7
good till countermanded - g.t.c.                              8
good-bye - gb                                                 9
goods - gds.                                                 10
goofballs - gb's                                             11
Gothic - Goth.                                               12
government - gov.; govt.                                     13
Government and Relief in Occupied Areas - GARIOA             14
government bill of lading - g/bl                             15
Government Issue - GI                                        16
Government Printing Office - GPO                             17
governor - Gov.; gov.                                        18
Governor General - Gov. Gen.                                 19
grade(s) - gr.                                               20
grade - grd.                                                 21
graded allowance (horse racing) - Alw. A-B-C, etc.          22
graded handicap (horse racing) - Hcp. A-B-C, etc.           23
gradient - grad                                              24
grading - grad                                               25
graduate - grad.                                             26
Graduate in Pharmacy - G.P.; Ph.G.                          27
graduated - grad.                                            28
grain(s) - gr.                                               29
a grain (L, granum) - gr.                                   30
grains - grs.                                                31
gram(s) - g; gm                                              32
gram atomic weight - gm-aw                                  33
gram-calories - g.-cal.                                     34
grammar - gr.; gram.                                        35
grammarian - gram.                                          36
grammatical - gram.                                         37
grammatical terms - grt                                     38
grammatically - gram.                                       39
grammes - g.                                                 40
grams - g.; gm.                                              41
grams per denier - g.p.d.                                    42
grams per gallon - g.p.g.                                    43
Granada - Gran                                               44
grand - gr.                                                  45
Grand Army of the Republic - GAR                             46
Grand Marshal - G.M.                                         47
Grand Master - G.M.                                          48
grand master keyed - GMK                                     49
Grand Old Party (Republican) - G.O.P.                        50
Grand Scribe - G.S.                                          51
Grand Trunk (RR) - GT                                        52
granddaughter - grdau.                                       53
grandson (L, Nepos) - grs.; (N.)                             54
granite - G; gran                                            55
Granolithic - Grano.                                         56
```

grass - grs   1
Grass minimum temperatures - T_gT_g 2
grating - grtg.   3
gravitation - grav   4
gravity - grav   5
gravity (specific) - G.   6
gravity pressures - G Forces   7
gray - g; gr.; gy.   8
Graysonia, Nashville & Ashdown (RR) - GN&A   9
grease trap - GT   10
great - g; gt.   11
Great Atlantic & Pacific Tea Company - A&P   12
Great Britain - Brit.; G.B.; Gt.Br.   13
great granddaughter - ggd   14
great gross - gg; g.gr.   15
Great Lakes Express (trucking) - GLX   16
Great Northern (RR) - GN   17
Great Western (RR) - GW   18
Greater Birmingham Alliance to Stop Pollution - GASP, Inc.   19
greatest common divisor - G.C.D.; g.c.d.   20
greatest common factor - G.C.F.; g.c.f.   21
greatest common measure - G.C.M.; g.c.m.   22
Grecian - Gr.   23
Greece - Grc.   24
Greek - Gk.   25
green - g; gn.; grn.   26
Green Bay & Western (RR) - GB&W   27
greenish blue - gB   28
greenish yellow - gY   29
Greenland - Green.; Grnld.   30
Greenwich civil time - G.c.t.   31
Greenwich mean astronomical time - G.m.a.t.   32
Greenwich mean time - G.m.t.   33
Gregory - Greg   34
grille - G; gr.   35
grille, bottom - BG   36
grille, ceiling - CR   37
grille, center - CG   38
grille, top - TG   39
grille, top & bottom - T&BG   40
grind - grd   41
gritty - gty.   42
grocer - groc   43
grocery - groc   44
gross - g; gr.; gro.   45
gross national product - GNP; g.n.p.   46
gross weight - gr. wt.   47
Gross World Product - GWP   48
ground - gd.; gnd.; grd.   49
ground based - g/b   50
ground control - GC   51
ground control approach - GCA   52
ground control intercept - GCI   53
Ground Elapsed Time - G.E.T.   54
ground speed - g.s.   55
ground zero - gz   56

```
grounded into double plays (baseball) - GIDP            1
grounded into double plays (no. of times by a given player) - 2
     Gr. into DP                                        3
ground-elapsed time - g.e.t.                            4
ground-to-air - G/A                                     5
ground-to-ground - G/G                                  6
group - gp.; GRP                                        7
Group on Advanced Leadership - GOAL                     8
grown diffused - GD                                     9
Grus (the Crane) - Gru                                 10
Guadeloupe - Guad.                                     11
guaranteed - gtd.                                      12
guaranteed annual wage - GAW                           13
guaranty - guar.                                       14
guard - gd.                                            15
guard (football) - G                                   16
guard rail - gdr                                       17
guardian - gd                                          18
guards - gds.                                          19
guardsman - gdsm                                       20
Guatemala - Guat.                                      21
Guatemala Airlines - AVIATECA                          22
Guiana - Gui.                                          23
guidance - gdnce; guid                                 24
Guidance and Navigation - G&N                          25
Guide to Catholic Literature - GCL                     26
guided missile - gm                                    27
guilder - gld.                                         28
guinea - g.                                            29
Guinea - Guin.                                         30
guineas - gns.                                         31
guitar - git                                           32
Gulf - G.                                              33
Gulf, Mobile & Ohio (RR) - GM&O                        34
gun - gn                                               35
gunner - Gnr                                           36
gunnery sergeant - Gunnery Sgt.                        37
Gunther - Gth.                                         38
guppies - gups                                         39
guppy - gup                                            40
gutta - gt.                                            41
guttae - gtt.                                          42
gutter - gut.                                          43
Gwendolyn - Gwen                                       44
gymnasium - gym.                                       45
gymnastic(s) - gym.                                    46
gynecological - gynecol.                               47
gynecology - gyn.; gynecol.                            48
Gypsum - Gyp.                                          49
gypsy - gyp                                            50
gyration - gyr.                                        51
gyro - gy                                              52
gyrocompass - gyro                                     53
gyroplane - gyro                                       54
gyroscope - gyro                                       55
Habakkuk - Hab.                                        56
```

```
habeas corpus (have the body - a writ) - hab. corp.    1
habitat - hab.                                         2
habitation - hab.                                      3
Hafnium - HF                                           4
Haggai - Hag.                                          5
hagiology - hagiol                                     6
hairdresser - hairdrsr.                                7
Haiti - Hai.                                           8
half (L, semi) - hf; (s.)                              9
half add - ha                                         10
half adder - ha                                       11
half hard - HH                                        12
half pay - h.p.                                       13
half subtracter - HS                                  14
halfbound - hb                                        15
half-bound - hf. bd.                                  16
half-calf - hf.cf.                                    17
half-cloth - hf. cl.                                  18
half-hard - hfh; hh                                   19
half-morocco - hf. mor.                               20
half-round - H Rd                                     21
halftime - ht                                         22
halftone - ht                                         23
Halifax - Hfx                                         24
halogen - hal; hlg                                    25
halt - H; HLT                                         26
Hamburg - Ham                                         27
Hamlet - Ham                                          28
hamlet - hmlt                                         29
Hampton & Branchville (RR) - H&B                      30
hand - hd.                                            31
hand control - hc                                     32
handbook - h/b; hdbk.                                 33
handful (L, manipulus) - M.                           34
handhole - hh                                         35
handicap - hcap.; hcp.                                36
handicap (horse racing) - Hcp.                        37
handicap stake (horse racing) - Hcp.S.                38
handily (horse racing) - h.                           39
handkerchief - hdkf.                                  40
handle - hdl.                                         41
handling - hdlg.                                      42
handrail - hdr; H.R.                                  43
handset - HS                                          44
hangar - hgr                                          45
hangars - hgs                                         46
hanger - hgr                                          47
hangers - hgs                                         48
hanging closet - H Cl                                 49
Hanover - Han.                                        50
harbor - h.; har.                                     51
hard - h.; hrd.                                       52
hard-drawn - hd                                       53
harden - hdn                                          54
hardness - h.                                         55
hardship - hdsp                                       56
```

```
hardware - H; hdw.; hdwe.                                          1
hardwood - Hdwd                                                    2
harmonic - har.; harm.                                             3
harmony - harm.                                                    4
harness - harn                                                     5
Harold - Hal; Har.                                                 6
harpoon - harp.                                                    7
harpsichord - harp.                                                8
harpsicordist - harp.                                              9
Harriet - Ht.                                                     10
Hartford - Hart                                                   11
Harvard - Harv.                                                   12
Hausa - Hau                                                       13
have the body - a writ (L, habeus corpus) - hab. corp.           14
Hawaii - Haw.                                                    15
Hawaiian - Haw.                                                  16
Hawaiian Airlines - HAL                                          17
hazard - haz                                                     18
hazy - h; hzy                                                    19
he does not prosecute (L, non prosequitur) - non pros.          20
he or she carved or engraved it (L, sculpsit) - sc.             21
he or she died (L, obiit) - ob.                                  22
he or she painted it - pinxit                                    23
he or she speaks (L, loquitur) - loq.                            24
head (L, caput) - (cap.); hd.                                    25
head (horse racing) - hd.                                        26
headless - hdls.                                                 27
headquarters - hdqrs.; H.Q.; h.q.                                28
headwaiter - hw                                                  29
Health Education and Welfare - HEW                               30
heartwood - hrtwd                                                31
heat - ht.                                                       32
heat resistant - h.r.                                            33
heat treat - ht                                                  34
heated - htd                                                     35
heater - H                                                       36
heater room - HR                                                 37
heater, water - WH                                               38
heat-treated - ht                                                39
heavy - hy.                                                      40
heavy (horse racing, condition of the track) - hy.              41
Hebrew - Heb.                                                    42
Hebrides - Hebr                                                  43
hectare - ha.                                                    44
hecto - h                                                        45
hectograph - hg.; hgm.                                           46
hectoliter - hl.                                                 47
hectometer - hm.                                                 48
Hector - Hect.                                                   49
Hefner lumens - Hlm.                                             50
heifer - hef                                                     51
height - h.; ht.; hgt.                                           52
height, above ground, of the base of lowest cloud seen - h      53
height of the waves - Hw                                         54
Heights - Hts                                                    55
heilig(e) - hl.                                                  56
```

```
heir(s) - her.                                                      1
heir apparent - heir app.                                           2
helicopter - hcptr; heli                                            3
heliogram - helio; hg                                               4
heliograph - helio                                                  5
heliostat - helio                                                   6
heliotrope - helio                                                  7
Helium - He                                                         8
Hellenic - Hel.                                                     9
Hellenic People's Army of Liberation - E.L.A.S.                    10
Hellenistic - Hel.                                                 11
helper - hlpr                                                      12
Helvetia - Hel.                                                    13
hemoglobin - Hb; Hg.                                               14
hemorrhage - hem.                                                  15
hemorrhoid - hem.                                                  16
Henry - Hen.                                                       17
henry; henries - H; h                                              18
Henry (unit of inductance) - hy                                    19
Henry Draper - HD                                                  20
herald - her.                                                      21
heraldic - her.                                                    22
heraldry - her.                                                    23
Herbert - Herb                                                     24
Hercules - Her                                                     25
here is buried (L, hic sepultus) - H.S.                            26
here lies (L, hic jacet) - H.J.                                    27
here lies (L, hic situs) - H.S.                                    28
here lies buried (L, hic jacet sepultus) - H.J.S.                  29
here rests in peace (L, his requiescat in pace) - H.R.I.P.         30
Herefordshire - Heref.                                             31
Herman - Hrm.                                                      32
hermetic - herm                                                    33
hermetically - herm                                                34
Heroin - H                                                         35
herpetological - herp.                                             36
herpetologist - herp.                                              37
herpetology - herp.                                                38
Herr (Mister) - Hr                                                 39
heterogeneous - heterog                                            40
hexachord - hex.                                                   41
hexagon - hex.                                                     42
hexagonal head - hex hd                                            43
hic est (this is) - h.e.                                           44
hic requiescat in pace (here rests in peace) - H.R.I.P.            45
hic sepultus (here is buried) - H.S.                               46
hic situs (here lies) - H.S.                                       47
hieroglyphics - hier                                               48
high - H; h; HI                                                    49
high (common stock rating) - A                                     50
high (music) - alt                                                 51
high altitude - ha                                                 52
high carbon - hc                                                   53
high cost of living - H.C.; h.c.; H.C.L.; h.c.l.                   54
high density - h.d.                                                55
high explosive - HE                                                56
```

high fidelity - hi-fi 1
high frequency - HF; H-F; H.-F.; H.F. 2
High German - H.G. 3
high grade (preferred stock rating) - AA 4
high level, single ended - HLSE 5
high point - H.P.; H Pt 6
High Point, Thomasville & Denton (RR) - HPT&D 7
high/positive - hp 8
high pressure - h.p.; h-press 9
high pressure metal vapor - HPMV; H.P.M.V. 10
high run (billiards) - HR 11
High School - H.S. 12
high(er) social class - HSC 13
high speed printer - HSP 14
high speed reader - HSR 15
high(er) status - Hs 16
high tensile bolts - H.T.Bolts 17
high tensile steel - HTS 18
high velocity - h.v. 19
high voltage - HV; hv; h-v 20
high water - h.w. 21
high water mark - h.w.m. 22
high-capacity - hc 23
high-capacity communications - HICAPOM 24
high-carbon steel - hcs 25
high-density data system - HDDS 26
highest (common stock rating) - A+ 27
highest common factor - H.C.F.; h.c.f. 28
highest possible frequency - HPF 29
high-fidelity - hi-fi 30
High-Frequency Current - H.F.C. 31
high-speed - h.s. 32
high-speed data acquisition - HSDA 33
high-speed printer - hsp 34
high-speed reader - hsr 35
high-voltage power supply - HVPS 36
high-water line - hwl 37
high-water mark - hwm 38
Highway - Hwy; Hy 39
hiking - hik 40
Hilary - Hil. 41
Hindu - Hind. 42
Hinduism - Hind. 43
Hindustan - Hind. 44
Hindustani - Hind. 45
His (or Her) Britannic Majesty - H.B.M. 46
His Eminence - H.E. 47
His Excellency - H.E. 48
His (or Her) Grace - H.G. 49
His (or Her) Imperial Highness - H.I.H. 50
His (or Her) Imperial Majesty - H.I.M. 51
His (or Her) Majesty - H.M. 52
His (or Her) Majesty's Service - H.M.S. 53
His (or Her) Majesty's Ship - H.M.S. 54
his (or her) mark - X 55
His (or Her) Royal Highness - H.R.H. 56

His (or Her) Serene Highness - H.S.H.   1
His (or Her) Serene Majesty - H.S.M.   2
Hispanic - Hispan   3
Hispaniola - Hisp   4
Historiae Societatis Socius (Fellow of the Historical   5
    Society) - H.S.S.   6
historical - hist.   7
history - hist.   8
hit and miss - h&m   9
hit batsmen (baseball) - HB   10
hit by a pitcher (baseball) - HP   11
Hitler Youth (Hitler Jugend) - H.J.   12
Hoboken - Hobo   13
hoc anno (in this year) - h.a.   14
hoc est (that is) - h.e.   15
hoc mense (in this month) - h.m.   16
hoc quaere (look for this) - h.q.   17
hoc sensa (in this sense) - H.S.   18
hoc tempore (at this time) - h.t.   19
hoc titulo (in or under this title) - h.t.   20
hogshead - hhd.   21
hoist - ho; hst   22
hold - HLD   23
holiday - hl; hol   24
Holland - Holl   25
hollow - hol   26
hollow metal - H.M.   27
hollow metal door - HMD   28
hollow metal frame - HMF   29
Hollow Metal-Painted - H.M./Pt.   30
holly - hol   31
Holmium - Ho   32
holograph - holo   33
holy (L, pius) - p.   34
Holy Communion - H.C.   35
Holy Cross Canons - O.S.C.   36
Holy Ghost Fathers - C.S.Sp.   37
Holy Virgin (L, Sancta Virgo) - S.V.   38
Home Economics - Home Ec   39
Home Guard - HG   40
Home Owners' Loan Corporation - HOLC   41
Home Rule - H.R.   42
home run (scoring) - ≡   43
home runs (baseball) - HR   44
Home Secretary - H.S.   45
Home Visit - H.V.   46
homeopath - homo   47
homeopathic - homo   48
homeopathy - homo   49
Homer - Hom.   50
Homeric - Hom.   51
homestead - hmstd   52
homonym - hom   53
homosexual - homo   54
homosexuality - homo   55
Honduras - Hond.   56

```
honey - hon                                                    1
Honeywell Corp. - H                                            2
Honolulu - Hono                                                3
Honolulu Stock Exchange - HON; Ho                              4
honor - hon.                                                   5
Honorable - Hon.                                               6
honorably - hon.                                               7
honorarium - hon.                                              8
honorary - hon.; hor.                                          9
honored - hond.                                               10
honors - hnrs.; hons.                                         11
hoodlum - hood.                                               12
Hoosac Tunnel & Wilmington (RR) - HT&W                        13
hora (hour) - H.                                              14
Horace - Hor                                                  15
Horatio - Hor                                                 16
horizon - H; hor.                                             17
horizontal - H; hor.; horiz.                                  18
Horo Logium (the Pendulum Clock) - Hor                        19
horology - hor.; horol.                                       20
horse (uncastrated male aged 5 or more) - h.                  21
horsepower - HP; H.P.; hp                                     22
horsepower-hour - hp.-hr.                                     23
horticultural - hort.                                         24
horticulture - hort.                                          25
hose bibb - H.B.                                              26
Hosea - Hos                                                   27
hosiery - hose.                                               28
hospital - hosp                                               29
Hospital Care - H.C.                                          30
Hospital Corps - H.C.                                         31
hospital sergeant - Hosp. Sgt.                                32
hospital steward - Hosp. Steward                              33
hot and cold - h. and c.                                      34
hot rolled steel - HRS                                        35
hot water (L, aqua fervens) - aq. ferv.; HW                   36
hot water, circulating - HW C                                 37
hot water heater - HWH                                        38
hot water tank - HWT                                          39
hot-rolled steel - HRS; hs                                    40
hour (L, hora) - H.; h.                                       41
hour(s) - hr.(s.)                                             42
house - h.; ho.; hse.                                         43
House bill - H.R.                                             44
House concurrent resolution - H.Con.Res.                      45
House document - H.Doc.                                       46
House joint resolution - H.J.Res.                             47
House of Commons - H.C.                                       48
House of Lords - H.L.                                         49
House of Representatives - H.R.                               50
House report - H.Rept.                                        51
House resolution - H.Res.                                     52
Household Finance Corporation - HFC                           53
housekeeper - hskpr                                           54
housekeeping - hskpg                                          55
housing - hsg.                                                56
```

Housing and Home Finance Agency - HHFA   1
Housing and Urban Development - HUD   2
Houston - Hous.   3
Howard - How.   4
Howitzer - How   5
Hubert - Hub.   6
Hubert H. Humphrey - HHH   7
Hugh - Hu.   8
Hugo - Hu.   9
huius mensis (this month's) - h.m.   10
hujus anni (this year's) - h.a.   11
human - hum.   12
human behavior - HB   13
humane - hum.   14
humanism - hum.   15
humanitarian - hum.   16
humanities - hum.   17
Humble Oil and Refining Company - HO&RC   18
humerous - hum.   19
humid - hmd   20
humidity - H; hum.   21
humidity index - h.i.   22
Humphrey - Hum.   23
hundred - C   24
hundredweight - cwt.   25
Hungarian - Hung.   26
Hungary - Hung.   27
Hungary's New Economic Mechanism - NEM   28
Huntingdon & Broad Top Mountain Railroad & Coal Co. (RR) -   29
   H&BTM   30
Huron-Clinton Metropolitan Authority - HCMA   31
hurricane - hur   32
husband - h.   33
husbandry - husb.   34
hybrid computer link - HYCOL   35
hybrid computer translator - HYCOTRAN   36
hybrid electromagnet wave - HEM   37
Hydra (the Water Snake) - Hya   38
hydrant - hydt.   39
hydrate - hyd.   40
hydraulic(s) - hyd; hydraul   41
hydrocyanic acid - AC   42
hydrodynamics - hydro; hydrodyn   43
hydroelectric - hydro; hydroelec   44
hydroelectric units - heu   45
hydroelectrical - hydro   46
Hydrogen - H   47
hydrogen bomb - H-bomb   48
hydrogen ion (positive or negative) - H+; H-   49
hydrogen line of solar spectrum - g   50
hydrogen-ion concentration - pH   51
hydrographic - hydrog.   52
hydrography - hydrog.   53
hydrology - hydro; hydrol   54
hydrolysis - h   55
hydromechanics - hydrom   56

```
hydrostatic - hydro                                            1
hydrostatic(s) - hydros.                                       2
Hydrus (the Lesser Water Snake) - Hyi                          3
hygiene - hyg                                                  4
hygienic - hyg                                                 5
Hyman - Hy                                                     6
hymnologist - hymnol                                           7
hymnology - hymnol                                             8
hyperbola - hyp                                                9
hyperbolic - hyp                                              10
hyperbolic cosecant - csch                                    11
hyperbolic cosine - cosh                                      12
hyperbolic cotangent - coth                                   13
hyperbolic secant - sech                                      14
hyperbolic sine - sinh                                        15
hyperbolic tangent - tanh                                     16
hyphen - hyp                                                  17
hypnotism - hypno                                             18
hypochondria - hypo                                           19
hypochondriac - hypo                                          20
hypodermic - hypo                                             21
hypotenuse - hyp.                                             22
hypothesis - hyp.                                             23
hypothetical - hyp.                                           24
hysteria - hyst                                               25
I beam - I                                                    26
I condemn (L, condemno) - C.                                  27
I owe you - IOU                                               28
Iberia AirLines of Spain - IB                                 29
ibidem (in the same place) - ib.; ibid.                       30
ice (water) (L, aqua astricta) - aq. astr.                    31
Iceland - Ice.                                                32
Icelandic - Ice.; Icel.                                       33
Icelandic Airlines - IAL                                      34
ichthyologists - ichs                                         35
ichthyology - ich; ichth; ichthyol                            36
icing - icg                                                   37
iconic - icon.                                                38
iconoclasm - icon.                                            39
iconoclast - icon.                                            40
iconographic - icon.                                          41
iconographical - icon.                                        42
iconography - icon.                                           43
iconoscope - ike                                              44
id (that) - i.                                                45
id est (that is) - i.e.                                       46
Idaho - Ida.                                                  47
Idaho State College - ISC                                     48
Idaho State University - ISU                                  49
idea - id.                                                    50
idem (the same) - id.                                         51
idem quod (the same as) - i.q.                                52
identification - I.D.; ident                                  53
identification card - ID-card                                 54
identification, friend or foe - IFF                           55
identification of position - IP                               56
```

```
identification point - IP                                1
identification section - IDS                             2
identify - ident                                         3
identity - ident                                         4
the Ides (L, Idus) - I                                   5
Ignatius - Ign.                                          6
ignite(s) - ign.                                         7
ignition - ign.                                          8
Illinois - Ill.                                          9
Illinois Central (RR) - IC                              10
Illinois Northern (RR) - IN                             11
Illinois Terminal (RR) - IT                             12
illiterate - illit.                                     13
illuminate - illum                                      14
Illuminating Engineering Society - IES                  15
illumination - illum                                    16
illustrated - ill.; illus.; illust.                     17
illustrated parts breakdown - IPB                       18
illustration - ill.; illust.                            19
illustrations - illus.                                  20
illustrator - illus.                                    21
image motion compensation - IMC                         22
imaginary - imag                                        23
imitate - imit.                                          24
imitation - imit.                                        25
imitative - imit.                                        26
Immaculate Heart of Mary Missioners - I.H.M.            27
immature - im                                            28
immediate - immed                                        29
immediate access storage - ias                          30
immediate operation use - IOU                            31
immediately (L, statim) - immy.; (stat.)                32
immigrant - immig.                                       33
immigration - immig.                                     34
Immigration and Naturalization - I&N                    35
immortal (L, immortalis) - i.                            36
immunity - immun                                         37
Immunization - IMM.                                      38
immunization - immun                                     39
immunology - immun.; immunol.                            40
imparted - imp.                                          41
impedance - Z                                            42
impedance angle - ia                                     43
imperative - imp.; imper.; impv.                         44
imperfect - imp.; imperf.; impf.                         45
imperforate - imperf.                                    46
imperial - imp.                                          47
imperial bushel - i.bu.                                  48
imperial gallon - i.gal.                                 49
imperial measure - im                                    50
imperial standard gallon - isg                           51
Imperial Wire Gauge - IWG                                52
impersonal - imp.; impers.                               53
implement - imp.; impl.                                  54
import(s) - imp.                                         55
important - impt.                                        56
```

```
imported - imp.                                                    1
importer - imp.; imptr.                                            2
Impost - I                                                         3
impregnate - impg.; impreg.                                        4
impregnated - impreg.                                              5
impregnating - impreg.                                             6
imprimatur (let it be printed) - imp.                              7
imprint - imp.                                                     8
improper - improp.                                                 9
improve - imv.                                                    10
improved - imp.                                                   11
improved data interchange - IDI                                  12
improvement - improv.                                            13
impulses per minute - IPM                                        14
in accordance with - IAW                                         15
in charge of - i.c.                                              16
in divided doses - fract. dos.                                   17
in equal parts - p.a.                                            18
in fine (at the end) - in f.                                     19
in its place (L, in loco) - in loc.                              20
in lieu of - i.l.o.                                              21
in limine (at the outset) - in lim.                              22
in loco (in the place of) - in loc.                              23
in loco citato (in the place cited) - in loc. cit.              24
in memory - in mem.                                              25
in nomine Dei (in the name of God) - I.N.D.                      26
in or of the next month (L, proximo) - prox.                     27
in or under this title (L, hoc titulo) - h.t.                    28
in order - i.o.                                                  29
in part (L, partim) - p.                                         30
in principio (in the beginning) - in pr.                         31
in proportion to the value (L, ad valorem) - ad val.            32
in quod erat demonstrandum (what was to be proved) - i.q.e.d. 33
in regard to - in re                                             34
in secret (L, incognito) - incog.                                35
in the beginning (L, in principio) - in pr.                      36
in the beginning (L, initio) - init.                             37
in the meantime (L, ad interim) - ad int.                        38
in the name of God (L, in nomine Dei) - I.N.D.                   39
in the place above cited (L, loco supra citato) - l.s.c.        40
in the place above mentioned (L, ubi supra) - u.s.              41
in the place cited (L, in loco citato) - in loc. cit.; l.c.;   42
    loc. cit.                                                    43
in the place cited (L, loco laudato) - ll.                       44
in the place of (L, in loco) - in loc.                           45
in the same place (L, ibidem) - ib.; ibid.                       46
in the time of (L, tempore) - t.; temp.                          47
in the work cited (L, opere citato) - o.c.; op. cit.            48
in the year (L, anno) - an.                                      49
in the year before Christ (L, anno ante Christum) - A.A.C.      50
in the year of our Lord (L, anno Domini) - A.D.                  51
in the year of the discovery (L, anno inventionis) - A.I.       52
in the year of the founding of the city (L, anno urbis          53
    conditae) - A.U.C.                                           54
in the year of the Hegira (L, anno Hegirae) - A.H.               55
in the year of the world (L, anno mundi) - A.M.; a.m.            56
```

119

```
indefinitely (L, sine die) - s.d.                              1
indemnity - indem.; indm.                                      2
indention - inden.                                             3
indenture - inden.                                             4
indentured - inden.                                            5
Independent - I.                                               6
independent - ind.; indep.                                     7
Independent Mutual Insurance Agent - IMA                       8
Independent Order of Foresters - I.O.F.                        9
Independent Order of Odd Fellows - I.O.O.F.                   10
index - ind.                                                  11
Index Medicus - IM                                            12
index of performance - IP                                     13
index of refraction - n                                       14
Index of Status Characteristics - ISC                         15
India - Ind.                                                  16
Indian - Ind.                                                 17
Indian Ocean - Ind O                                          18
Indian reservation - Indian res.                              19
Indiana - Ind.                                                20
Indiana Harbor Belt (RR) - IHB                                21
Indiana State College - ISC                                   22
indicate - ind.                                               23
indicated - ind.                                              24
indicated airspeed - ias                                      25
indicated altitude - ia                                       26
indicated horse power - i.h.p.; i.hp.                         27
indicated horsepower hour - ihph                              28
indicated mean effective pressure - imep                      29
indicating - I; indic.                                        30
indicating device - ID                                        31
indication - ind.                                             32
indicative - ind.; indic.                                     33
indicator - I; ind.; indic.                                   34
Indies - Ind.                                                 35
indigo - ind.                                                 36
indirect - ind.                                               37
indirect addressing - IA                                      38
indirect object - ind. obj.                                   39
indirectly - ind.                                             40
Indium - In                                                   41
individual - indiv.; individ.                                 42
individual system operation - ISO                             43
Indochina - Indoc                                             44
indoctrinate - indoc                                          45
indoctrination - indoc                                        46
Indo-European - IE; Indo-Eur                                  47
Indonesia - Indo; Indon.                                      48
indorse - ind.                                                49
indorsed - ind.                                               50
indorsement - ind.                                            51
inductance - L; induc.                                        52
inductance-capacitance-resistance - lcr                       53
induction - induc.                                            54
induction regulator - ind. reg.                               55
inductive reactance - $X_L$                                   56
```

```
inductor - L                                                    1
induline - ind.                                                 2
Indux (the Indian) - Ind                                        3
industrial - I; ind.; indus.                                    4
industrial data processing - IDP                                5
Industrial Engineer - Ind Eng                                   6
industrial process control - IPC                                7
industrial production - IP                                      8
Industrial Workers of the World - I.W.W.                        9
industry - ind.; indus.                                        10
inertia - I                                                    11
infant - i                                                     12
infantry - inf.                                                13
infectious - inf.                                              14
infectious bronchitis - i.b.                                   15
infectious disease - id                                        16
infectious mononucleosis - i.m.                                17
inferior - inf.                                                18
infielder (baseball) - if.                                     19
infinitive - inf.; infin.                                      20
infirmary - infmry                                             21
in-flight - i-f                                                22
inflight refueling - ifr                                       23
influence(s) - infl.                                           24
influenza - flu                                                25
information - IFN; inf.; info                                   26
information distributor - ID                                   27
information overload testing apparatus - IOTA                  28
information processing center - IPC                            29
information retrieval - ir                                     30
information storage and retrieval - isr                        31
infra (below) - inf.                                           32
infrared - ifr                                                 33
inhalation - inhal                                             34
initial - init.                                                35
initial appearance - IA                                        36
initial boiling point - IBP; I.B.P.; i.b.p.                    37
Initial Engine Test - IET                                      38
Initial Office Visit - I.O.V.                                  39
initial point - i.p.                                           40
initial receiving point - IRP                                  41
initial teaching alphabet - i.t.a.                             42
initial velocity - IV; I.V.; i.v.                              43
initio (in the beginning) - init.                              44
injection - inj.; inject.                                      45
injure - inj                                                   46
injury - inj                                                   47
inlet - in                                                     48
inlet manhole - IMH                                            49
Inner City Business Improvement Forum - ICBIF                  50
inning - inn.                                                  51
innings - inns.                                                52
innings pitched (baseball) - IP                                53
inoperative - inop                                             54
inorganic - inorg.                                             55
input - IN                                                     56
```

institution - inst.; instn.   1
instruction - instn.   2
instruction book - ib   3
instruction counter - IC   4
Instructional Resources Center - IRC   5
instructions - instns.   6
instructor - instr.   7
instrument - INST; instm   8
instrument(s) - instr.   9
instrument approach system - ias   10
instrument landing approach - ILA   11
instrument landing approach system - ILAS; I.L.A.S.   12
instrument landing system - ILS; I.L.S.   13
instrumental - instr.   14
instrumentation - instm.   15
insufficient - insuf.   16
insulate - insul.   17
insulated - ins.; insul.   18
Insulated Metal Panels-Porcelain Enameled - Ins.Met.Pa./P.E.   19
insulating - insulg.   20
insulation - ins.; insul.   21
insulator - ins.   22
Insurance - INS.   23
insurance - ins.; insur.   24
insure - ins.   25
intake - int   26
integer - J   27
integral - int   28
integrated chopper - INCH   29
integrated circuit - ic   30
integrated computer/telemetry - IC/T   31
integrated data file - IDF   32
integrated data processing - IDP   33
integrated data store - IDS   34
intelligence - intel.; intell.   35
Intelligence Department - I.D.; i.d.   36
intelligence quotient - IQ; I.Q.   37
intensified - intens.   38
intensifier - intens.   39
intensity of magnetic field - H   40
intensive - intens.   41
Inter Record Gap - IRG   42
Inter-American Defense Board - IADB   43
interbank - i   44
intercept - incpt   45
interchange center - IC   46
intercoastal - intcl   47
intercommunication - interm   48
intercommunication flip-flop - ICF   49
intercontinental ballistic missile - I.C.B.M.; ICBM   50
Interdenominational - Inter.   51
Interdepartment Radio Advisory Committee - IRAC   52
interest - i; int.   53
interference - INTEC; interf   54
interference rejection unit - IFRU   55
Intergovernmental Maritime Consultative Organization - IMCO   56

123

```
interim - int.                                                    1
interior - int.                                                   2
interior decorator - int dec                                      3
interjection - int.; interj.                                      4
interlinear - il                                                  5
intermediate - inter                                              6
intermediate frequency - IF; I-F; I.-F.; I.F.; i.f.              7
intermediate range ballistic missile - I.R.B.M.; IRBM           8
interment - intrmt                                                9
intermittent - intmt                                             10
internal - int.; intern.                                         11
internal combustion - ic                                         12
internal connection - IC                                         13
internal function register - IFR                                 14
internal gauge - it. ga.                                         15
internal pipe thread - ipt                                       16
Internal Revenue - I.R.                                          17
Internal Revenue Officer - I.R.O.                                18
Internal Revenue Service - I.R.S.                                19
internal thread - i.t.                                           20
internal-combustion engine - ICE                                 21
internally specified index - ISI                                 22
international - int.; int'l                                       23
International - Internat.                                         24
International Annealed Copper Standard - IACS; I.A.C.S.          25
International Association of Machinists - IAM                     26
International Association of Poets, Playwrights, Editors,         27
    Essayists, and Novelists - P.E.N.                            28
International Astronomical Union - I.A.U.                         29
International Atomic Energy Agency - IAEA                         30
International Brotherhood of Teamsters - IBT                      31
International Business Machines Corporation - IBM                 32
International Catholic Truth Society - I.C.T.S.                   33
International Civil Aviation Organization - ICAO                  34
International Court of Justice - ICJ                              35
International Development Association - IDA                       36
international distress frequency - idf                            37
International Finance Corporation - IFC                           38
International Geophysical Year - IGY                              39
International Labor Organization - ILO                            40
International Longshoremen's Association - ILA                    41
International Meteorological Organization - IMO                   42
International News Photos - INP                                   43
International News Service - INS                                  44
International Phonetic Alphabet - IPA                             45
International Refugee Organization - IRO                          46
international standard atmosphere - isa                           47
International Telecommunication Union - ITU                       48
International Telephone and Telegraph - IT&T                      49
international tolerance - i.t.                                    50
International Trade Organization - ITO                            51
International Typographical Union - ITU                           52
International Unit(s) - I.U.; i.u.                                53
International Whaling Commission - IWC                            54
internationally - internat.                                      55
interphone - inph; INT                                           56
```

Iowa State University - ISU	1
Ipanema - Ip	2
Ipswich - Ips	3
Iranian - Iran.	4
Iraq - Iq	5
Ireland - Ire.	6
iridescent - irid	7
iridium - Ir	8
Irish - Ir.	9
Irish Christian Brothers - F.S.C.H.	10
Irish Free State - I.F.S.	11
Irish International Airlines - IIA	12
Irish Republican Army - IRA; I.R.A.	13
Iron - Fe	14
iron - I	15
iron pipe - i.p.	16
iron pipe size - IPS; I.P.S.	17
ironical - iron.	18
ironically - iron.	19
ironing machine - IM	20
iron-pipe size - IPS	21
irredeemable - irred.	22
irregular - irreg.	23
irregularly - irreg.	24
irrigation - irrig	25
Irvin - Irv	26
Irving - Irv	27
Isabella - Isab.	28
Isaiah - Is; Isa.	29
Ishmael - Ish.	30
Islam - Is	31
Island(s) - I.	32
Island - Is.; is.	33
island - i; isl.	34
islands - is.; isls.	35
Isle - Is.	36
Isle(s) - I.	37
isle - isl.	38
Isle of Man - I. of Man	39
Isle of Wight - I.W.	40
isolate - iso	41
isometric - isom.	42
isotopic weight - i.w.	43
Israel - Is; Isr.	44
Israel Airlines - EL-AL; EI-AI	45
issue - iss.	46
isthmus - Isth.; isth.	47
it does not follow (L, non sequitur) - non. seq.	48
it is not clear or evident (L, non liquet) - n.l.	49
it is not permitted (L, non licet) - n.l.	50
Italian - It.; Ital.	51
italic(s) - ital.	52
italic (type) - ital.	53
italics - itlx	54
Italy - It.; Ital.	55
item - it.	56

```
item description - ID                                               1
item processing - IP                                                2
item transfer - IT                                                  3
itemize - it.                                                       4
itinerant - itin.                                                   5
itinerary - itin.                                                   6
Ivan - Iv                                                           7
Ivory Coast - I.C.                                                  8
izzard - z                                                          9
jack - j                                                           10
Jackson - Jack                                                     11
Jacob - Ja; Jac.                                                   12
Jacobean - Jac.                                                    13
Jacobite - Jac.                                                    14
Jacque - J                                                         15
Jacques - Ja.                                                      16
Jaguar - Jag                                                       17
Jahrbuch - Jahrb.                                                  18
Jahresbericht - Jahresb.                                           19
Jakarta - Jak                                                      20
Jamaica - Jam.                                                     21
James - Ja; Jas.                                                   22
jam-template machine screws - JTMS                                 23
janitory - jan                                                     24
janitorial - jan                                                   25
janitor's closet - J.C.; Jan. Clos.                                26
January - Ja.; Jan.                                                27
Japan - Jap.                                                       28
Japan Air Lines - JAL                                              29
Japanese - Jap.                                                    30
Japanese industrial standard - JIS                                 31
jargon - jarg                                                      32
Jasper - Jasp.                                                     33
jasper - jasp                                                      34
jaundice - jaund                                                   35
Javanese - Jav.                                                    36
Jean-Jacques Servan-Schreiber - JJSS                               37
Jeffrey - Jef                                                      38
Jehovah - JHVH                                                     39
Jemima - Jem                                                       40
Jeremiah - Jer                                                     41
Jerome - Jer.                                                      42
Jersey - Jer.                                                      43
Jesuit Educational Association - JEA                               44
Jesus Christ - J.C.                                                45
Jesus, Mary, and Joseph - J.M.J.                                   46
Jesus of Nazareth, King of the Jews (Iesus Nazareuus, Rex          47
    Iudaeorum) - I.N.R.I.                                          48
Jesus, the Savior of Men (Iesus Hominum Salvator) - IHS            49
jet pilot - j.p.                                                   50
jet power - jp                                                     51
jet propulsion - JP                                                52
Jet Propulsion Laboratory - JPL                                    53
jet-assisted take-off - JATO                                       54
jetsam - jet.                                                      55
jettison - jett.                                                   56
```

```
jewel - jwl.                                           1
jeweler - jwlr.                                        2
jewelry - jew.; jwlry.                                 3
Job - Jb                                               4
Job Opportunities in Business - JOBS                   5
job order - JO                                         6
job processing word - JPW                              7
jockey - jock                                          8
jockey strap - jock                                    9
jocose - joc.                                         10
jocular - joc.                                        11
jocularly - joc.                                      12
Joel - Jl.; Jo.                                       13
Joel Levis - JL                                       14
John - Jn; Jno                                        15
1 John - 1 Jn                                         16
2 John - 2 Jn                                         17
3 John - 3 Jn                                         18
John Crerar Library - JCL                             19
John Fitzgerald Kennedy - JFK                         20
join - jn                                             21
joined - jd.                                          22
joint - jnt; jt.                                      23
joint account - j/a; j.a.                             24
joint author - jt. author                             25
joint editor - jt. ed.                                26
joint occupancy date - jod                            27
joint operations center - JOC                         28
joint stock - jnt.stk.                                29
joint stock company (Swed, aktiebolag) - A/B          30
jointly - jtly                                        31
Jonah - Jon                                           32
Jonathan - Jona.                                      33
Jordan - Jord                                         34
Joseph - Jo; Jos.                                     35
Josepha - Josa.                                       36
Josephine - Jo; Jose                                  37
Joshua - Jos; Josh                                    38
joule - J; j                                          39
Journal - J.; Jour.                                   40
journalist - jnlst; jour.                             41
journals - jnls                                       42
journey - jour.                                       43
journeyman - jour.                                    44
judex (judge) - J.                                    45
Judge - J.                                            46
Judge Advocate - J.A.                                 47
Judge Advocate General - JAG; Judge Adv. Gen.         48
judgement(s) - jud.                                   49
Judges - Jgs; JJ; Judg.                               50
judicial - jud.                                       51
Judith - Jdt; Jud.                                    52
judo - jud                                            53
Judson - Jud                                          54
julep - jul.                                          55
Jules - Jul.                                          56
```

```
Julia - Jla.                                                    1
Julian - Jul.                                                   2
Juliet - Jlt.                                                   3
Julius - Jul.                                                   4
Julius Caesar - J.C.                                            5
July - Jl.; Jul.; Jy.                                           6
jump address - JA                                               7
Junction - Jc.; Junc.                                           8
junction - jct.; jctn.                                          9
junction box (outlet) - J                                      10
junction gate number - JGN                                     11
junction point - jct pt                                        12
juncture - jnt                                                 13
June - Je.; Jun                                                14
Juneau - Jun                                                   15
junior - j                                                     16
Junior - Jr.; jr.; Jun                                         17
Junior Achievement - JA                                        18
Junior Association of Commerce - J.A.C.                        19
Junior Chamber of Commerce - JC; jaycee; JCC                   20
Junior College - JC                                            21
Junior College Journal - JCJ                                   22
Junior College Research Review - JCRR                          23
junior grade - JG; jg.                                         24
junior high school - JHS                                       25
junior partner - JP                                            26
junior varsity - J.V.                                          27
Jupiter - Jup.                                                 28
Juris Doctor - J.D.                                            29
jurisconsult - J.C.                                            30
jurisdiction - juris.                                          31
jurisprudence - jurisp.                                        32
juror - jr.                                                    33
jury duty - j.d.                                               34
just as they come; average quality (L, talis qualis) -        35
   tal. qual.                                                  36
Justice - J.                                                   37
justice - jus.                                                 38
Justice of the Peace - J.P.                                    39
Justices - JJ.                                                 40
justification - just.                                          41
Justin - Just.                                                 42
Justinian - Just.                                              43
Justus - Just.                                                 44
Juvenal - Juv                                                  45
juvenile - J; juv                                              46
juvenile delinquency - JD'cy                                   47
juvenile delinquent - j.d.                                     48
juxtapose - jux                                                49
juxtaposition - jux                                            50
kaffir - kaf                                                   51
kalamein - kal                                                 52
kalamein door - KD                                             53
Kalamein Frame - KF                                            54
kalends - kal.                                                 55
Kalsomine - K.                                                 56
```

```
Kansas - Kan.; Kans.                                            1
Kansas City - KC                                                2
Kansas City Southern (RR) - KCS                                 3
Kansas, Oklahoma & Gulf (RR) - KO&G                             4
Kansas State College - KSC                                      5
Kansas State University - KSU                                   6
karat, carat - k.; kt.                                          7
Kashmir - Kash                                                  8
Katharine - Kath.                                               9
Katherine - Kath.                                              10
kayak - k                                                      11
keel - k                                                       12
keeper - kpr.                                                  13
keeper of the privy seal (L, custos privati sigilli) -         14
   C.P.S.                                                      15
keeper of the seal (L, custos sigilli) - C.S.                  16
keg(s) - kg.                                                   17
Kelvin - K                                                     18
Kelvin calorie temperature - Kcal.                             19
Kent State University - KSU                                    20
Kentucky - Ken.; Ky.                                           21
Kentucky State College - KSC                                   22
Kenya - Ken.                                                   23
Kenyon College - KC                                            24
key word in context - kwic                                     25
key word in text - kwit                                        26
keyboard - KB                                                  27
keyboard common contact - KCC                                  28
keyboard send/receive - KSR                                    29
keyboard typing reperforator - KTR                             30
keyed alike - KA                                               31
keyed alike & grand master keyed - KAGMK                       32
keyed alike & master keyed - KAMK                              33
keying device - KY                                             34
keypunch operator - kpo                                        35
keystone - K                                                   36
kick plate - kp; K.Pl.                                         37
kidney - kid.                                                  38
kidney, spleen, liver - k.s.l.                                 39
kilderkin - kild                                               40
killed - kd.                                                   41
killed in action - KIA                                         42
kiln dried - kd                                                43
kiln-dried - KD                                                44
kilo - k                                                       45
kilo british thermal unit - kbtu                               46
kilo electron volts - kev                                      47
kilobar(s) - kb.; kbar                                         48
kilocalorie(s) - kcal                                          49
kilocycle - kc                                                 50
kilocycles = kiloHertz - k.c.p.s.                              51
kilocycles per second - kc.s.; kc./s.                          52
kiloelectron volts - kev; k.e.v.                               53
kilogauss - kg.                                                54
kilograin - kgr.                                               55
kilogram - k.                                                  56
```

```
kilogram(s) - kg                                                    1
kilogram-calories - kg.-cal.                                        2
kilogram-force - kgf                                                3
kilogram-meters - kg.-m.                                            4
kilograms - kg                                                      5
kiloHertz - kHz                                                     6
kiloliter(s) - kl                                                   7
kilomegacycle(s) - KMC                                              8
kilometer(s) - km                                                   9
kilometers per second - km/sec                                     10
kiloton - kt.                                                      11
kilovolt - kv.                                                     12
kilovolt ampere - kv-a.                                            13
kilovolt-ampere - kva; kv.-a.; k.v.a.                              14
kilovolt-amperes - kv.-a.                                          15
kilovolts - kv.                                                    16
kilovolts peak - kvp.; kv.p.; k.v.p.                               17
kilowatt(s) - kw                                                   18
kilowatt electrical - kwe.                                         19
kilowatt hour(s) - kwh                                             20
kilowatt thermal - kwt.                                            21
kilowatthour - kwhr                                                22
kilowatt-hour - kw.-hr.                                            23
kilowatts - kw.                                                    24
kindergarten - k                                                   25
kinematic viscosity - KV; K.V.                                     26
kinetic energy - ke                                                27
King (Rex) - K; (R)                                                28
King and Emperor (L, Rex et Imperator) - R.I.; R.&I.               29
King James Version - KJV                                           30
kingdom - kdm.; km.                                                31
1 Kings - 1 Kgs.                                                   32
2 Kings - 2 Kgs.                                                   33
King's Bench - K.B.                                                34
King's Bishop - KB                                                 35
King's Counsel - K.C.                                              36
King's Knight - KN                                                 37
King's Rook - KR                                                   38
Kip (1000 lbs.) - K                                                39
kitchen - k                                                        40
kitchen police - KP                                                41
kitchen sink - KS                                                  42
kleptomania - klepto                                               43
kleptomaniac - klepto                                              44
Knight - K.; k.; knt.; kt.                                         45
Knight Bachelor - K.B.                                             46
Knight Commander - K.C.                                            47
Knight Commander of the Bath - K.C.B.                              48
Knight Grand Cross - G.C.                                          49
Knight of Malta - K.M.                                             50
Knight of Pius IX - K.P.                                           51
Knight of Saint Gregory - K.S.G.                                   52
Knight of Saint Sylvester - K.S.S.                                 53
Knight of the Garter - K.G.                                        54
Knight of the Order of St. Patrick - K.P.                          55
Knight of the Order of the Garter - K.G.                           56
```

```
lavatory - lav.                                              1
lavatory, dental - DL                                        2
lavatory, medical - ML                                       3
lavatory, pedestal - PL                                      4
lavatory, wall - WL                                          5
law - L.; l.                                                 6
law agent - l.a.                                             7
Law Reports - L.R.                                           8
Lawrence - Lawr.                                             9
laws - LL.                                                  10
lawyer - law.; lwyr.                                        11
Lawyer's edition - L.Ed.                                    12
layer - LYR                                                 13
Lazarus - Laz.                                              14
lazy - lzy                                                  15
lead - ld                                                   16
lead (L, plumbum) - Pb                                      17
lead and oil - LO                                           18
lead covered - LC                                           19
leader - L; ldr.                                            20
leader drain - LD                                           21
leading - ldg.                                              22
leading edge - LE                                           23
leaf - l.                                                   24
league - l.                                                 25
league(s) - lea.                                            26
League of Nations - L.N.                                    27
League of Women Voters - LWV                                28
Learning Media Center - LMC                                 29
least common factor - lcf                                   30
least common multiple - L.C.M.; l.c.m.                      31
least fatal dose - l.f.d.                                   32
least significant bit - LSB                                 33
least significant digit - LSD; L.S.D.                       34
least voltage coincidence detection - LVCD                  35
least-preferred co-worker - L-PC                            36
leather - lea.                                              37
leave(s) - lv.                                              38
leave of absence - loa                                      39
leave with pay - lwp                                        40
leave without pay - lwop                                    41
Lebanese - Leb                                              42
Lebanon - Leb                                               43
Lector of Sacred Theology - S.T.Lr.                         44
lecture - lect.                                             45
lecturer - lect.; lectr.                                    46
ledger - ldr.; led.                                         47
ledger folio - l.f.                                         48
Leeward Islands - Le.Is.                                    49
left - L.; l.; lt.                                          50
left center - l.c.                                          51
left defense (ice hockey) - LD                              52
left end (football) - LE                                    53
left eye - l.e.; O.L.; O.S.                                 54
left field (baseball) - lf.                                 55
left fielder - 7                                            56
```

```
left foot (figure skating) - L.                                      1
left forward (basketball) - lf.                                      2
left fullback (field hockey) - LB; LFB                               3
left fullback (soccer) - LB                                          4
left guard (basketball) - lg.                                        5
left guard (football) - lg.                                          6
left halfback (field hockey) - LH, LHB                               7
left halfback (football) - LH, LHB                                   8
left halfback (soccer) - LH, LHB                                     9
left hand - LH; l.h.                                                10
left hand reverse - LHR                                             11
left inside backward edge (figure skating) - LIB                    12
left inside forward (field hockey) - LI                             13
left inside forward edge (figure skating) - LIF                     14
left on base (on a baseball scorecard) - L, LB                      15
left outside backward edge (figure skating) - LOB                   16
left outside forward edge (figure skating) - LOF                    17
left side - l.s.                                                    18
left tackle (football) - LT                                         19
left wing (field hockey) - LW                                       20
left wing (ice hockey) - LW                                         21
lefthand thread - lh th                                             22
left-to-right - l-to-r                                              23
leg before wicket (Cricket) - l.b.w.                                24
legal - leg.                                                        25
Legal Aid Society - LAS                                             26
legate - leg.                                                       27
legation - leg.                                                     28
legato - leg.                                                       29
legend - leg.                                                       30
legislation - leg.; legisl.                                         31
legislative - leg.; legisl.                                         32
Legislative Reference Service (Library of Congress) - LRS           33
legislature - leg.                                                  34
legitimate - legit                                                  35
Lehigh & Hudson River (RR) - L&HR                                   36
Lehigh & New England (RR) - L&NE                                    37
Lehigh Valley (RR) - LV                                             38
Leicestershire - Leics.                                             39
Leipsig - Leip.                                                     40
lemonade - lemo                                                     41
Lemuel - Lem                                                        42
Lend-Lease - L.L.                                                   43
length - L; l; LG; lgth                                             44
length (Physics) - L                                                45
length overall - LOA                                                46
length to diameter ratio - l/d ratio                                47
Leningrad - Len                                                     48
Leo (the Lion) - Leo                                                49
Leo Minor (the Lesser Lion) - LMi                                   50
Leonard - Leo; Leon                                                 51
Leopold - Leo                                                       52
Lepus (the Hare) - Lep                                              53
lesbian - les                                                       54
lesbianism - les                                                    55
less than carload lot - L.C.L.; l.c.l.                              56
```

135

```
Lester - Les                                            1
let a mixture be made (L, fiat mistura) - ft. mist.     2
let a powder be made (L, fiat pulvis) - ft. pulv.       3
let it be given to - d.d.                               4
let it be made (L, fiat) - f.                           5
let it be printed (L, imprimatur) - imp.                6
let it stand - stet                                     7
let pills be made - f. pil.                             8
let the buyer beware (L, caveat emptor) - c.e.          9
let there be added (L, adde) - ad.                     10
let there be made - ft.                                11
lethal dose - l.d.                                     12
letter(s) - let.                                       13
letter - ltr.                                          14
Letter of Aristeas to Philocrates - Aristeas           15
letter of authority - l/a                              16
letter of credit - L/C; l/c; l.c.                      17
letter signed - l.s.                                   18
letterhead - lett.hd.                                  19
letters and cards - LC mail                            20
level - lev; lvl                                       21
level control - LC                                     22
level recorder - LR                                    23
level switch - LS                                      24
lever - lev                                            25
Leviticus - Lv                                         26
levo- - l                                              27
Lewis - Lew                                            28
lexicographer - lex; lexicog.                          29
lexicographical - lexicog.                             30
lexicography - lex; lexicog.                           31
lexicon - lex.                                         32
Lexington - Lex                                        33
liaison - ln.                                          34
liber (a book) - L.                                    35
Liberal - L.; Lib.                                     36
Liberation - Lib.                                      37
Liberia - Lib.                                         38
liberty - lib                                          39
libra (pound) - lb.                                    40
Libra (the Balance) - Lib                              41
librarian - LBR; lib.; libr.                           42
library - lib.; libr.                                  43
Library Journal - LJ                                   44
Library of Congress - LC                               45
Libya - Lib                                            46
Licentiate in Midwifery - L.M.                         47
Licentiate of Canon Law - J.C.L.                       48
Licentiate of Oriental Languages - Ling.Or.L.          49
Licentiate of Sacred Scripture - S.S.L.                50
Licentiate of Sacred Theology - S.T.L.                 51
lid - ld                                               52
Liechtenstein - Liech.                                 53
lien - ln.                                             54
Lieutenant - Lieut.; Lt.                               55
lieutenant colonel - Lt. Col.                          56
```

lieutenant commander - Lt.Comdr.; Lt.Commander 1
lieutenant general - Lt.Gen. 2
lieutenant governor - Lt.Gov. 3
lieutenant junior grade - Lt.(jg.) 4
life insurance policy - L.I.P. 5
Life Saving Station - L.S.S. 6
life-boat - lb. 7
lifeguard - L.G. 8
Lifesaving Service - L.S.S. 9
ligament - lig 10
light (L, lux) - lt.; (lx.) 11
light amplification by stimulated emission of radiation - 12
  laser 13
light detection and ranging - lidar 14
light face - l.f. 15
light foot quantizer - LFQ 16
light transmission index - LTI 17
light weight concrete - LWC 18
light weight insulating concrete - LWIC 19
lighter - ltr. 20
lighter-than-air - LTA 21
lightface - lf. 22
lighting - light. 23
lightning - ltng. 24
lights - lgts. 25
limestone - LS 26
limit - lim 27
Limited - Ld. 28
limited - Ltd.; ltd. 29
limited edition - ltd. ed. 30
limiting date - lim. dat. 31
limousine - limo 32
Lincolnshire - Lincs. 33
line - l. 34
line buffer - LB 35
line by line - l/l 36
line connector - LC 37
line gate number - LGN 38
line generator - LG 39
line of departure - LD 40
line of duty - ld; lod 41
line of least resistance - l.l.r. 42
line relay - LR 43
Linea Aerea Nacional de Chile - LAN 44
lineal - lin 45
linear - lin 46
linear accelerator - LINAC 47
linear decision - LD 48
linear feet - lin. ft. 49
linear power controller - LPC 50
linear programming - LP 51
Lineas Aereas de Nicaragua - LANICA 52
lineman - lmn 53
linen chute - L CH 54
linen closet - L CL 55
line-of-position - l-o-p 56

137

```
line-of-sight - l-o-s                                     1
lines - ll                                                2
lines per inch - lpi                                      3
lines-per-minute - LPM                                    4
Ling-Temco-Vought - LTV                                   5
linguistic(s) - ling.                                     6
liniment - linim.                                         7
lining - lng                                              8
link - l.                                                 9
link(s) - li.                                            10
link alloter - LA                                        11
link circuit - LC                                        12
linoleum - lino.; linol.                                 13
linoleum base - LB                                       14
linoleum floor - LF                                      15
linotype - lino.                                         16
lintel - lntl                                            17
liquefied petroleum gas - LPG; L.P.G.                    18
liquid - liq.                                            19
liquid hourly space velocity - LHSV; L.H.S.V.            20
liquidation - liquid.                                    21
liquor - liq.                                            22
lira - L.                                                23
lira(s) - l.                                             24
Lisbon - Lis                                             25
listed - L                                               26
liter(s) - l                                             27
liter - lit.                                             28
literal - lit.                                           29
literally - lit.                                         30
literary - lit.                                          31
literature - lit.                                        32
Lithium - Li                                             33
lithograph - lith.; litho.; lithog.                      34
lithographical - lithog.                                 35
lithography - lith.; litho.; lithog.                     36
lithology - lithol.                                      37
Lithuanian - Lith.                                       38
litter - lit.                                            39
little - lil; lit.                                       40
Little League - LL                                       41
liturgical - liturg.                                     42
liturgy - liturg.                                        43
Live Oak, Perry & Gulf (RR) - LOP&G                      44
liver - liv                                              45
Liverpool - Liv                                          46
living room - LR                                         47
livre(s) - lv.                                           48
lizard - liz                                             49
load - ld                                                50
load accumulator - LAC                                   51
load accumulator with magnitude - LAM                    52
load cell - LC                                           53
load limit - ld. lmt.                                    54
load memory lockout register - LMLR                      55
load waterline - l.w.l.                                  56
```

```
load-compensated diode-transistor logic - LCDTL          1
loading - ldg.                                           2
loading point - ldg.pt.                                  3
loads - lds                                              4
loan - ln.                                               5
local - loc.                                             6
local purchase order - lpo                               7
local standard time - l.s.t.                             8
local time - l.t.                                        9
locality - lcty                                         10
locate - loc.                                           11
location - loc.                                         12
locker - lkr.                                           13
locker room - LKR R                                     14
lockwasher - lkwash                                     15
loco citato (in the place cited) - loc. cit.            16
loco supra citato (in the place above cited) - l.s.c.   17
locomotive - loco.                                      18
locus (a place) - L.                                    19
locus sigilli (the place of the seal) - L.S.           20
lodging - ldg                                           21
lodgings - ldgs                                         22
logarithm - log.                                        23
logging - logg.                                         24
logic - Log.; log.                                      25
logic corporation - LC                                  26
logic driver - LD                                       27
logic theory - LT                                       28
logical - log.                                          29
logical commands - LOGANDS                              30
logical equipment table - LET                           31
logical program - LOGRAM                                32
logistical support - log sup                            33
London - Lon.                                           34
long - lg                                               35
long calcined ton - l.c.t.                              36
long distance Xeroxography - LDX                        37
long dry ton - l.d.t.                                   38
Long Island (RR) - LI                                   39
long leg vertical - L.L.V.                              40
long meter - L.M.                                       41
long playing - l.p.                                     42
long playing, monaural - LPM                            43
long playing, stereo - LPS                              44
long range - lr                                         45
long range input monitor - LRIM                         46
long ton - l.t.; lt                                     47
long-distance call - ldc                                48
longevity - longv                                       49
Longfellow - Longf.                                     50
longitude (terrestrial) - L                             51
longitude - long.                                       52
longitudinal - long.                                    53
long-playing - LP                                       54
long-range data - LRD                                   55
long-range navigation - loran                           56
```

```
long-range search - LRS                              1
look for this (L, hoc quaere) - h.q.                 2
lookout - lkt                                        3
looper - L                                           4
looseleaf - l.l.                                     5
loquitur (he or she speaks) - loq.                   6
Lord (L, Dominus) - (D.); Ld.                        7
Lord Mayor - L.M.                                    8
Lorenzo - Lor.                                       9
Los Angeles - LA                                    10
loss factor - LF.                                   11
loss of signal - los                                12
loss on ignition - LOI; L.O.I.                      13
lost (no. of games) - L                             14
a lotion (L, lotio) - lot.                          15
louder (It, pin forte) - p.f.                       16
loudness level - LL                                 17
loudspeaker - ls                                    18
Louis - Ls                                          19
Louisiana - La.                                     20
Louisiana & Arkansas (RR) - L&A                     21
Louisiana & North West (RR) - L&NW                  22
Louisiana Midland (RR) - LM                         23
Louisiana Southern (RR) - LS                        24
Louisville & Nashville (RR) - L&N                   25
Louisville & Wadley (RR) - L&W                      26
louver - louv.                                      27
louver opening - L.O.                               28
louvered door - Louv. Dr.                           29
low - L.; l.; lo                                    30
low (common stock rating) - B-                      31
low altitude - l.a.                                 32
low and medium frequency - L/MF                     33
low blood pressure - l.b.p.                         34
low frequency - LF                                  35
Low German - LG.                                    36
Low Latin - LL.                                     37
low level - LL                                      38
low level logic - LLL                               39
low pass - LP                                       40
low point - L.P.                                    41
low pressure - LP                                   42
low tension - LT                                    43
low to high - L/H                                   44
low torque - lt                                     45
low voltage - LV                                    46
low watermark - l.w.m.                              47
low-alloy steel - l.a.s.                            48
low-density - l-d                                   49
lower - lr; lwr                                     50
lower case - l.c.                                   51
lower class - Lc                                    52
lower dead center - ldc                             53
lower deck - l.d.                                   54
lower echelon automatic switchboard - LEAS          55
lower grade (preferred stock rating) - BB           56
```

```
lower left - 1/1                                              1
lower left center - llc                                       2
lower limit - ll                                              3
lower right - 1/r                                             4
lower right center - lrc                                      5
lowest (common stock rating) - C                              6
lowest common denominator - l.c.d.                            7
lowest common multiple - lcm                                  8
low-frequency current - l-f.c.                                9
low-voltage - LV                                             10
low-watermark - lwm                                          11
Loyal Order of Moose - L.O.O.M.                              12
loyalty - loy                                                13
Loyola University - LU                                       14
lubricant - lub; lubric.                                     15
lubricate - lub; lubric.                                     16
lubricating oil - lub oil                                    17
lubrication - lub; lubric.                                   18
Lucius - L.                                                  19
Lucretius - Luc.; Lucr.                                      20
Lufthansa - LH                                               21
Luke - Lk                                                    22
lumbago - lum                                                23
lumber - lbr                                                 24
lumen - L; l                                                 25
lumen(s) - lm                                                26
luminosity - lum                                             27
luminous - lum                                               28
lunar - lun                                                  29
Lunar Equipment Conveyer - LEC                               30
lunar excursion module - LEM                                 31
Lunar Module - LM                                            32
Lunar Orbit Insertion - LOI                                  33
Lunar Receiving Laboratory - LRL                             34
Lupus (the Wolf) - Lup                                       35
lupus erythematosus - L.E.                                   36
Lutetium - Lu                                                37
Lutheran - Luth.                                             38
lux (light) - lx.                                            39
Luxembourg - Lux.                                            40
Lydia - Lyd                                                  41
lymph - lym                                                  42
Lyndon B. Johnson - LBJ                                      43
Lynx (the Lynx) - Lyn                                        44
Lyra (the Lyre) - Lyr                                        45
lyric(s) - lyr.                                              46
lyrical - lyr.                                               47
lyricism - lyr.                                              48
lyricist - lyr.                                              49
lysergic acid diethylamide - Acid; LSD                       50
Mabel - Mab                                                  51
1 Maccabees - 1 Mc                                           52
2 Maccabees - 2 Mc                                           53
Macedonia - Maced                                            54
macerate (L, macera) - mac.                                  55
mach speed - M                                               56
```

141

1 Maccabees - 1 Mc
2 Maccabees - 2 Mc
Macedonia - Maced
macerate (L, macera) - mac.
mach speed - M
machine - mach.
machine direction - MD; M.D.
machine finish - M.F.
machine language - ml
machine room - MACH R
machine screw - m.s.; Msc
machine steel - m.s.
machine translation - MT
machine unit - MU
machinery - mach.
machinist - mach.
Mackey Airlines - MK
mackinaw - mack
mackintosh - mack
Macomb County Community College - MCCC
Macon, Dublin & Savannah (RR) - MD&S
Madagascar - Madag.
Madame - Mme. (no period in French)
Madeira Islands - Mad. Is.
Mademoiselle - Mlle. (no period in French)
Mademoiselles - Mlles. (no period in French)
Madrid - Madr.
magazine - mag.
magister (master) - M.
magister artium (master of arts) - M.A.
magister chirurgiae (mastery of surgery) - M.Ch.
magnesia - mag
magnesia black - MB
magnesium - mag
Magnesium - Mg
magnet - M; mag.
magnetic - M; mag.
magnetic drum module - DM
magnetic field intensity - H
magnetic field strength - H
magnetic flux density - B; b
Magnetic Ink Character Recognition - MICR
magnetic tape - MT; mag tape
magnetic tape control unit - MTCU
magnetic tape field search - MFS
magnetic tape module - TM
magnetism - mag.; magn.
magneto - mag.
magneto hydrodynamics - MHD
magnetohydrodynamic device - MHD; M.H.D.
magnetohydrodynamic generator - MHD generator
magnetomotive force - MMF; M.M.F.; m.m.f.
magneton - M; mag.
magnitude - mag.
magnitude - magnit.
magnum - mag.

1
2
3
4
5
6
7
8
9
10
11
12
13
14
15
16
17
18
19
20
21
22
23
24
25
26
27
28
29
30
31
32
33
34
35
36
37
38
39
40
41
42
43
44
45
46
47
48
49
50
51
52
53
54
55
56

```
mahogany - mah.; mahog.                                    1
Maiden (horse racing) - M                                  2
maiden allowance (horse racing) - Alw.M.                   3
Maiden race (horse racing) - Mdn.                          4
mail - ml.                                                 5
mail chute - MC                                            6
mail order - m.o.                                          7
mail order department - M.O.D.                             8
main - mn                                                  9
main communications center - MCC                          10
main line of resistance - m.l.r.                          11
main memory - MM                                          12
Maine Central (Me.-N.H.-Vt.)(RR) - MC                     13
maintenance - maint.                                      14
maintenance and repairs - M&R                             15
maintenance and supply - M&S                              16
maintenance point - MP                                    17
maintenance repair and operating - MRO                    18
Majesty - M.                                              19
Major - Maj.                                              20
major - maj.                                              21
major general - Maj. Gen.                                 22
majority - maj.                                           23
make (L, fiant) - ft.                                     24
Make-a-Picture Story Test - MAPS                          25
make-before-break - MBB                                   26
make-break - M-B                                          27
Malachi - Mal.                                            28
Malagasy - Malag.                                         29
Malay - Mal.                                              30
Malaya - Mala.                                            31
Malayan - Mal.                                            32
male - m.                                                 33
male(s) - M                                               34
malfunction detection system - MDS                        35
malignant - malig                                         36
malleable - mall.                                         37
malleable iron - MI                                       38
malleable iron pipe - MIP                                 39
Malta - Mal                                               40
mammalogy - mammal.                                       41
management - mgmt.; mgt.                                   42
management information systems - MIS                      43
manager - man.; mgr.                                      44
Manchuria - Manch                                         45
maneuvering - manuv                                       46
Manganese - Mn                                            47
Manhattan - Man.; Manh.                                   48
manhole - M.H.                                            49
manhour - manhr                                           50
manifest - man.; manif.; mfst.                            51
manifold - manf.                                          52
Manila - Man.                                             53
manipulus (handful) - M.                                  54
Manistee & Northeastern (RR) - M&NE                       55
Manistique & Lake Superior (RR) - M&LS                    56
```

```
Manitoba - M.; Man.                                              1
manual - m; man.                                                 2
manual of operation - MANOP                                      3
manual word - MW                                                 4
manually operated - m.o.; man.op.                                5
manually operated plotting board - MOPB                          6
manufacture - mfr.                                               7
manufactured - mfd.                                              8
manufacturer - mfr.                                              9
manufacturers - mfrs.                                           10
manufacturing - mfg.                                            11
manure - man.                                                   12
manuscript - MS                                                 13
manuscript(s) - ms.(s.)                                         14
manuscripts - MSS                                               15
map reference - MR                                              16
Marathon Oil Company - M                                        17
marble - mar.; MR                                               18
Marble Window Stools - MarW.Stl.                                19
marbled edges - m.e.                                            20
March - Mar.; Mr.                                               21
Marchioness - March.                                            22
Marcus - M.; Marc.; Mcs.                                        23
mare (horse racing) - m.                                        24
Margaret - Mag.; Marg.                                          25
Margery - Marg.                                                 26
margin - marg.                                                  27
margin of safety - M.S.                                         28
marginal - marg.                                                29
marginal credit - M/C                                           30
marginalia - marg.                                              31
Maria - Mar.                                                    32
Marian Fathers - M.I.C.                                         33
MarianHill Fathers - C.M.M.                                     34
marijuana - J; juana; THC                                       35
marijuana's unpredictable element - tetrahydrocannabinol -      36
    THC                                                         37
marine - mar.                                                   38
Marist Brothers - F.M.S.                                        39
Marist Fathers - S.M.                                           40
maritime - mar.                                                 41
Maritime Administration - MA                                    42
Mark - Mk                                                       43
mark (L, signa) - mk.; (S)                                      44
mark well (L, nota bene) - N.B.                                 45
marked - mkd.; MRKD                                             46
marker - mrkr                                                   47
marker light indicator - MLI                                    48
market - mar.; mkt.                                             49
market value - m.v.                                             50
marksman - mkm                                                  51
Marquess - Marq.                                                52
Marquette University - MU                                       53
Marquis - Marq.                                                 54
married - m.; mar.                                              55
Martin Luther King - MLK                                        56
```

Martin thin-film electronic circuit - MARTEC   1
Martinique - Mart.   2
martyr - M.   3
martyrology - Mart.   4
Martyrs - MM.   5
Marygrove College - MC   6
Maryknoll Missioners - M.M.   7
Maryland - Md.   8
Maryland & Pennsylvania (RR) - M&P   9
masculine - m.; masc.   10
mask index register - MXR   11
masonry - mas.; msry.   12
masonry opening - M.O.   13
mass - M.; m.   14
Mass Concentrations - MASCON   15
mass over energy - m/e   16
Massachusetts - Mass.   17
Massachusetts Institute of Technology - M.I.T.   18
master (L, magister) - M.   19
Master Commandant - M.C.   20
master control - MC   21
master control program - MCP   22
master control routine - MCR   23
master control system - MCS   24
master drum sender - MDS   25
master gunnery sergeant - M. Gunnery Sgt.   26
Master in Surgery - M.S.   27
master instruction tape - MIT   28
master keyed - MK   29
master mechanic - mstr. mech.   30
master monitor - MM   31
Master of Agriculture - M.Agr.   32
Master of Arts (L, Artium Magister) - A.M.   33
Master of Arts (L, Magister Artium) - M.A.   34
Master of Arts in Social Work - A.M.S.W.   35
Master of Business Administration - M.B.A.   36
master of ceremonies - emcee   37
Master of Ceremonies - M.C.   38
Master of Civil Law - M.C.L.   39
Master of Dental Surgery - M.D.S.   40
Master of Education - Ed.M.; M.Ed.   41
Master of Fine Arts - M.F.A.   42
master of foxhounds - M.F.H.   43
Master of Laws (L, Legum Magister) - LL.M.   44
Master of Library Science - M.L.S.   45
Master of Music (L, Musicae Magister) - Mus.M.   46
Master of Pedagogy - M.Pd.; Pd.M.   47
Master of Pharmacy - Pharm.M.   48
Master of Physical Education - M.P.E.   49
Master of Sacred Theology - S.T.M.   50
Master of Science (L, Scientiae Magister) - M.S.; M.Sc.   51
    (S.M.; Sc.M.)   52
Master of Science in Engineering - M.S.E.   53
Master of Surgery (L, Chirurgiae Magister) - C.M.   54
Master of Surgery (L, Magister Chirurgiae) - M.Ch.   55
master oscillator-power amplifier - MOPA   56

```
master sergeant - M.Sgt.                                          1
Master-at-Arms - MAA                                              2
masurium - Ma                                                     3
match race (horse racing) - Mtch.                                 4
material - matl.; mtrl.                                           5
material handling - m.h.                                          6
mathematical - math.                                              7
mathematical constant expressing acceleration of a body          8
    due to gravitation - g                                       9
mathematics - math.                                              10
matinee - mat.                                                   11
matins - mat.                                                    12
matriculate - matric.                                            13
matriculation - matric.                                          14
Mattachine Society - MS                                          15
Matthew - Mt                                                     16
maturity - mat.                                                  17
Maurice - Maur.                                                  18
Mauritania - Maur.                                               19
maxilla - maxill                                                 20
maxillary - maxill                                               21
maxim - max.                                                     22
maximal - max                                                    23
Maximilian - Max                                                 24
maximum - max.; mxm.                                             25
maximum allowable concentration - MAC                            26
maximum capacity - max. cap.                                     27
maximum effort - m.e.                                            28
maximum likelihood estimate - MLE                                29
maximum torque - m.t.                                            30
maximum usable frequency - MUF                                   31
May - My.                                                        32
may he, she, or they rest in peace (L, requiescat, or            33
    requiescant in pace) - R.I.P.                                34
mayonnaise - mayo                                                35
mean acrodynamic chord - MAC; M.A.C.                             36
mean blood pressure - m.b.p.                                     37
mean corpuscular hemoglobin - MCH                                38
mean corpuscular hemoglobin concentration - MCHC                 39
mean corpuscular volume - MCV                                    40
mean deviation - m.d.                                            41
mean down time - MDT                                             42
mean effective pressure - MEP; M.E.P.; m.e.p.                    43
mean high tide - MHT                                             44
mean sea level - m.s.l.                                          45
mean square - MS                                                 46
mean temperature difference - MTD; M.T.D.                        47
mean time between failures - MTBF                                48
mean time to repair - MTTR                                       49
mean value - MV                                                  50
mean variation - m.v.                                            51
mean-time-to-failure - MTTF                                      52
measurable - meas.                                               53
measure - m; meas.                                               54
Measure of Undesirable Respirable Contaminants (air              55
    pollution) - MURC Index                                      56
```

```
measured value - MV                                                   1
measurement - meas.; mst.                                             2
mechanic - mec.                                                       3
mechanical - mech.                                                    4
mechanical efficiency - ME                                            5
Mechanical Engineer - M.E.                                            6
mechanical part - MP                                                  7
mechanical translation - MT                                           8
mechanics - m; mech.                                                  9
mechanism - mech.                                                    10
mechanized - mech.; mecz.                                            11
medal - med.                                                         12
medalist - med.                                                      13
medallion - med.                                                     14
median - med                                                         15
medic - med                                                          16
medical - med                                                        17
medical care - medicare                                              18
medical corpsman - medic                                             19
medical discharge - MD                                               20
medical lavatory - ML                                                21
Medical Literature Analysis and Retrieval System - MEDLARS           22
Medical Unit Self-contained Transportable - MUST                     23
Medication - MED.                                                    24
medicinae (of medicine) - M.                                         25
medicinae baccalaureus (bachelor of medicine) - M.B.                 26
medicine - med.                                                      27
medicine cabinet - MC; Med. Cab.                                     28
Medieval - M; med.                                                   29
Medieval Greek - MGk; MGr                                            30
Medieval Latin - ML                                                  31
Mediterranean - Medit.                                               32
medium - m.; med.                                                    33
medium frequency - MF; m.f.; mf                                      34
medium grade (preferred stock rating) - BBB                          35
medium power - M                                                     36
meeting - mtg.                                                       37
mega - M                                                             38
mega roentgen equivalent physical - megarep; megareps                39
megacycle - mc.                                                      40
megacycles per second = Mega-Hertz - m.c.p.s.                        41
Mega-Hertz - MHz                                                     42
megajoules - mj.                                                     43
megarads - mr.                                                       44
megasecond - ms.                                                     45
megaton - mt.                                                        46
megawatt - Mw                                                        47
megawatt-days - mwd.; mw.d.                                          48
megawatt-days per ton - MWD/T                                        49
megawatts electrical - MWE                                           50
megohm - MEG                                                         51
Melanesia - Melan.                                                   52
Melanesian - Melan.                                                  53
Melba - Mel                                                          54
melodrama - melo                                                     55
melting point - M.P.; m.p.                                           56
```

147

```
Melvil - Mel                                                         1
Melville - Mel                                                       2
Melvin - Mel                                                         3
member - mbr.; mem.                                                  4
Member of Congress - M.C.                                            5
Member of Parliament - M.P.                                          6
Member of Parliament (Canada) - MPC; M.P.C.                          7
Member of the House of Representatives - M.H.R.                      8
Member of the Royal College of Physicians - M.R.C.P.                9
Member of the Royal College of Surgeons - M.R.C.S.                  10
a member of the Women's Army Corps - WAC                            11
a member of the Youth International Party - YIPPIE                  12
a member of women in the Air Force - WAF                           13
membrane - memb                                                    14
memento - mem.                                                     15
memoir(s) - mem.                                                   16
memorandum - mem.; memo.                                           17
memorandum of deposit - M/D; m.d.                                  18
memorial - mem.                                                    19
Memorial University of Newfoundland - MUN                          20
memory - mem.                                                      21
memory address - MA                                                22
memory buffer - MB                                                 23
memory buffer register - MBR                                       24
memory buffer register, even - MBR-E                               25
memory buffer register, odd - MBR-O                                26
memory information register - MIR                                  27
memory lockout register - MLR                                      28
memory multiplexor - MM                                            29
memory register - MR                                               30
memory system - MS                                                 31
memory-address register - MAR                                      32
memory-address register storage - MARS                             33
memory-data register - MDR                                         34
Men Our Masters - MOM                                              35
Mennonite - Men.; Mennon.                                          36
Men's rest room - MRR                                              37
Men's toilet - MT                                                  38
Men's Wash Room - MWR                                              39
Mensa (the Table Mountain) - Men                                   40
menses - men.                                                      41
menstruation - men.                                                42
mental - ment                                                      43
mercantile - mer.; merc.                                           44
merchandise - mdse.                                                45
merchantable - merch                                               46
mercurial - merc.                                                  47
Mercury - Hg; Mer                                                  48
mercury - merc.                                                    49
Mercury Redstone 3 (rocket) - MR-3                                 50
Mercury Redstone 4 (rocket) - MR-4                                 51
Mericana de Aviacion - CMA                                         52
meridian - m; mer.                                                 53
Meridian & Bigbee River (RR) - M&BR                                54
meridies (noon) - m.                                               55
Merionethshire - Merions.                                          56
```

```
Mesa - M                                                         1
Mesdames - Mmes. (no period in French)                           2
mesothorium - Ms-Th                                              3
message - msg.                                                   4
message waiting - MSG/WTG                                        5
message-waiting indicator - MWI                                  6
messenger - msgr.                                                7
Messieurs - MM.                                                  8
mestizo - mest                                                   9
meta- - m-                                                       10
metabolic index - m.i.                                           11
metabolic rate - m.r.                                            12
metabolism - metab                                               13
metal - met.                                                     14
Metal Acoustical Panels - M.Ac.Pan.                              15
Metal Acoustical Pans - M.Ac.P.                                  16
Metal Baluster/Painted - Met.Bal./Pt.                            17
metal base - MB                                                  18
metal clad - met.cl.                                             19
metal covered wood - mcw                                         20
Metal Deck Closure-Painted - Met.De.Cl./Pt.                      21
metal divider strip - M.D.S.                                     22
metal edge strip - M.E.S.                                        23
Metal Hand Railing/Painted - Met.H.Rail/Pt.                      24
metal lath - M.L.                                                25
Metal Lockers - Met.Loc.                                         26
Metal Siding - Met.Sid.                                          27
Metal Siding Painted - Met.Sid./Pt.                              28
Metal Stringer & Risers/Painted - Met.Str.&Ri./Pt.              29
metallurgical - metal.                                           30
Metallurgical Engineer - Met.E.                                  31
metallurgy - metal.; metall.                                     32
metaphor - met.                                                  33
metaphysic(s) - metaph.                                          34
metaphysical - metaph.                                           35
metaphysics - met.; metaphys.                                    36
meteorological - meteor.; meteorol.                              37
meteorological satellite - METSAT                                38
meteorology - meteor.; meteorol.                                 39
meter(s) - m                                                     40
meter (instrument) - M                                           41
meter kilogram - mk.                                             42
metering - mtrg                                                  43
meter-kilograms - m-kg.                                          44
meter-kilogram-second system - MKS system                        45
meters per second - m/s                                          46
methane - meth                                                   47
method - meth.                                                   48
Methodist - Meth                                                 49
Methodist Episcopal - ME                                         50
methyl - Me                                                      51
metric ton - M.T.; t.                                            52
Metro-Goldwyn-Mayer - MGM                                        53
metronome - met.                                                 54
metropolis - metrop.                                             55
metropolitan - met.; metrop.                                     56
```

149

```
Metropolitan Police - M.P.                                         1
Metropolitan Transit Authority - MTA                               2
Mexican - Mex.                                                     3
Mexican pesetas - Mptas.                                           4
Mexico - Mex.                                                      5
mezzanine - mezz.                                                  6
mezzo forte (moderately loud) - mf; m.f.                           7
Miami University - MU                                              8
Micah - Mi.; Mic.                                                  9
Michael - Mich.; Michl.                                           10
Michael J. Heffernan - MJH                                        11
Michaelmas - Mich.                                                12
Michigan - Mich.                                                  13
Michigan Committee Against Repression - MCAR                      14
Michigan Council of Cooperative Nurseries - MCCN                  15
Michigan International Speedway - MIS                             16
Michigan Library Association - M.L.A.                             17
Michigan State University - MSU                                   18
microalloy diffused-base transistor - MADT                       19
microalloy transistor - MAT                                      20
microampere - mu a                                               21
microelectronic - ME                                             22
microfarad - mf; Mfd.                                            23
microfilm - mcflm                                                24
Microfunctional circuit - MFC                                    25
microgram(s) - mcg.                                              26
micro-inch - micro-in.                                           27
micrometer - mike                                                28
micromicrofarad - Mmf; Mmfd                                      29
micromicron - mu mu                                              30
micron - mu                                                      31
Micronesia - Micron                                              32
microphone - mic; mike                                           33
microscope - micros.                                             34
microscopic - micros.                                            35
Microscopium (the Microscope) - Mic                              36
microscopy - micros.                                             37
microsecond - mu sec.                                            38
microvolt - mu v                                                 39
microwatt - mu w                                                 40
microwave amplification by stimulated emission of radiation      41
    maser                                                        42
Middle - M.; m.; mid.                                            43
middle class - Mc                                                44
Middle Creek (W.Va.)(RR) - MC                                    45
Middle Dutch - MD                                                46
Middle English - ME                                              47
Middle Flemish - MFl.                                            48
Middle French - MF; MFr.                                         49
Middle Greek - MGr.                                              50
Middle High German - MHG                                         51
middle initial - m.i.                                            52
Middle Irish - MIr.                                              53
Middle Italian - MIt.                                            54
Middle Low German - MLG.                                         55
middle of the month - m.o.m.                                     56
```

```
Middle Scottish - MScot                                        1
Midland Continental (RR) - MCO                                 2
Midland Valley (RR) - MV                                       3
midnight - mdnt.                                               4
Midshipman - Mid.; midn.                                       5
Midwest Stock Exchange - MSE; MW                               6
midwestern - midw                                              7
milage - mil.                                                  8
Milan - Mil                                                    9
mile - m.                                                     10
mile(s) - mi.                                                 11
mileage - mil.                                                12
miles per gallon - MPG; mpg; m.p.g.                           13
miles per hour - mph                                          14
miles per hour per second - mi. per hr. per sec.              15
military - mil.; milit.; MLTY                                 16
Military Academy - M.A.                                       17
Military Advisory Group - MAG                                 18
Military Assistance Command, Vietnam - MACV                   19
military exchange - MEX                                       20
military occupational specialty - MOS                         21
military personnel - mil pers                                 22
Military Police - M.P.                                        23
military press (weight lifting) - M.P.                        24
military specification - milspec                              25
Military Standard - Mil-Std; MIL-STD                          26
Military Test Space Station - MTSS                            27
militia - mil.                                                28
mill(s) - mi.                                                 29
mill annealed - ma                                            30
mill arbor - ml ar                                            31
mill cutter - ml cu                                           32
mill finish - M.F.                                            33
mill run - M.R.; m.r.                                         34
milliampere(s) - ma.                                          35
millibar - mb.                                                36
millibarns - mb.                                              37
millicurie(s) - mc.                                           38
millicycles per second = milli-Hertz - m.c.p.s.              39
millidarcies - md.                                            40
milliequivalent - me; m.eq.; meq.; mEq.                       41
millifarad - mf.; mfd.                                        42
milli-foot-lamberts - mftl                                    43
milligals - mgals.                                            44
milligauss - mG                                               45
milligram(s) - mg.                                            46
milligram atoms per gram - mats./g.                           47
milligrams - mg.                                              48
millihenry - mh.                                              49
milli-Hertz - mHz                                             50
millijoules - mj.                                             51
milliliter(s) - ml                                            52
millimeter(s) - mm                                            53
millimicron - m mu                                            54
millimoles - mM.                                              55
milliner - mlnr.                                              56
```

```
Missile Defense Alarm System - MIDAS                                1
missing - mis; misg                                                 2
missing in action - MIA                                             3
mission - miss.                                                     4
Missionaries of the Holy Family - M.S.F.                            5
Missionaries of the Sacred Heart - M.S.C.                           6
missionary - miss.                                                  7
Missionary Church Association - MCA                                 8
Missionary Servants of the Most Holy Trinity - M.S.S.S.T.           9
Mississippi - Miss.                                                10
Mississippi Central (Miss.)(RR) - MC                               11
Mississippi Export (RR) - MEX                                      12
Mississippi State University - MSU                                 13
Missouri - Mo.                                                     14
Missouri Illinois (RR) - MI                                        15
Missouri Pacific (RR) - MP                                         16
Missouri Valley Authority- MVA                                     17
Missouri-Kansas-Texas (RR) - MKT                                   18
Missus - Mrs.                                                      19
Mister - Mr.                                                       20
Mister (Fr, Monsieur) - M.                                         21
Mister (Ger, Herr) - Hr.                                           22
Mister, Miss, Mistress (Port, Dom, Dona) - D.                      23
Mister, Miss, Mistress (Sp, Don, Dona) - D.                        24
Misters - Messrs.                                                  25
Mistress - Mrs.                                                    26
Mitchell - Mitch                                                   27
mix (L, misce) - M.; m.                                            28
mixed - mxd.                                                       29
mixing - mix.                                                      30
mixture - mixt.                                                    31
mixture of smoke and fog - smog                                    32
mobile - M; mbl.; mob.                                             33
Mobile (Bell Telephone) - M                                        34
Mobile & Gulf (RR) - M&G                                           35
mobilization - mob.                                                36
mobilization day - M-day                                           37
mobilized - mob.                                                   38
mode transducer - MT                                               39
model - mod                                                        40
Model Cities - MC                                                  41
models - mods                                                      42
moderate - mdt.; mod.                                              43
moderately loud (It, mezzo forte) - mf.                            44
moderately slow and even (music) - andante                         45
moderato (music) - mod.                                            46
modern - mod.                                                      47
Modern English - MnE.                                              48
Modern English Usage (Fowler) - MEU                                49
Modern Greek - Mod.Gr.                                             50
Modern Language Association - M.L.A.                               51
Modern Latin - Mod. L.                                             52
Modern Provençal - Mod. Pr.                                        53
modern tips - MT                                                   54
Modern Woodmen of America - M.W.A.                                 55
moderns - mods                                                     56
```

```
modification - mod.                                         1
modification of - m.                                        2
modification of the stem of - m.s.                          3
modified - mod.                                             4
modifiers - mods.                                           5
modify - mod.                                               6
modular - mod.                                              7
Modularized Equipment Stowage Assembly - MESA               8
modulated continuous wave - MCW                             9
modulation-demodulation - M-D                              10
modulator - mod.                                           11
module - mod.                                              12
modules - mods.                                            13
modulus of elasticity - E                                  14
Mohawk Airlines - MO                                       15
moisture and ash free - m.a.f.                             16
molar - m.                                                 17
molar absorbancy - Am                                      18
molar ratio of phosphorus to lead - MR P/Ph                19
molded - mld.                                              20
molder - mldr.                                             21
molecular - mol.                                           22
molecular electronics - ME                                 23
molecular weight - M; mol.wt.                              24
molecule - mol.                                            25
molienisia (tropical fish) - mollie                        26
Molybdenum - Mo                                            27
Monaco - Mon                                               28
monastery - mon.                                           29
monaural - mono                                            30
Monday - M.; Mo.; Mon.                                     31
monetary - mon.                                            32
money - moy                                                33
money order - M.O.; m.o.                                   34
Mongolia - Mong.                                           35
Mongolian - Mong.; Mongol.                                 36
monitor - M; MNTR; mon                                     37
monitor out of service - MONOS                             38
monitor station reports - MOREPS                           39
monitoring - montrg                                        40
Monoceros (the Unicorn) - Mon                              41
monogram - monog.                                          42
Monographs - Monogr.                                       43
monolithic - monol.                                        44
mononucleosis - mono                                       45
monophonic - mono                                          46
monorail - mono                                            47
Monosodium Glutamate - MSG                                 48
monotonous - monot                                         49
monotony - monot                                           50
monotype - monot                                           51
Monseigneur - mgr.                                         52
monsieur (Mister) - M.                                     53
Monsignor - Mgr.; Mngr.; Mon.; Msgr.                       54
monsoon - mon                                              55
Montana - Mont.                                            56
```

Montana State University - MSU   1
Montecarlo method - MCM   2
month - m.; mo.   3
monthly - M; Month.   4
months - mos.   5
months after date - M/D; m.d.   6
months after sight - m/s   7
month's date - m.d.   8
Montour (RR) - MON   9
Montreal - Mont.   10
Montreal Stock Exchange - MON; MS   11
monument - mon   12
moon - m.   13
Moravian - Mor.   14
more - M   15
Morehouse College - MC   16
Mormon - Morm   17
morning - A.M.; a.m.; m.   18
Moroccan - Mor.   19
Morocco - Mor.   20
morocco - mor.   21
morphine - M; morph.   22
morphological - morph.   23
Morphologisches - Morphol.   24
morphology - morph.; morphol.   25
Morris - Mor.   26
mortal - mort   27
mortality - mort   28
mortar - mort   29
mortgage - mtg.; mtge.   30
mortgaged - mtgd.   31
mortgagee - mtgee.   32
mortgagor - mtgor.   33
mortician - mort.   34
Morton - Mort   35
mortuary - mort.   36
mosaic - mos   37
Moscow - Mos   38
mosque - Mq   39
Most Holy Lord (a title of the Pope) (L, Sanctissimus   40
    Dominus) - SS.D.   41
Most Reverend - Mt. Rev.   42
most significant bit - MSB   43
most valuable player (sports) - MVP   44
mother - m   45
motion - mtn   46
Motion Picture Association of America - MPAA   47
motivation research - MR; M.R.   48
motor - M; mot.   49
motor drive - MD   50
motor freight - m.f.   51
motor generator - MG   52
motor operated - mot.op.   53
motor vessel - MV   54
motorboat - m.b.   55
motorcycle - mtrcl.   56

```
motorize - mtz.                                                          1
motorized - mot.                                                         2
Motorized Section of the N.S.D.A.P. (Nationalsozialistis-                3
   cheskraftfahrerkorps) - N.S.K.K.                                      4
motorship - MS                                                           5
moulding - mldg.                                                         6
mount - Mt.; mt.; mtn.                                                   7
mountain - M.; Mt.; mt.; mtn.                                            8
mountain standard time - m.s.t.                                          9
mountain time - m.t.                                                    10
mountains - Mts.; mts.                                                  11
mounted - mtd.                                                          12
Mounted Police - M.P.; MP                                              13
mounting - mtg.                                                        14
mounts - Mts.                                                          15
mouth - mth.                                                           16
movable metal partition - M.M.P.                                       17
movable partition - M PART                                             18
movement - mvmt                                                        19
Movement for a Democratic Military - MDM                               20
moving mop display - MMD                                               21
Mozambique - Moz.                                                      22
mucilage - muc.                                                        23
mucous membrane - m.m.                                                 24
muddy (horse racing, condition of the track) - my.                     25
muffed fly (baseball) - O                                              26
mulatto - mulat                                                        27
mullion - mull.                                                        28
multiaperture device - MAD                                             29
multichannel data recorder - MDR                                       30
multicomponent circuits - MCC                                          31
multifrequency key pulsing - MFKP                                      32
multiple frequency-shift keying - MFSK                                 33
multiple independent re-entry vehicle - MIRV                           34
multiple independently targetable re-entry vehicles - MIRV             35
multiple module access - MMA                                           36
multiple sclerosis - m.s.                                              37
multiple transfer - MT                                                 38
multiple-access computer - mac                                         39
multiplex - mpx; MUX                                                   40
multiplex-automatic error correction - MUX-ARO                         41
multiplexer and terminal unit - MTU                                    42
multiplier quotient register - MQ                                      43
multiply - MLY                                                         44
multiply and round - MLR                                               45
multipurpose communications and signaling - MCS                        46
Munich - Mun                                                           47
municipal - mun.                                                       48
municipal police - M.P.                                                49
municipality - mun.                                                    50
munition(s) - mun.                                                     51
Musca (the [Southern] Fly) - Mus                                       52
Muscat & Oman - Oman.                                                  53
muscular dystrophy - m.d.                                              54
museum - mus.                                                          55
music - mus.                                                           56
```

```
music wire - muw                                               1
music wire gauge - m.w.g.                                      2
musicae magister (master of music) - Mus.M.                    3
musical - Mus.                                                 4
musician - Mus.                                                5
musicologist - musicol                                         6
musicology - musicol                                           7
Muslim - Mus                                                   8
muslin - musl.                                                 9
mutation - mut                                                10
mutatis mutandis (with the necessary changes) - m.m.          11
mutato nomine (the name being changed) - m.n.                 12
mutilate - mutil                                              13
mutilated - mut; mutil                                        14
mutilation - mutil                                            15
mutual - mut.; mutu.                                          16
mutual conductance - Gm, gm                                   17
mutual defense assistance program - MDAP                      18
mutual inductance - M                                         19
Mutual of New York - MONY                                     20
muzzle velocity - M.V.                                        21
mycological - mycol.                                          22
mycology - mycol.                                             23
myopia - My.                                                  24
myriagram - myg.                                              25
myrialiter - myl.                                             26
myriameter - mym.                                             27
myriare - mya.                                                28
mysteries - myst.                                             29
mystery - myst.                                               30
mythological - myth.; mythol.                                 31
mythology - myth.; mythol.                                    32
Nacogdoches & Southeastern (RR) - N&SE                        33
Nagasaki - Nag                                                34
Nahum - Na; Nah.                                              35
nail - N                                                      36
name (L, nomen) - N; nom.                                     37
the name being changed (L, mutato nomine) - m.n.             38
name unknown - n.u.                                           39
namely (L, scilicet) - sc.; scil.                             40
namely (L, scilicet) - SS.; ss.                               41
namely (L, videlicet) - viz.                                  42
names (L, nomina) - N                                         43
Nano - N                                                      44
nanofarad - Nf                                                45
nanohenry - nh                                                46
nanosecond - NSEC                                             47
napalm - nap.                                                 48
Naples - Nap                                                  49
Napoleon - Nap.                                               50
narcotic - narc                                               51
narcotic addict - narco                                       52
narcotics - cotics                                            53
narrow - nar                                                  54
narrow band frequency modulation - NBFM                       55
narrow gauge - n.g.                                           56
```

157

National Labor Relations Board - NLRB   1
National League (baseball) - NL   2
National Liberation Front - NLF   3
National Library of Canada - NLC   4
National Lumber Manufacturers Association - NLMA   5
National Mobilization Committee to End the War - MOB   6
National Office of Vital Statistics - NOVS   7
National Organization for Women - NOW   8
National Park - Nat Pk   9
National Peace Action Coalition - NPAC   10
National Petroleum Association - NPA; N.P.A.   11
National Railways of Mexico (RR) - NRM   12
National Recovery Administration - NRA; N.R.A.   13
National Research Council - N.R.C.   14
National Resistance Committee (WWII, Comité National de la   15
    Résistance) - CNR   16
National Safety Council - N.S.C.   17
National Science Foundation - NSF   18
National Security Council - NSC   19
National Shipping Authority - NSA   20
National Socialist German Workers' Party (Nationalsozialis- 21
    titsche Deutsche Arbeiter Partei) - N.S.D.A.P.   22
National Stock Exchange - NSE   23
National United Front of Kampuchea - FUNK   24
National Youth Organization - NYA; N.Y.A.   25
Nationalist - N.   26
Nationalsocialistische Deutsche Arbeiterpartei, see   27
    National Socialist German Workers' Party - NAZI   28
native - nat.   29
natural - nat.   30
natural history - nat. hist.   31
natural log - n.l.   32
natural order - nat. ord.   33
natural radioactivity - RN   34
natural science - nat. sci.   35
naturalist - nat.   36
naturalization - nat.   37
naturalized - nat.   38
nature - nat.   39
natus (born) - n.   40
naught - 0   41
nautical - n; naut.   42
nautical mile - n.m.   43
nautical miles - NMI   44
naval - nav.   45
Naval Engineer - N.E.   46
navigate - nav.   47
navigating - nav.   48
navigation - nav.; navig.   49
navigational satellite - NAVSAT   50
navigator - nav.; navig.   51
Navy - N.   52
Nazarene - Naz.   53
Nazi Conspiracy and Aggression - N.C.A.   54
near - nr.   55
Nebraska - Neb.; Nebr.   56

```
necessary - nec                                              1
neck - nk                                                    2
neck (horse racing) - nk.                                    3
necrology - necrol                                           4
necrosis - necr                                              5
negation - neg.                                              6
negative - n; neg.                                           7
negative electron - negatron                                 8
negative input, positive output -   NIPO                     9
negatively - neg.                                           10
Negro - N; Neg                                              11
Negroid - Neg                                               12
Nehemiah - Neh                                              13
Neighborhood Youth Corps - NYC                              14
Nelson - Nels                                               15
nemine contradicente (no one contradicting) - nem. con.     16
Neodymium - Nd                                              17
Neo-Latin - NL; NL.; N.L.                                   18
neological - neol.                                          19
neologism - neol.                                           20
neologist - neol.                                           21
neologistic - neol.                                         22
neologistical - neol.                                       23
neology - neol.                                             24
Neon - N                                                    25
neon - Ne                                                   26
Nepal - Nep.                                                27
nephew - n.                                                 28
Nepos (grandson) - N.                                       29
Neptune - Nep.                                              30
nested - nstd.                                              31
net - n.                                                    32
net proceeds - n.p.                                         33
net weight - n.wt.; nt.wt.                                  34
Netherlands - Neth.                                         35
Netherlands West Indies - Neth.W.I.                         36
nets (tennis) - N                                           37
network - net.                                              38
Network Election Service - N.E.S.                           39
neuralgia - neur                                            40
neuritis - neur                                             41
neurological - neurol                                       42
neurologist - neurol                                        43
neurology - neurol                                          44
neuropathology - neuropath                                  45
neurotic - neuro                                            46
neuter - n; neut.                                           47
neutral - n; neut.                                          48
neutral ion - neutron                                       49
neutral protein Hagedorn (insulin) - NPH                    50
neutrality - neut.                                          51
neutralization number - NN; N.N.                            52
neutron - n                                                 53
Nevada - Nev.                                               54
Nevada Northern (RR) - NN                                   55
new - n.; nu                                                56
```

night frequency - NFQ 1
night letter - NL 2
night letter telegram - NLT 3
night message - NM 4
nimbus - N; Nb. 5
nine - IX 6
nine hundred - CM 7
nineteen - XIX 8
ninety - XC 9
Niobium - Nb 10
nipple - nip 11
Nipponese - Nip 12
nisi prius (unless before) - ni.pri. 13
niton - Nt. 14
Nitrogen - N 15
nigrogen-free extract - n.-f.e. 16
nitroglycerin - ng 17
no account - N.A.; n/a 18
no appreciable disease - N.A.D. 19
No Charge - N.C. 20
no commercial value - n.c.v. 21
no connection - NC 22
no date - n.d. 23
no detect - ND 24
no funds - n/f; N.F.; n.f. 25
no further requirement(s) - n.f.r. 26
no go - n.g. 27
no good - N.G.; n.g. 28
no one contradicting (L, nemine contradicente) - nem. con. 29
no place - n.p. 30
no place or date - n.p. or d. 31
no price - NP 32
no protest - N.P. 33
no publisher - n.p. 34
No Ranking - N.R. 35
no risk - n.r. 36
no strength temperature- NST; N.S.T. 37
no time lost - n.t.l. 38
no title page - n.t.p. 39
no transmission - NT 40
Noah - No. 41
nobis (for [or on] our part) - nob. 42
nocte (at night) - n. 43
noise criterion - NC 44
noise load ratio - NLR 45
noise transmission impairment - NTT 46
noise-measuring equipment - NME 47
nolle prosequi (will not prosecute) - nol. pros. 48
no-load speed - NLS 49
nomen (name) - N.; nom. 50
nomenclature - nom. 51
nomina (names) - N. 52
nominal - nom. 53
nominal damages - nom dam 54
nominal horse power - N.H.P. 55
nominal pipe size - nps 56

nominate - nom	1
nominative - n.; nom.; nomin.	2
non culpabilis (not guilty) - non cul.	3
non licet (it is not permitted) - n.l.	4
non liquet (it is not clear) - n.l.	5
non longe (not far) - n.l.	6
non obstante (notwithstanding) - non obs.	7
non prosequitur (he does not prosecute) - non pros.	8
non sequitur (it does not follow) - non seq.	9
nonappropriated funds - naf	10
nonautomatic self-verification - N SV	11
Non-Callable - NC	12
noncommissioned - noncom.	13
Noncommissioned Officer - NCO; noncom.	14
nonconformist - noncon.	15
Non-Cumulative - non-cm	16
nondestructive readout (Burroughs) - NDRO	17
nondestructive testing - NDT	18
nonexpendable - nx	19
noninterference basis - NIB	20
nonlinear differential equations - NDE	21
nonprotein nitrogen - NPN	22
non-rapid eye movements - NREM	23
non-removable pin - NRP	24
nonresident - non-res	25
nonreturn to zero - NRZ	26
nonreturn-to-zero-change - NRZ-C	27
nonreturn-to-zero-mark - NRZ-M	28
non-slip - n.s.	29
nonstandard - non std; n.s.	30
nonstandard item - nsi	31
Non-voting - non-vtg; nv	32
Noon (L, meridies) - (M.; m.); N.; n.	33
Nordair - NDR	34
Norfolk - Norf.	35
Norfolk & Western (RR) - N&W	36
Norfolk Southern (RR) - NS	37
norm - n	38
Norma (the Level) - Nor	39
normal - N; n; nor.; norm.; nrml.	40
Normal (strength solution) - N.	41
normal pressure and temperature - npt	42
normal temperature and pressure - NTP; N.T.P.	43
normal working hours - NWH	44
normalize - NRM	45
normally closed - NC	46
normally open - NO	47
Norman - Nor.; Norm	48
Norman French - NF	49
Norse - N.	50
north - N; n; No.; Nor.	51
North America - N.A.	52
North Atlantic Treaty Organization - NATO	53
North Borneo - N.Bor.	54
North Carolina - N.C.	55
North Central Airlines - NO	56

North Central Association of Colleges and Secondary
    Schools - N.C.A.C.S.S.
North Dakota - N.D.; N.Dak.
north latitude - n.l.; n.lat.; N.Lat.; N.lat.
North Vietnamese Army - NVA
Northamptonshire - Northants.
northbound - NB
northeast - NE
Northeast Airlines - NE
north-easterly - NEly
northeastern - NE; ne
northerly - Nly
northern - N; n; No
Northern Alberta (Alta.-B.C.) (RR) - NA
Northern Consolidated Airlines - NC
Northern England - N.Eng.
Northern Ireland - N.I.; N.Ire.
Northern Pacific (RR) - NP
Northern Territory - N.T.
north-northeast - NNE; N.N.E.
north-northwest - NNW; N.N.W.
Northumberland - Northum.
northwest - NW; N.W.; n.w.
Northwest Community Organization - NCO
Northwest Orient Airlines - NW
Northwest Territories (Canada) - N.W.T.; N.W.Terr.
northwesterly - NWly
northwestern - NW; N.W.; n.w.
Northwestern Pacific (RR) - NWP
Norway - Nor.; Norw.
Norwegian - Nor.; Norw.
nose - n
nose (horse racing) - no.
nosing - nos.
noster (our) - N.
not applicable - n.a.
not assigned - NA
not at present - n.a.p.
not authorized - n.a.
not available - NA
not elsewhere classified - n.e.c.
not elsewhere mentioned - n.e.m.
not elsewhere specified - n.e.s.
not far (L, non longe) - n.l.
not for sale - n.f.s.
not guilty (L, non culpabilis) - non cul.
not in contract - N.I.C.
not in stock - n.i.s.
not included elsewhere - n.i.e.
not known - nk
not later than - n.l.t.
not less than - n.l.t.
not measured - NM
not otherwise herein provided - NOHP
not otherwise indexed by name - n.o.i.b.n.
not otherwise provided - n.o.p.

```
not otherwise provided for - n.o.p.                              1
not otherwise specified - N.O.S.; n.o.s.                         2
not provided for - n.p.f.                                        3
not published - NP                                               4
not specifically provided for - n.s.p.f.                         5
not specified - n.s.                                             6
not sufficient - n.s.                                            7
not sufficient funds - N.S.F.                                    8
not to scale - NTS; nts                                          9
not yet diagnosed - N.Y.D.                                      10
not yet published - n.y.p.                                      11
not yet returned - n.y.r.                                       12
nota bene (note well) - N.B.; NB; n.b.                          13
Notary Public - N.P.                                            14
note - n.                                                       15
Notes and Queries - N. & Q.                                     16
nothing - NIL                                                   17
notify - ntfy                                                   18
Notre Dame - ND                                                 19
Nottinghamshire - Notts.                                        20
notwithstanding (L, non obstante) - (non obs.); notwg.          21
noun - n.                                                       22
noun feminine - n.f.                                            23
noun masculine - n.m.                                           24
noun plural - n.pl.                                             25
noun singular - n.sing.                                         26
nouns - nn.                                                     27
Nova Scotia - N.S.                                              28
novelist - nov.                                                 29
November - N.; 9ber; Nov.                                       30
nozzle - noz                                                    31
nuclear detonations - NUDETS                                    32
nuclear ship - NS                                               33
nucleus - nucl.                                                 34
number - n.; No.; no.; NR                                       35
number of bits - N                                              36
number of turns - N                                             37
number one position (Polo) - 1                                  38
number three position (Polo) - 3                                39
number two position (Polo) - 2                                  40
numbering transmitter - NT                                      41
Numbers - Nm                                                    42
numbers - Nos.; nos.                                            43
numeral(s) - num.                                               44
numerical aperture - NA                                         45
Numerical Control - NCT; N/C                                    46
numismatic(s) - numis.; numism.                                 47
Nuremberg Documents - N.D.                                      48
Nuremberg Proceedings - N.P.                                    49
nursery - nurs.                                                 50
nutmeg - nm.                                                    51
nutrition - nutr                                                52
nylon - nyl                                                     53
nymphomania - nympho                                            54
nymphomaniac - nympho                                           55
oak - o                                                         56
```

165

```
Oakland Athletics - A's; Oakland A's                          1
Obadiah - Ob                                                  2
obbligato - obb.                                              3
obedient - obdt.                                              4
Oberbefehlshaber West - OB West                               5
Oberkommando der Wehrmacht - OKW                              6
obiit (he or she died) - ob.                                  7
obiit sine prole (died without issue) - ob. s.p.             8
obiter (incidentally) - ob.                                   9
obituary - obit.                                             10
object - obj.                                                11
objection - obj.; object.                                    12
objective - obj.; object.                                    13
Oblates of Mary Immaculate - O.M.I.                          14
Oblates of Saint Francis de Sales - O.S.F.S.                 15
Oblates of Saint Joseph - O.S.J.                             16
obligate - oblg                                              17
obligation(s) - oblig                                        18
oblique - obl.                                               19
oblong - obl.                                                20
oboe - ob.                                                   21
obscure - obsc.                                              22
obscure glass - ob. gl.                                      23
Obscure Tempered Glass - Ob.Te.Gl.                           24
obscured - obsc.                                             25
observation - Obs.; obsn.                                    26
observation post - OP                                        27
observatory - Obs.                                           28
observe - obs.                                               29
observed - obsd.                                             30
observer - obsr.                                             31
obsolescent - obsol.; obsoles.; obsolesc.                    32
obsolete - obs.                                              33
obstacle - obs.                                              34
obstetric(s) - obstet.                                       35
obstetrical - obstet.                                        36
obstetrician - O.B.; obstet.                                 37
obstetrics - O.B.; obstet.                                   38
obstruction - obstr                                          39
obverse - obv.                                               40
occasion - occ.                                              41
occasional - occ.; occas.                                    42
occasionally - occ.; occas.                                  43
occident - occ.                                              44
occidental - occ.                                            45
occultism - occult.                                          46
occupation - occup.                                          47
occupational therapy - O.T.                                  48
occurs - OC                                                  49
Ocean - O.; Oc.; oc.                                         50
oceanography - oceanog.                                      51
octagon - oct                                                52
octagonal - oct                                              53
octal - OCT                                                  54
octane - oct                                                 55
Octans (the Octant) - Oct                                    56
```

166

```
octarius (a pint) - O                                               1
Octavius - Oct.                                                     2
octavo - 8vo; 8º; O.; o.; Oct.                                      3
octodecimo - 18mo; 18º                                              4
October - 8ber; O.; Oct.                                            5
odd number - D                                                      6
odometer - odom                                                     7
of - o.                                                             8
of age (L, aetatis) - aet.                                          9
of each (Gr, ana) - Ā; ĀĀ; āā                                      10
of medicine (L, medicinae) - M.                                    11
of Oxford (Oxoniensis) - Oxon.                                     12
of the last month (L, ultimo) - ult.                               13
of the next month (L, proximo) - prox.                             14
off - o.                                                           15
offensive - offen                                                  16
offer - off.                                                       17
offered - off.; offd.                                              18
office - ofc.; off.                                                19
office copy - OC                                                   20
Office of Civil Defense - OCD                                      21
Office of Economic Opportunity - OEO                               22
Office of Emergency Planning - OEP                                 23
Office of Federal Contract Compliance - OFCC                       24
Office of Foreign Police (Auslands Politische Abteilung) -         25
    A.P.A.                                                         26
Office of International Trade - OIT                                 27
Office of Price Administration - OPA                               28
Office of Science and Technology - OST                             29
Office of Strategic Services - OSS                                 30
Office of the Secretary of Defense - OSD                           31
Office of War Information - OWI                                    32
Office Visit - O.V.                                                33
officer - off.                                                     34
officer in charge - OIC                                            35
officer of the day - OD                                            36
Officer of the Guard - O.G.                                        37
Officers' Reserve Corps - O.R.C.                                   38
Officers' Training Camp - O.T.C.                                   39
Officers' Training Corps - O.T.C.                                  40
official - ofcl.; off.                                             41
officiate - off.                                                   42
officiating - offg.                                                43
off-line operating simulator - OOPS                                44
Ohio - O.                                                          45
ohm - o                                                            46
oil in water - OIW                                                 47
ointment (L, unguentum) - ung.                                     48
okay - OK                                                          49
Oklahoma - Okla.                                                   50
Oklahoma City-Ada-Atoka (RR) - OCAA                                51
old - O.; o.                                                       52
Old Arabic - OAr.                                                  53
Old Celtic - OCelt.                                                54
Old Cymric - OCym.                                                 55
Old Danish - ODan.                                                 56
```

```
Old Dutch - OD                                                      1
Old English - OE; OE.; O.E.                                         2
Old French - OF; OF.; O.F.; OFr.                                    3
Old Frisian - OFris.                                                4
Old High German - OHG; OHG.; O.H.G.                                 5
Old Irish - OIr.                                                    6
Old Italian - OIt.                                                  7
Old Kinderhood - O.K.                                               8
Old Latin - OL.                                                     9
Old Low German - OLG                                               10
Old Norman French - ONorm.Fr.                                      11
Old Norse - ON; ON.; O.N.                                          12
Old Persian - OPer.                                                13
Old Saxon - OS; OS.; O.S.                                          14
Old Serbian - OSerb.                                               15
old series - o.s.                                                  16
Old Slavic - OSlav.                                                17
Old Spanish - OSp.                                                 18
Old Style (calendar) - O/S; o/s; O.S.                              19
Old Testament - OT; OT.; O.T.; Old Test.                           20
Old Tuberculin - OT                                                21
Old Welsh - OW.                                                    22
old-age and survivors insurance - OASI                             23
Older Women's Liberation - OWL                                     24
Oldsmobile - Olds                                                  25
oleomargarin - oleo                                                26
olfactory - olf                                                    27
olive drab - O.D.; o.d.                                            28
olive green - OlG                                                  29
olive oil - oliv.                                                  30
Oliver - Ol.                                                       31
Olympia - Olym.                                                    32
omission excepted - o.e.                                           33
on account - o/a                                                   34
on behalf of (L, per procurationem) - p.p.; p.pro.;               35
    per pro.                                                       36
on board - o.b.                                                    37
on center - O.C.                                                   38
on demand - o/d; o.d.                                              39
on dry basis - ODB; O.D.B.                                         40
on request - O/R                                                   41
on the back of the leaf (L, folio verso) - f.v.                    42
on the quiet -   QT                                                43
on the threshold, at the outset (L, in limine) - in lim.           44
on the way (L, in transitu) - in trans.                            45
on truck - o.t.                                                    46
on weight of fiber - OWF; O.W.F.                                   47
one - I                                                            48
one at a time - o.a.t.                                             49
one furlong - 220                                                  50
one hundred - C                                                    51
one hundred yard or meter race - 100                               52
one millionth - Micro                                              53
one strong (It. una corda) - u.c.                                  54
one tenth - DECI                                                   55
one thousand - M                                                   56
```
168

```
one thousand feet board measure - MBM                        1
one time only - o.t.o.                                       2
one-half - ss                                                3
Oneid & Western (RR) - O&W                                   4
one-seater canoe - c.1                                       5
one-seater kayak - k.1                                       6
one-side-coated sheet (paper art) - Cls                      7
on-line real time - OLRT                                     8
only - o.                                                    9
only child - o.c.                                           10
onomatopoeia - onomat.                                      11
onomatopoeic - onomat.                                      12
Ontario - O.; Ont.                                          13
Ontario Northland (Ont.) (RR) - ON                          14
open account - c.o.                                         15
open circuit voltage - ocv; o.c.v.                          16
open hearth - OH                                            17
open-circuit - O/C                                          18
opening - O.; opng.                                         19
opera - op.                                                 20
opera (words) - op.                                         21
operate - opr                                               22
operating - OPERG; optg.                                    23
operating characteristics - OC                              24
operation - op.; opn.                                       25
operational fixed - OF                                      26
operational readiness inspection - ORI                      27
operational training unit - OTU                             28
operations and checkout - O&C                               29
operations control center - OCC                             30
operations/logistics - O/L                                  31
operations maintenance - OM                                 32
operations research - OR                                    33
operator - oper.; opr.                                      34
operator distance calling - ODD                             35
operator programming method - OPM                           36
opere citato (in the work cited) - o.c.; op. cit.           37
Ophiuchus (the Serpent-Holder) - Oph                        38
ophthalmology - ophthal.                                    39
opinion - opn.                                              40
Opinion Research Center - ORC                               41
opinions - ops.                                             42
Opinions of the Attorney General - Op. Atty. Gen.           43
opponents' runs (baseball) - OR                             44
opportunity - oppor.; oppy.                                 45
oppose - opp.                                               46
opposed - opp.                                              47
opposed to - opp.                                           48
opposite - op.; opp.                                        49
optative - opt.                                             50
optic - opt.                                                51
optical - opt.                                              52
optical character recognition - OCR                         53
optical pulse transmitter using leaser - OPTUL             54
optical rotary dispersion - ORD                             55
optician - opt.; optn.                                      56
```

```
optics - opt.                                                          1
optimus (best) - opt.                                                  2
option - opt.                                                          3
optional - opt.                                                        4
optometrist - optom                                                    5
optometry - optom                                                      6
opus (work) - op.                                                      7
opus citatum (the work cited) - op. cit.                               8
Or gate - OG                                                           9
ora pro nobis (pray for us) - o.p.n.                                  10
orange - o; orn                                                       11
orange juice - oj                                                     12
orator - orat.                                                        13
Oratorians - Cong. Orat.                                              14
oratorical - orat.                                                    15
oratory - orat.                                                       16
orbiting astronomical observatory - OAO                               17
orbiting geophysical observatory - OGO                                18
orbiting solar observatory - OSO                                      19
orchestra - orch.                                                     20
orchestral - orch.                                                    21
ordained - ord.                                                       22
order - o.; ord.                                                      23
order bill of lading - O.B/L; ob/l                                    24
order of - o/o                                                        25
Order of Merit - O.M.                                                 26
Order of Minims - O.M.                                                27
Order of our Lady of Mercy - O.D.M.                                   28
Order of Preachers (Dominicans) - O.P.                                29
Order of St. Augustine - O.S.A.                                       30
Order of Saint Basil the Great - O.S.B.M.                             31
Order of St. Benedict (Benedictines) - O.S.B.                         32
Order of Saint Camillus - O.S.Cam.                                    33
Order of St. Dominic - O.S.D.                                         34
Order of Saint Francis - O.S.F.                                       35
Order of the Most Holy Trinity - O.S.S.T.                             36
orderly - Odly                                                        37
orderly sergeant - Orderly Sgt.                                       38
ordinal - ord.                                                        39
ordinance(s) - ord.                                                   40
ordinarily - ord.                                                     41
ordinary - ord.                                                       42
an ordinate - Y                                                       43
ordnance - ord.; ordn.                                                44
ordnance sergeant - Ord. Sgt.                                         45
Oregon - Oreg.                                                        46
Oregon & Northwestern (RR) - O&N                                      47
Oregon, California & Eastern (RR) - OC&E                              48
Oregon Electric (RR) - OE                                             49
Oregon Trunk (RR) - OT                                                50
organ - org.                                                          51
organic - org.                                                        52
organism - org.                                                       53
organization - org.; orgn.                                            54
Organization for Economic Cooperation and Development -               55
    OECD                                                              56
```

```
our memorandum - ormen                          1
out of print - o.p.                              2
out of service - o/s                             3
out of stock - o/s; o.s.                         4
out to out - o/o                                 5
outboard - otbd.                                 6
outfielder (baseball) - of.                      7
outgoing line circuit - OLC                      8
outlet - out                                     9
outlet contact - OC                             10
outpatient department - O.P.D.                  11
output - OUT                                    12
output control pulses - OCP                     13
outs (tennis) - O                               14
outs or put-outs (baseball) - o.                15
outside - os                                    16
outside diameter - OD; O.D.                     17
outside edge (figure skating) - O               18
outside home (lacrosse) - OH                    19
outside left (soccer) - OL                      20
outside radius - o.r.                           21
outside right (soccer) - OR                     22
outstanding - o/s                               23
oval head - ovhd                                24
oval headed screw - OHS                         25
oven dry basis - ODB; O.D.B.                    26
overall - OA; o.a.                              27
overall depth - o.a.d.                          28
overall height - o.a.h.                         29
overall length - o.a.l.                         30
overall width - o.a.w.                          31
overcast - O.; ocst                             32
overcharge - o/c                                33
overdose (drugs) - O.D.                         34
overdraft - O.D.                                35
overdrawn - O.D.                                36
overflow - ovfl                                 37
overhaul - ovhl                                 38
overhead - ovhd                                 39
overhead door - O.H. Door                       40
overheat - ovht                                 41
overkill - ovk                                  42
overlap - OL                                    43
overload - ovld                                 44
overpaid - ovpd                                 45
Overseas (Bell Telephone) - O                   46
oversize - os                                   47
over-the-counter - O-C                          48
"Over-the-Counter" - UNL                        49
overtime - OT; o.t.                             50
overture - overt.                               51
Ovid - Ov                                       52
ovum - ov.                                      53
Owly Bird (air travel) - OB                     54
owner's risk - o.r.                             55
Oxford - Ox.                                    56
```

173

```
papers - prs.                                                     1
Papua - Pap.                                                      2
papyrus - pap.                                                    3
par value - p.v.                                                  4
parabola - parab                                                  5
parachute - prcht.                                                6
paragraph - par.                                                  7
paragraphs - pars.                                                8
Paraguay - Par.; Para.                                            9
parallel - p.; par.                                              10
parallel with - p/w                                              11
paralysis - paral                                                12
parameter - PAR                                                  13
parasite - paras                                                 14
parasitic - paras                                                15
parcel - pcl.                                                    16
parcel air lift - P.A.L.                                         17
parcel post - P.P.; p.p.                                         18
parcel post insured - p.p.i.                                     19
parchment - parchm.                                              20
paregoric - P.G.; P.O.                                           21
Parent Cooperative Preschool International - PCPI                22
parental generation - P                                          23
Parental guidance suggested (all ages admitted) (movie          24
     code) - GP                                                  25
parentheses - parens.                                            26
parenthesis - par.; paren.                                       27
Parents Opposed to Pornography in Schools - POPS                28
Parents Without Partners - PWP                                   29
Parent-Teacher Association - PTA                                 30
Paris & Mount Pleasant (RR) - P&MP                               31
parish - par.                                                    32
Parish Priest - P.P.                                             33
parity switch - PS                                               34
park - pk.                                                       35
parks - pks.                                                     36
Parks and Recreation - Parks and Rec.                           37
parkway - pkwy                                                   38
Parliament - Parl.                                               39
Parliamentary - Parl.                                            40
parliamentary procedure - parl. proc.                           41
part - p.; pt.                                                   42
part number - PN; pn; p/n                                       43
part of - p/o                                                    44
part paid - p.p.                                                 45
partes aequales (equal parts) - p.ae.                           46
partial - part.                                                  47
partial loss - p.l.                                              48
participating - part.; Ptc                                      49
participating preferred - pt. pf.                               50
participial - part.; p.pl.; ppl.                                51
participial adjective - p.a.                                    52
participial adjective - part. adj.                              53
participle - p.; part.;                                         54
particle - part.                                                55
particular - part.                                              56
```

```
particular average - p.a.                                              1
particularly - part.                                                   2
partim (in part) - p.                                                  3
partition - part.; partn.; pn.                                         4
partly - part.                                                         5
partner - part.                                                        6
parts - pts.                                                           7
parts by weight per 100 parts of resin - phr.                          8
parts per billion - ppb                                                9
parts per hour - pts/hr                                               10
parts per hundred million - p.p.h.m.                                  11
parts per million - ppm                                               12
party - p.                                                            13
Party Organization for Abroad (Auslands Organization) -               14
    A.O.                                                              15
passage - pass.                                                       16
passbook - p.b.                                                       17
passed - pd.                                                          18
passed assistant surgeon - Passed Asst. Surg.                         19
passed ball (on a baseball score card) - B                            20
passed balls (baseball) - PB                                          21
passenger - pass.; psgr.                                              22
Passenger Agent - P.A.                                                23
passim (everywhere) - pass.                                           24
passing (grading) - D                                                 25
Passionist Fathers - C.P.                                             26
passive - pass.                                                       27
Passive Seismic Experiment Package - PSEP                             28
Passive Thermal Control - PTC                                         29
past - p.                                                             30
Past Commander - P.C.                                                 31
Past Master - P.M.                                                    32
past medical history - p.m.h.                                         33
past participle - p.p.; pp.                                           34
past tense - p.t.                                                     35
past weather - W                                                      36
pastor - P.                                                           37
patent - pat.                                                         38
Patent Office - Pat. Off.                                             39
patented - pat.; patd.                                                40
patents - pats.                                                       41
pater (father) - P.                                                   42
pathological - path.; pathol                                          43
pathologist - pathol                                                  44
pathology - path.; pathol                                             45
Patricia - Pat                                                        46
Patrick - Pat                                                         47
patrol - pat.                                                         48
pattern - pat.; PATN; patt.                                           49
pattern correspondence index - PCI                                    50
patternmaker - ptrnmkr.                                               51
patternmaking - patmkg.                                               52
Paul - Pl.                                                            53
Paulist Fathers - C.S.P.                                              54
pavement - pvmt.                                                      55
Pavo (the Peacock) - Pav                                              56
```

175

```
Pawn - P                                                        1
pay - p.                                                        2
pay on delivery - P.O.D.; p.o.d.                                3
pay on return - P.O.R.; p.o.r.                                  4
payable-on-receipt - p.o.r.                                     5
paycheck - pc                                                   6
payload - pld                                                   7
Paymaster - P.M.; Paymtr.                                       8
Paymaster General - P.M.G.                                      9
payment - payt.; pmt.; pt.; pymt.                              10
payments - pts.                                                11
payroll - PR; P/R                                              12
Peace Corps - PC                                               13
peak - pk.                                                     14
peak reverse voltage - PRV                                     15
peaks - pks.                                                   16
peak-to-peak - P-P                                             17
peck - pk.                                                     18
pecks - pks.                                                   19
Pecos Valley Southern (RR) - PVS                               20
pectoral - p                                                   21
peculiar - pq                                                  22
peculiar test equipment - PTE                                  23
pedagogy - ped.                                                24
pedal - ped.                                                   25
pedestal - ped.                                                26
pedestal lavatory - PL                                         27
pedestrian - ped.                                              28
pediatrics - pediat                                            29
Pegasus - Peg                                                  30
Pekinese - Pek.                                                31
Peking - Pek                                                   32
pellagra preventive - PP                                       33
pellet - pel                                                   34
pelvis - pel                                                   35
pence (L, denarii) - d.                                        36
pending - pndg                                                 37
peninsula - Pen.; pen.                                         38
penitent - pen.                                                39
penitentiary - pen.                                            40
Penn-Central (RR) - P-C; PC                                    41
Pennsylvania - Pa.; Penn.; Penna.                              42
Pennsylvania (RR) - PA                                         43
Pennsylvania & Atlantic (RR) - P&A                             44
Pennsylvania Central (RR) - PC; Penn.Cent.                     45
Pennsylvania-Reading Seashore (RR) - PRS                       46
penny - p.                                                     47
penny (Brit, L, denarius) - d.                                 48
penny nail - d                                                 49
pennyweight - dwt.; pwt.                                       50
penology - penol.                                              51
Pentacostal Holiness - Pent. Hol.                              52
Pentagon - Pent                                                53
people (L, populus) - (P.); peo.                               54
People for the Enjoyment of Eyeballing Knees - PEEK            55
per (by, for) - p.                                             56
```

```
per annum (per year) - p.a.; per an.                        1
per cent rated wattage - PRW                                2
per centum (by the hundred) - per cent; per ct.             3
per diem - P.D.; p.d.                                       4
per procurationem (on behalf of) - p.p.; p.pro.; per pro.   5
per thousand - per mil.                                     6
per year (L, per annum) - p.a.; per an.                     7
perambulator - pram                                         8
Perceived Noise-level in decibels (measure of sound pollu-  9
    tion) - PNdB                                            10
percent - p.c.; pct.                                        11
percentage - PC                                             12
percentage by weight - w/o                                  13
perception of light - PL                                    14
percussion - perc                                           15
Père - P.; PP.                                              16
perfect - perf.; pf.                                        17
perfection - perf.                                          18
perforate - perf.                                           19
perforated - perf.                                          20
perform - perf.                                             21
performance - perf.                                         22
performance index - PI                                      23
performer - perf.                                           24
perfume - perf.                                             25
perhaps - perh.                                             26
perimeter - peri                                            27
period - p.; per.                                           28
period of the waves - Pw                                    29
periodical requirements - PR                                30
peripheral buffer - PB                                      31
peripheral command indicator - PCI                          32
permanent - perm                                            33
permanent magnet - PM                                       34
peroxide value - PV                                         35
perpendicular - perp.                                       36
perpetual - perp.                                           37
Perseus - Per                                               38
Persia - Pers.                                              39
Persian - Per.; Pers.                                       40
Persic - Per.                                               41
person - p.; per.; pers.                                    42
Person (Bell Telephone) - P                                 43
Person Call Back (Bell Telephone) - K                       44
persona non grata (unacceptable person) - p.n.g.           45
personal - pers.                                            46
personal analog computer - PAC                              47
personal income - p.i.                                      48
personal property - p.p.                                    49
Personal Service - PS; ps                                   50
personal signalling system - PSS                            51
personality quotient - PQ                                   52
personally - pers.                                          53
Personnel - Pers                                            54
Persons under 18 not admitted (movie code) - X             55
perspective - persp.                                        56
```

```
pertaining - pert.                                                    1
pertaining to - in re                                                 2
Peruvian - Peruv.                                                     3
peseta - p.                                                           4
peseta(s) - pta(s)                                                    5
peso - p.                                                             6
Pesticide Regulation Division - PRD                                   7
pet cock - PC                                                         8
Peter - Pet.; Pete                                                    9
1 Peter - 1 Pt                                                       10
2 Peter - 2 Pt                                                       11
Peters - Pet.                                                        12
petition - petn.                                                     13
petrography - petrog.                                                14
petroleum - pet.; petro                                              15
petrology - petrol.                                                  16
petty cash - P/C; p/c; P.C.; p.c.                                    17
petty officer - P.O.; PO                                             18
petty officer first class - Petty Officer 1c                         19
petty officer second class - Petty Officer 2c                        20
petty officer third class - Petty Officer 3c                         21
pfennig - pf.; pfg.                                                  22
pharmaceutic - Pharm.; pharm.                                        23
pharmaceutical - Phar.; phar.                                        24
Pharmaceutical Chemist - Ph.C.                                       25
pharmacist - pharm.                                                  26
pharmacological - pharmacol.                                         27
pharmacologist - pharmacol.                                          28
Pharmacology - Pharmacol.                                            29
pharmacopoeia - Ph.; Phar.; phar.; Pharm.; pharm.                    30
pharmacy - Phar.; phar.; Pharm.; pharm.                              31
phase - ph.                                                          32
phase modulation - PM                                                33
phase-shift-keyed - PSK                                              34
phenomena - phenom                                                   35
phenomenon - phenom                                                  36
phenosulfonphthalein (test) - PSP                                    37
phenyl - Ph                                                          38
Philadelphia - Phila.                                                39
Philadelphia-Baltimore-Washington Stock Exchange - PBS;              40
    PB                                                               41
Philemon - Phil.; Philem.; Phlm.                                     42
Philip - Phil                                                        43
Philippians - Phil.; Philip.                                         44
Philippine - Phil.                                                   45
Philippine Air Lines - PAL                                           46
Philippines - Phil.                                                  47
philological - philol.                                               48
philology - philol.                                                  49
philosopher - philos.                                                50
philosophical - phil.; philos.; philosoph.                           51
philosophy - phil.; philos.                                          52
Phoenix - Phoen.                                                     53
Phoenix (constellation) - Phe                                        54
phone - ph.                                                          55
phonetic(s) - phon.                                                  56
```

178

```
phonetical - phon.                                      1
phonetically balanced - PB                              2
phonetics - phonet.                                     3
phonics - phon.                                         4
phonograph - phono                                      5
phonology - phonol.                                     6
phosphate - phos                                        7
phosphor - ph                                           8
phosphorus - P                                          9
phosphorus protein (diets) - P                         10
photoconductor - PC                                    11
photoelectric cell - PEC                               12
photoelectromagnetic - PEM                             13
photograph(s) - photo                                  14
photographer - photog                                  15
photographic - photog                                  16
photography - photog                                   17
photometry - photom.                                   18
photon - ph                                            19
photo-optical recorder tracker - PORT                  20
photostat - stat                                       21
phototube - PHT                                        22
phrase - phr.                                          23
phraseology - phr.                                     24
phrenological - phren.; phrenol.                       25
phrenologist - phren.                                  26
phrenology - phren.; phrenol.                          27
Physical - Phys.                                       28
physical - phys.                                       29
physical chemistry - phys. chem.                       30
physical equipment table - PET                         31
physical geography - phys. geog.                       32
physician - phys.                                      33
physicist - phys.                                      34
physics - phys.                                        35
Physikalische - Physikal.                              36
physiognomy - physiog                                  37
physiological - phys.; physiol.                        38
physiologist - physiol.                                39
physiology - phys.; physiol.                           40
pianissimo - pp.                                       41
piano - p.                                             42
pickled and oiled - p&o                                43
pickup - pu                                            44
pickup and delivery - p&d                              45
picofarad - pf                                         46
picosecond - PSEC                                      47
Pictor (the Painter) - Pic                             48
pictorial - pict.                                      49
picture - PC                                           50
picture(s) - pict.                                     51
pictures - pics                                        52
Pidgin English - Pid.Eng.                              53
piebald - p.b.                                         54
piece - pc.                                            55
pieces - pcs.; ps.                                     56
```

pieces per hour - pcs/hr
Piedmont Airlines - PI
pigment - pig.
pill(s) (L, pilula) - pil.
pilot - plt
pilot punch - PP
pink - Pk
pint - p.; pt.
a pint (L, octarius) - O.; o.
pints - pt.; pts.
pinxit - pinx.; pnxt.; pxt.
pioneer - pion.
Pious Society of Missions - P.S.M.
Pious Society of St. Paul - SS.P.
Pious Society of the Missionaries of Saint Charles -
    P.S.S.C.
pipe - p.
pipe shaft - PS
pipe sleeve - P SL
Pisces - Pis
Pisces (the Fishes) - Psc
Piscis Austrinus (the Southern Fish) - Ps A
pitch circle - pc
pitch diameter - P.D.; p.d.
pitcher (baseball) - p.; 1
Pittsburgh - Pit.; Pitt.
Pittsburgh & Lake Erie (RR) - P&LE
Pittsburgh & Shawmut (RR) - P&S
Pittsburgh & West Virginia (RR) - P&WV
pius (holy) - p.
pizzicato - pizz.
place - pl.
a place (L, locus) - L.
place (horse racing) - Pl.
place of the seal (L, locus sigilli) - L.S.
placements (tennis) - P
plaintiff - plf.; plff.; pltff.
plaintiffs - pltffs.
plan position indicator - PPI; P.P.I.
planning and scheduling - PS
planning control sheet - PCS
plan-position indicator - PPI
plaster - plas.; plstr.
plasterer - plstr.
Plaster-Painted - Pl./Pt.
Plaster-Sand Finish-Painted - Pl.S.F./Pt.
Plaster Vinyl Wall Covered - Plas.V.W.C.
plastic - plast.
Plastic Covered Acoustical Tile - P.C.Ac.T.
Plastic Luminous - Pl.Lum.
plate - pl.; plt.
plateau - plat.
plates - pl.
platform - plat.; platf.
Platinum - Pt
platoon - plat.

1
2
3
4
5
6
7
8
9
10
11
12
13
14
15
16
17
18
19
20
21
22
23
24
25
26
27
28
29
30
31
32
33
34
35
36
37
38
39
40
41
42
43
44
45
46
47
48
49
50
51
52
53
54
55
56

```
played (total games) - P                                          1
please - PSE                                                      2
please exchange - p.x.                                           3
please note - p.n.                                               4
please omit flowers - p.o.f.                                     5
please reply (Fr, répondez sil vous plaît) - R.S.V.P.            6
please turn over - p.t.o.                                        7
plenipotentiary - plen.                                          8
Plinth - P                                                       9
plug - P                                                        10
plug-in electronics - PIE                                       11
plumber - plb.; plbr.                                           12
plumbing - plb.; plbg.; plmb.                                   13
plumbing stack - ST                                             14
pluperfect - plupf.                                             15
plural - pl.; plu.; plur.                                       16
plurality - plur.                                               17
Pluto - P.                                                      18
Plymouth - Ply                                                  19
plywood - plywd                                                 20
pneumatic(s) - pneum.                                           21
poetic - poet.                                                  22
poetical - poet.                                                23
Poetics - Poet.                                                 24
Poetry - Poet.                                                  25
poetry - poet.                                                  26
Poetry Society of America - PSA                                 27
point - pt.                                                     28
point (lacrosse position) - P                                   29
point of shipment - P/S                                         30
point of tangent - PT                                           31
point of view - pv                                              32
points - P; pts.                                                33
points after touchdown (football) - PAT                         34
point-to-point - PTP                                            35
Poland - Pol.                                                   36
Polar Orbiting Geophysical Observatory - POGO                   37
pole - p.                                                       38
Police aux Questions Juives (French Organization) - P.Q.J.      39
Police Constable - P.C.                                         40
Police Department - P.D.                                        41
Police Magistrate - P.M.                                        42
Police Superintendent - Police Supt.                            43
policy - plcy                                                   44
policy proof of interest - p.p.i.                               45
Polish - Pol.                                                   46
polish - pol.                                                   47
polished - pol.                                                 48
polished plate glass - PPGL                                     49
polished wire glass - PWGL                                      50
political - pol.; polit.                                        51
Political Action Committee - P.A.C.; PAC                        52
political district - pol. dist.                                 53
political economy - Pol. Econ.; pol. econ.                      54
Political Organization (Politische Organisation) - P.O.         55
political science - poli. sci.                                  56
```

181

```
politician - polit.                                    1
politics - pol.; polit.                                2
pollen index - pol ind                                 3
pollution - poll.                                      4
polyethylene - POLY                                    5
Polynesia - Poly                                       6
polytechnic - poly.                                    7
polytechnical - poly.                                  8
polyvinyl chloride (plastic bottles) - PVC             9
pomeranian - pom                                      10
pondere (by weight) - p.                              11
Pontiac - Pont                                        12
pontifex (bishop) - P.                                13
pontoon - pont.                                       14
Pope (L, papa) - P.                                   15
popular - pop.                                        16
popular edition - pop.ed.                             17
popularly - pop.                                      18
population - p.; pop.                                 19
populus (people) - P.                                 20
porcelain - porc.                                     21
porcelain enamel - Porc. Enam.                        22
porch - P                                             23
port - pt.                                            24
Port Angeles Western (RR) - PAW                       25
port of call - POC                                    26
portable - P; port.; ptbl.                            27
portable camera-transmitter - PCT                     28
Portable Life Support System - PLSS                   29
portrait(s) - port(s)                                 30
ports - pts.                                          31
Portugal - Pg.; Port.                                 32
Portuguese - Pg.; Port.                               33
Portuguese Guinea - Port. Gui.                        34
Portuguese Timor - Port. Timor                        35
position - pn.; pos.; posn.; psn.                     36
position indicator - p.                               37
position-event-time - PET                             38
positional tolerance - PT                             39
positive - pos.                                       40
positive crankcase ventilation valve - PCV Valve      41
positive infinity variable - PIV; P.I.V.              42
positive input-negative output - PINO                 43
positive real number - RE+                            44
positive-negative - p-n                               45
possession - poss.                                    46
possessive - pos.; poss.                              47
possessive pronoun - pos pron                         48
possible - poss.                                      49
possibly - poss.                                      50
post - p.                                             51
post (after) - p.                                     52
Post Adjutant - P.A.                                  53
post card - p.c.                                      54
Post Commander - P.C.                                 55
post date - pd                                        56
```

```
post exchange - PX                                                    1
post meridiem (afternoon) - P.M.; p.m.                                2
post mortem (after death) - P.M.                                      3
post mortem dumps - PMD                                               4
post office - P.O.                                                    5
Post Office Box - POB; P.O.B.                                         6
Post Office Department - POD; P.O.D.                                  7
post script - p.s.                                                    8
post scripts - p.ss.                                                  9
post scriptum (post script) - p.s.                                   10
postage paid - pp                                                    11
postal - post.                                                       12
postal card - p.c.                                                   13
postal district - P.D.                                               14
Postal Laws and Regulations - P.L.&R.                                15
postal order - P.O.                                                  16
postal receipts - post. rcts.                                        17
posterior - poster.                                                  18
postgraduate - postgrad                                              19
posthumous - posth                                                   20
postmark - pmk.                                                      21
postmarked - pmkd.                                                   22
Postmaster - P.M.                                                    23
Postmaster General - P.M.G.                                          24
post-mortem - P.M.; p.m.                                             25
postpaid - p.p.; ppd.                                                26
postscript - P.S.; p.s.                                              27
postscripts - P.SS.; p.ss.                                           28
Potassium - K                                                        29
potatoes - potats                                                    30
potential - pot.                                                     31
potential difference - p.d.                                          32
potter - pot.                                                        33
pottery - pot.                                                       34
poultry - poul                                                       35
pound (L, libra) - L; lb.                                            36
pound, apothecaries' - lb. ap.                                       37
pound, apothecary's - lb. ap.                                        38
pound, avoirdupois - lb. av.                                         39
pound, troy - lb. t.                                                 40
pounder - pdr.                                                       41
pounds per base box (tin) - lb./bb.                                  42
pounds per cubic foot - lb. per cu. ft.; LB/CU FT; LBS/FT$^3$        43
pounds per linear inch - p.l.i.                                      44
pounds per minute - p.p.m.; p/m                                      45
pounds per square foot - p.s.f.; LB/FT$^2$                          46
pounds per square inch - p.s.i.; LB/SQ IN                           47
pounds per square inch absolute - p.s.i.a.                          48
pounds per square inch gauge - p.s.i.g.                             49
pounds per thousand barrels - ptb; p.t.b.                          50
pour prendre congé (to take leave) - P.P.C.; p.p.c.                51
powder (L, pulvis) - powd.; (pulv.)                                52
powder room - PR                                                    53
power - P; pow.; pr.; pwr.                                          54
power factor - PF                                                   55
power house - PH                                                   56
```

power of attorney - P.A.; p/a 1
power supply - PS 2
power-pack single-unit A and B battery (computer) - AB 3
powers - prs. 4
practice - prac 5
Praemonstratensians - O. Praem. 6
pragmatic - prag 7
Praseodymium - Pr 8
pray for us (L, ora pro nobis) - o.p.n. 9
Prayer Book - P.B.; Pr. Bk. 10
Pre-Anglo-Saxon - Pre-AS. 11
precast - prcst.; prec. 12
Precast Concrete - Pre. Con. 13
Precast Concrete-Painted - Pre.Con./Pt. 14
preceded - prec. 15
precedence - prec. 16
preceding - prec. 17
precipitate - ppt. 18
precipitation - ppn.; pre. 19
precision - prec. 20
precision graph recorder - PGR 21
precision graphic recorder - PGR 22
precision interactive operation - PIO 23
precision voltage reference - PVR 24
predicate - pred. 25
predication - pred. 26
predicative - pred. 27
prediction - pred. 28
preempt - pre-em 29
preemptor - pre-em 30
prefabricated - prefab. 31
preface - pref. 32
prefaced - pref. 33
prefatory - pref. 34
prefecture - pref. 35
prefer - pref. 36
preferably - pref. 37
preference - pr.; pref. 38
preferences - prs. 39
preferred - pf.; pfd.; pref. 40
preferred (stock) - Pr.; pr. 41
prefix - pfx.; pref. 42
prefixed - pref. 43
pregnant - pg 44
prehistoric - prehist 45
prejudice - prej. 46
preliminary - prelim. 47
Preliminary (stock) - P 48
preliminary data report - PDR 49
premium - pm; prem 50
premolded - prmld 51
prepaid - P.P.; ppd. 52
preparation - prep. 53
preparatory - prep. 54
prepare - prep. 55
prepared - prep. 56

```
preposition - prep.                                              1
Presbyterian - Presb.                                            2
Preschool - Pre-S; ps                                            3
prescription - Rx                                                4
present - pr.; pres.                                             5
present participle - p.pr.; ppr.; pres. part.                    6
present position - PPSN                                          7
present weather - WW                                             8
presents - prs.                                                  9
Preservation of our Femininity and Finances - POOFF             10
preserve - presv                                                11
presidency - pres.                                              12
President - P.; Pres.                                           13
presidential - presdl.                                          14
President's Science Advisory Committee - PSAC                   15
Presiding Elder - P.E.                                          16
presiding judge - P.J.                                          17
press agent - PA; P.A.; p.a.                                    18
press release - P.R.                                            19
pressed metal - P.M.; Pr. Met.                                  20
pressfeeder - prsfdr.                                           21
pressman - prsmn.                                               22
pressure - P; pres.; press.                                     23
pressure change - PP                                            24
pressure reducing valve - PRV                                   25
pressure silver ion - pAg                                       26
pressure-sensitive - P-S                                        27
presumption - pres.                                             28
presumptive - pres.                                             29
preterit - pret.; pt.                                           30
previous - prev.                                                31
previous orders - po                                            32
previous question - p.q.                                        33
previously - prev.                                              34
price - pr.                                                     35
price current - P/C; p/c; p.c.                                  36
Price-Earnings Ratio - P-E Ratio                                37
prices - pc.; prs.                                              38
prices current - pc                                             39
priest - pr.                                                    40
priests - prs.                                                  41
primary - PRI; prim.                                            42
primate - prim.                                                 43
prime (preferred stock rating) - AAA                            44
Prime Minister - P.M.                                           45
primeval - prim.                                                46
primitive - prim.                                               47
primus (first) - p.                                             48
Prince - P.; pr.                                                49
Prince Consort - P.C.                                           50
Prince Edward Island - P.E.I.                                   51
Princeton University - PU                                       52
principal(s) - prin.                                            53
principal parts - prin. pts.                                    54
principally - prin.                                             55
principle(s) - prin.                                            56
```

```
print alphamerically - PRA                                      1
print numerically - PRN                                         2
print octal - PRO                                               3
print register 1 - PR-1                                         4
printed - pr.; prtd.                                            5
printed circuit lamp - PCL                                      6
printed circuits - Pc                                           7
printer - pr.; PRT; ptr.                                        8
printer dump - PRD                                              9
printing - pr.; print.; prtg.; ptg.                            10
print-out - p.o.                                               11
prior - pr.                                                    12
prior notice required - p.n.r.                                 13
prior preferred - pr. pf.                                      14
prism - pr.                                                    15
prisoner of war - POW                                          16
Private - Pvt.                                                 17
private - pvt.                                                 18
private account - p.a.                                         19
private automatic branch exchange (AT&T) - PABX                20
private automatic exchange - PAX                               21
private branch exchange - PBX; P.B.X.                          22
Private First Class - Pfc                                      23
private resolution - Private Res.                              24
privately owned vehicle - p.o.v.                               25
privately printed - pp.                                        26
privative - priv.                                              27
Privy Countil - P.C.                                           28
Privy Seal - P.S.                                              29
pro (for) - p.                                                 30
pro forma (stock) - p                                          31
pro tempore (for the time being) - p.t.; pro tem.             32
probability distribution analyzer - PDA                        33
probability distribution function - PDF                        34
probable - prob.                                               35
problem error - P.E.                                           36
probably - prob.                                               37
probate - P.; prob.                                            38
probation - prob.                                              39
problem - prob.                                                40
problem-oriented language - POL                                41
procedure - prc; proc                                          42
Proceedings - Proc.; proc.                                     43
proceeds - proc.                                               44
process - prcs.; proc.                                         45
process branch indicator - PBI                                 46
process interrupt status word - PISW                           47
process operator console - POC                                 48
processor controller - P-C                                     49
processor state register - PSR                                 50
proclamation - proc.                                           51
proctor - proc.                                                52
procure - proc.                                                53
procurement - proc.                                            54
procurement division - PD                                      55
produce - prod.                                                56
```

```
proportion - ppn                                                    1
Proportional Representation - P.R.                                  2
proposed - prop.                                                    3
proposition - prop.                                                 4
proprietary - propr.                                                5
proprietor - propr.                                                 6
prosecuting attorney - Pros. Atty.                                  7
prosody - pros.                                                     8
prostate - prost                                                    9
protamine zinc insulin - PZI                                        10
protected cast box strike - PCBX                                    11
protected strike - PX                                               12
protected wrought box strike - PWBX                                 13
Protective Squads (Schutzstaffel) - S.S.                            14
protectorate - prot.                                                15
Protein-Bound Iodine - P.B.I.                                       16
Protestant - Prot.                                                  17
Protestant Episcopal - P.E.                                         18
Protistenkunde - Protistenk.                                        19
protoactinium - Pa                                                  20
proton - p                                                          21
prototype - Y                                                       22
Provençal - Pr.; Prov.                                              23
Provence - Prov.                                                    24
proverb - prov.                                                     25
proverbial - prov.                                                  26
Proverbs - Prov.; Prv.                                              27
providence - prov.                                                  28
provident - prov.                                                   29
Province - Prov.                                                    30
province - prov.                                                    31
Province of Quebec - P.Q.; Que                                      32
Provincetown-Boston Airline - PT                                    33
provincial - prov.                                                  34
Provincial English - Prov. Eng.                                     35
Provincial Scottish - Prov. Scot.                                   36
provision - prov.                                                   37
provisional - prov.                                                 38
provisional costs - PC                                              39
Provisional Revolutionary Government of South Vietnam -             40
     PRG                                                            41
Provost - Prov.                                                     42
Provost Marshal - P.M.                                              43
Provost Marshal General - P.M.G.                                    44
proximo (next month) - prox.                                        45
Prussia - Prus.                                                     46
Prussian - Prus.                                                    47
Psalm - Ps.; Psa.                                                   48
Psalms - Ps.; Psa.; Pss.                                            49
pseudonym - pseud.                                                  50
psychic - psych.                                                    51
psychical - psych.                                                  52
psychokinesis - PK                                                  53
psychological - psychol.                                            54
psychology - Psychol.; psychol.                                     55
pubic - pub.                                                        56
```

```
public - pub.                                                      1
Public Affairs Information Service - PAIS                          2
Public Buildings Service - PBS                                     3
Public Health - P.H.                                               4
Public Health Service - PHS                                        5
Public Housing Administration - PHA                                6
Public Opinion - PO                                                7
public relations - PR; p.r.                                        8
public resolution - Public Res.                                    9
public sale - P.S.; p.s.                                          10
Public School - P.S.; PS                                          11
Public Works Administration - P.W.A.; PWA                         12
Public Works Department - P.W.D.                                  13
public-address system - PA; p-a system                            14
publication - Pub.; pub.; publ.; pubn.                            15
Publication of the Modern Language Association - PMLA             16
published - pub.; publ.                                           17
publisher - pub.; publ.                                           18
publisher's library binding - PLB                                 19
Publishers' Weekly - PW                                           20
publishing - pub.; publ.                                          21
Publius - P.                                                      22
Puerto Rico - P.R.                                                23
pull chain - PC                                                   24
pulse - P.                                                        25
pulse amplifier - PA                                              26
pulse code modulation - PCM; P.C.M.                               27
pulse controller - PC                                             28
pulse counter - P-C                                               29
pulse driver - PD                                                 30
pulse duration - PD                                               31
pulse repetition rate - p.r.r.                                    32
pulse shaper - PS                                                 33
pulse time modulation - PTM                                       34
pulse width - PW                                                  35
pulse-amplitude modulation - PAM                                  36
pulse-duration modulation - PDM                                   37
pulse-repetition frequency - PRF                                  38
pulse-repetition rate - PRR                                       39
pulses per second - pps                                           40
pulse-width coded - PWC                                           41
pulse-width discriminator - PWD                                   42
pulse-width encoder - PWE                                         43
pulse-width modulation - PWM                                      44
pulverize - pulv.                                                 45
pulverized - pulv.                                                46
punch - P                                                         47
punched card - PC                                                 48
punched card system - PCS                                         49
punched tape block reader - PTBR                                  50
punctuate - punct.                                                51
punctuation - p; punt.                                            52
pupil - P                                                         53
Puppis (the Stern [of Argo]) - Pup                                54
purchase - pchs.; purch.                                          55
purchase order - PO                                               56
```

```
purchasing - purch.                                              1
Purchasing Agent - P.A.                                          2
Purdue University - PU                                           3
pure water (L, aqua pura) - aq. pur.                             4
Purified Protein Derivative (tuberculin) - PPD                   5
purplish blue - pB                                               6
purplish pink - pPk                                              7
purplish red - pR                                                8
pursuit - pur.                                                   9
push button - PB                                                10
push button panel - PBP                                         11
put and call - p&c; P.a.C.                                      12
put-outs (baseball) - po.                                       13
Pyxis (the Compass) - Pyx                                       14
quadrangle - quad.                                              15
quadrant - QUAD                                                 16
quadruplets - quads                                             17
qualification maintainability inspection - QMI                 18
qualified - qual.                                               19
quality - qlty.; qual.                                          20
quality control - qc                                            21
quality factor - QF                                            22
quality reliability assurance - QRA                             23
Quanah, Acme & Pacific (RR) - QA&P                             24
Quantas Empire Airways - QUANTAS                               25
quantity - qnty; qt; qty; quan                                 26
quantity not sufficient - q.n.s.                               27
quantity of electricity - Q                                    28
quantity sufficient to make - q.s.ad                           29
quantizer - QNT                                                30
quantum libet (as much as you please) - q.l.                   31
quantum placet (as much as seems good) - q.pl.                 32
quantum sufficit (sufficient quantity) - q.s.                  33
quantum vis (as much as you will) - q.v.                       34
quarry - qry                                                   35
quarry tile - Q.T.                                             36
quarry tile base - QTB                                         37
quarry tile floor - QTF                                        38
quarry tile roof - QTR                                         39
quart(s) - q.                                                  40
quart - qt.; qu.                                               41
quarter - qr.; qu.; quart.                                     42
quarter section - q.s.                                         43
quarterback (football) - QB                                    44
quartered - qtd.                                               45
quartering - Qr                                                46
quarterly - qrtly.; qu.; Quart.; quart.                        47
Quartermaster - QM; Q.M.                                       48
Quartermaster Corps - Q.M.C.                                   49
Quartermaster General - Q.M.G.; Q.M. Gen.                      50
Quartermaster sergeant - Q.M.Sgt.                              51
quarters - qrs.                                                52
quarto - 4mo; 4°; 4to; Q.                                      53
quartos - Qq.; qq.                                             54
quarts - qts.                                                  55
quartz - qtz.                                                  56
```

```
quasi - q.                                                        1
quasi dicat (as if one should say) - q.d.                         2
quasi dictum (as if said) - q.d.                                  3
quasi dixisset (as if he had said) - q.d.                        ·4
Quebec - Q.; Qbc.; Que.                                           5
Quebec Central (RR) - QC                                          6
Quebecair - QBA                                                   7
Queen - Q.; Qn.                                                   8
queen (L, regina) - qu.; (R.)                                     9
Queen and Empress (L, Regina et Imperatrix) - R.I.; R.&I.        10
Queen Victoria (L, Victoria Regina) - V.R.                       11
Queen's Bench - Q.B.                                             12
Queen's Bishop - QB                                              13
Queen's Counsel - QC                                             14
Queen's Knight - QN                                              15
Queen's Rook - QR                                                16
queer - qr                                                       17
query - q.; qu.; Qy.; qy.                                        18
question - Q.; q.; qn.; qu.; ques.                               19
question and answer - Q&A                                        20
questionably - ques.                                             21
questionnaire - qstnr                                            22
questions - qq                                                   23
Queuing theory - QT                                              24
quick - qk                                                       25
quick dependable communications - QDC                            26
quick reaction - QR                                              27
quickly ends dandruff - Q.E.D.                                   28
quick-make, quick-break - QMQB                                   29
quiet - q.t.                                                     30
quintal - q.; ql.                                                31
quintuple - quint                                                32
quintuplet - quint                                               33
quintuplets - quints                                             34
Quintus - Q                                                      35
quire - q.; qr.;                                                 36
quires - qrs.                                                    37
quod erat demonstrandum (which was to be demonstrated) -         38
     Q.E.D.; q.e.d.                                              39
quod erat faciendum (which was to be done) - Q.E.F.; q.e.f.      40
quot erat inveniendum (which was to be found out) - Q.E.I.       41
     q.e.i.                                                      42
quod est (which is) - q.e.                                       43
quod vide (which see) - q.v.                                     44
quorum - quor.                                                   45
quotation - qn.; quot.                                           46
quotation marks - quotes                                         47
quoted - quot.                                                   48
rabbi - R.                                                       49
rabbinical - rabb.                                               50
Rachel - Ra.                                                     51
radar - rad                                                      52
radar beacon - racon                                             53
radial - rad                                                     54
radian - rad                                                     55
radiant - rad                                                    56
```

```
radiate - rad.                                                      1
radiation - rad.                                                    2
radiator - rad.                                                     3
radiator enclosed - RAD ENCL                                        4
radiator recess - RAD REC                                           5
Radical - R.                                                        6
radical (chemical) - R                                              7
radical (math) - rad.                                               8
radio - R; rad.                                                     9
Radio Corporation of America - RCA                                 10
radio detection and ranging - radar                                11
radio direction finder - RDF                                       12
radio direction finding - RDF                                      13
radioactive - r/a                                                  14
radiofrequency - RF; R-F; R.-F.; R.F.; r.f.                        15
radio magnetic indicator - RMI                                     16
radio teletype - RATT                                              17
radio-frequency choke - RFC                                        18
radiotelephone - RTF                                               19
radius - r.; rad.                                                  20
radix - rad.                                                       21
Raleigh - Ral                                                      22
railhead - rhd.                                                    23
railroad - R.; RR                                                  24
railroad post office - RPO; R.P.O.                                 25
Railroad Retirement Board - RRB                                    26
railway - R.; Ry.                                                  27
Railway Express - REA                                              28
Railway Mail Service - R.M.S.                                      29
railways - rys.                                                    30
rain water (L, aqua pluvialis) - aq. pluv.                         31
rallentando - rall.                                                32
random - rdm                                                       33
random access discrete address - RADAS                             34
random access memory - RAM                                         35
random access nondestructive advanced memory - RANDAM              36
random access plan position indicator - RAPPI                      37
random access programming and checkout equipment -                 38
    RAPCOE                                                          39
random lengths - r.l.                                              40
random widths - r.w.                                               41
range - rg.; rge.                                                  42
range finding - rf                                                 43
range height indicator - RHI                                       44
rank - R                                                           45
rapid - rap.                                                       46
rapid access disc - RAD                                            47
rapid alphanumeric digital indicating device memory -              48
    RANDID                                                         49
rapid circuit etch - RCE                                           50
rapid eye movements - REM                                          51
rapid fire - r.f.                                                  52
rare - r.                                                          53
rarissime (very rarely) - rr.                                      54
rate - rt                                                          55
rate of change - rc                                                56
```

```
rate of energy loss - REL                                              1
rate of exchange - R.E.; r/e                                           2
rate of interest - r                                                   3
rate of turn - r.t.                                                    4
ratio - R                                                              5
ratio of circumference to diameter of a circle - pi                    6
ratio transformer unit - RT                                            7
ration(s) - rat.                                                       8
Raymond - Ray                                                          9
reactance - X                                                         10
Reaction Control System - RCS                                         11
read - R                                                              12
read and compute - RC                                                 13
read backward - RB                                                    14
read buffer - RB                                                      15
read channel continue - RCC                                           16
read channel initialize - RCI                                         17
read check - RD CHK                                                   18
read forward - RF                                                     19
read, write, and compute - RWC                                        20
read, write, and continue - RWC                                       21
read, write, and initialize - RWI                                     22
readability, strength, tone - RST                                     23
readable - RDBL                                                       24
read-around-numbers - RAN                                             25
reader code - RC                                                      26
reader common contact - RCC                                           27
reader control relay - RCR                                            28
reader tape contact - RTC                                             29
Reading (RR) - READ                                                   30
reading level(s) - RL                                                 31
reading, 'riting, and 'rithmetic - three R's                          32
ready - rdy                                                           33
real estate - R.E.; real est; rl est                                  34
real estate owner - R.E.O.                                            35
real-time communications (RCA) - REALCOM                              36
realtor - rltr                                                        37
realty - rlty                                                         38
ream - rm.                                                            39
reams - rms.                                                          40
reappoint - reapt.                                                    41
reappointed - reaptd.                                                 42
rear - rr.                                                            43
Rear Admiral - R.A.; Rear Adm.                                        44
rear view - r.v.                                                      45
rearward communications system - RCS                                  46
reason - rsn                                                          47
reassemble - reasm                                                    48
reassign - rsg                                                        49
Réaumur (thermometer) - R.                                            50
Réaumur - Réaum.                                                      51
recall finder - RCF                                                   52
recapitulate - recap.                                                 53
recapitulation - recap.                                               54
receipt - rcpt.; rec.; rect.; rept.                                   55
receipt of goods - r.o.g.                                             56
```

194

```
recurrence rate - RR                              1
red blood cell(s) - rbc                           2
red blood cell count - R.B.C.                     3
red blood count - R.B.C.                          4
Red Cross - R.C.                                  5
redactor - R.                                     6
reddish brown - rBr                               7
reddish orange - rO                               8
reddish purple - rP                               9
Redemptorist Fathers - C.S.S.R.                  10
redesign - redsg                                 11
reduce - red.                                    12
reduced - red.                                   13
reducer - red.                                   14
reducing - red.                                  15
reduction - red.                                 16
reduplicate - redup.                             17
reduplicated - redup.                            18
reduplication - redup.; redupl.                  19
reduplicative - redupl.                          20
reenlist - Reenl                                 21
reenlistment - Reenlmt                           22
Reeve Aleutian Airways - RV                      23
refashion - refash.                              24
refashioned - refash.                            25
referee - ref.                                   26
reference - ref.                                 27
reference - refer.                               28
referred - ref.; refd.                           29
refine - ref.                                    30
refined - ref.                                   31
refining - ref.                                  32
reflect - refl.                                  33
reflected - refl.                                34
reflection - refl.                               35
reflective - refl.                               36
reflector - refl.                                37
reflex - refl.                                    38
reflexive - refl.                                39
reflexive pronoun - refl pron                    40
reform - ref.                                    41
reformation - ref.                               41
Reformed - Ref.                                  42
reformed - ref.                                  43
Reformed Episcopal - R.E.                        44
Reformed Presbyterian - R.P.                     45
reformer - ref.                                  46
refraction - ref                                 47
refractive index - ri                            48
refrigerant discharge (pipe) - RD               49
refrigerate - refg.                              50
refrigerating - refrig.                          51
refrigeration - refg.                            52
refrigerator - fridge; refg.                     53
refrigerator suction - RS                        54
refund - ref.; refd.                             55
refunding - ref.; rfg.                           56
```

```
regarding - re                                                    1
regarding our letters - reourlets                                 2
regarding our telegram - reourtel                                 3
regarding telegram - retel                                        4
regarding your telegram - reurtel                                 5
regent - Regt.                                                    6
Regiae Societatis Sodalis (Fellow of the Royal Society)          7
    R.S.S.                                                         8
regiment - reg.; regt.; rgt.                                      9
regimental - regtl.                                              10
regina (queen) - R.                                              11
Reginald - Reg                                                   12
region - reg.; rgn.                                              13
regional center - RC                                             14
register - reg.; regis.; RG                                      15
register, bottom - BR                                            16
register, ceiling - CR                                           17
register, center - CR                                            18
register (N) stages - RG(N)                                      19
register, top - TR                                               20
register, top & bottom - T&BR                                    21
registered - reg.; regd.                                         22
Registered Nurse - R.N.                                          23
registrar - reg.; regr.                                          24
registry - reg.; regis.                                          25
Regius Professor - R.P.                                          26
regular - reg.                                                   27
Regular Army - RA; R.A.                                          28
regularly - reg.                                                 29
regulate - reg.                                                  30
regulation - reg.                                                31
regulator - reg.                                                 32
Reich Security Main Office (Reichssicherheitshauptamt) -         33
    R.S.H.A.                                                      34
reichsmark - RM; r.m.                                            35
reigned - rgd                                                    36
reimburse - reimb                                                37
reincorporate - reincorp                                         38
reinforce - reinf.                                               39
reinforced - reinf.                                              40
reinforcing - reinf.                                             41
Reisskilometer - Rkm.                                            42
reject failure rate - RFR                                        43
rejoin - rej.; rejn.                                             44
rejoined - rejd.                                                 45
relate - rel.                                                    46
relating - rel.                                                  47
relation - rel.                                                  48
relative - rel.; rltv.                                           49
relative centrifugal force - RCF; R.C.F.                         50
relative humidity - rel hum; RH; R.H.                            51
relative pronoun - rel. pron.                                    52
relatively - rel.                                                53
relay - rly; RY                                                  54
relay logic - RL                                                 55
release - rel.                                                   56
```

```
release clause - r.c.                                              1
released - rel.                                                    2
reliability improvement factor - RIF                               3
reliability index - RI                                             4
reliability test assembly - RTA                                    5
relic(s) - rel.                                                    6
relief - rlf                                                       7
relief valve - RV                                                  8
religion - rel.; relig.                                            9
religious - rel.                                                  10
relocate - reloc                                                  11
remaining on board - r.o.b.                                       12
remark - rem.                                                     13
remarkable - rem.                                                 14
remittance - rem.                                                 15
remote - rmte                                                     16
remote communications complex - RCC                               17
remote control - RC                                               18
remote data transmitter - RDT                                     19
remote position control - RPC                                     20
remote station - RS                                               21
remote station alarm - RSA                                        22
remote terminal unit - RTU                                        23
remote transfer point - RTP                                       24
remote-control oscillator - RCO                                   25
removable - remov.                                                26
remove - rem.                                                     27
Renaissance - Ren                                                 28
rendered - rd.                                                    29
rendezvous evaluation pod - REP                                   30
Rendus - Rend.                                                    31
renegotiate - rngt                                                32
Renegotiation Board - RB                                          33
renovate - renv                                                   34
reorganize - reorg                                                35
repair - rep.; repr.                                              36
repeat - rep.; rpt.                                               37
repeater - RP                                                     38
reperforator - REPERF                                             39
repertory - rep.                                                  40
repetition - rep.                                                 41
repetition rate - RR                                              42
repetitive operation - REP-OP                                     43
replace - repl                                                    44
replacing - r.                                                    45
replica - rplca                                                   46
reply paid - RP                                                   47
répondez s'il vous plaît (please reply) - R.S.V.P.; r.s.v.p.     48
report - rep.; rept.; rprt.; rpt.                                 49
Report Program Generator - RPG                                    50
reportage - reptge.                                               51
reported - rep.                                                   52
reporter - rep.                                                   53
represent - repr.                                                 54
Representative - Rep.                                             55
representative calculating operation - RCO                        56
```

```
representatives - reps.                              1
represented - repr.                                  2
representing - repr.                                  3
reprint - repr.; rp.                                 4
reprinted - repr.                                    5
reprinting - repr.                                   6
reproduce - repro.                                   7
reproduced - repr.                                   8
reproduction - repro.                                9
reptile - rept                                      10
Republic - Rep.; rep.; Repub.                       11
Republic of New Africa - RNA                        12
Republican - R.; Rep.; Repub.                       13
Republican from Alabama - R.-Ala.                   14
Republican from Alaska - R.-Alaska                  15
Republican from Arizona - R.-Ariz.                  16
Republican from Arkansas - R.-Ark.                  17
Republican from California - R.-Calif.              18
Republican from Colorado - R.-Colo.                 19
Republican from Connecticut - R.-Conn.              20
Republican from Delaware - R.-Del.                  21
Republican from Florida - R.-Fla.                   22
Republican from Georgia - R.-Ga.                    23
Republican from Hawaii - R.-Hawaii                  24
Republican from Idaho - R.-Idaho                    25
Republican from Illinois - R.-Ill.                  26
Republican from Indiana - R.-Ind.                   27
Republican from Iowa - R.-Iowa                      28
Republican from Kansas - R.-Kans.                   29
Republican from Kentucky - R.-Ky.                   30
Republican from Louisiana - R.-La.                  31
Republican from Maine - R.-Maine                    32
Republican from Massachusetts - R.-Mass.            33
Republican from Maryland - R.-Md.                   34
Republican from Michigan - R.-Mich.                 35
Republican from Minnesota - R.-Minn.                36
Republican from Mississippi - R.-Miss.              37
Republican from Missouri - R.-Mo.                   38
Republican from Montana - R.-Mont.                  39
Republican from Nebraska - R.-Nebr.                 40
Republican from Nevada - R.-Nev.                    41
Republican from New Hampshire - R.-N.H.             42
Republican from New Jersey - R.-N.J.                43
Republican from New Mexico - R.-N.Mex.              44
Republican from New York - R.-N.Y.                  45
Republican from North Carolina - R.-N.C.            46
Republican from North Dakota - R.-N.Dak.            47
Republican from Ohio - R.-Ohio                      48
Republican from Oklahoma - R.-Okla.                 49
Republican from Oregon - R.-Oreg.                   50
Republican from Pennsylvania - R.-Pa.               51
Republican from Rhode Island - R.-R.I.              52
Republican from South Carolina - R.-S.C.            53
Republican from South Dakota - R.-S.Dak.            54
Republican from Tennessee - R.-Tenn.                55
Republican from Texas - R.-Tex.                     56
```

```
Republican from Utah - R.-Utah                              1
Republican from Vermont - R.-Vt.                            2
Republican from Virginia - R.-Va.                           3
Republican from Washington - R.-Wash.                       4
Republican from West Virginia - R.-W.Va.                    5
Republican from Wisconsin - R.-Wis.                         6
Republican from Wyoming - R.-Wyo.                           7
reputation - rep                                            8
request - req                                               9
request for price quotation - RPQ                          10
requiescat, or requiescant in pace (may he, she, or they   11
   rest in peace) - R.I.P.                                 12
require - req.; rqr.                                        13
required - req.; reqd.                                      14
required delivery date - r.d.d.                            15
requirement - rqmt.                                        16
requisition - req.; reqn.                                  17
rerum politicarum doctor (doctor of political science) -   18
   R.P.D.                                                   19
rescue - rsq                                               20
research - res.; rsch.                                     21
Research and Development - R. & D.                         22
Research and Development Board - RDB                       23
research and technology - RT                               24
research, development, test, and evaluation - RDT&E        25
Research in Education - RIE                                26
Research Selected Vote Profile - R.S.V.P.                  27
Reservation - Res                                          28
reserve - res.                                             29
Reserve Corps - R.C.                                       30
Reserve Officers' Training Corps - ROTC                    31
reservoir - rsvr                                           32
reset - R; RE                                              33
reset gate - RG                                            34
residence - r.; res.                                       35
resident - res.                                            36
resident physician - Res. Phys.                            37
resides - res.                                             38
residue - res.                                             39
resignation - resig.                                       40
resigned - res.; resgd.                                    41
resilient - res.                                           42
resin emulsion - RE                                        43
resistance - R; res.                                       44
resistance (electrical) - R; r                             45
resistance bulb thermometer - RBT                          46
resistance capacitance - RC; R-C; R.-C.; R.C.              47
resistant - res.                                           48
resistor - R; res.                                         49
resolution - res.                                          50
resort - res.                                              51
respective - resp.                                         52
respectively - resp.                                       53
respelling - resp.                                         54
respiration - resp.                                        55
respiratory quotient - R.Q.                                56
```

```
respond - resp.                                              1
respondent - R; resp.                                        2
respondents - R's                                            3
response - R.                                                4
responsible - resp                                           5
respublica (commonwealth) - R.                               6
Resurrection - Resurr.                                       7
rest and recreation - r & r                                  8
rest and recuperation - R and R                              9
rest in peace - R.I.P.                                       10
restaurant - restr.                                          11
restored - rest.                                             12
restrict - rest.                                             13
restricted - rstr.                                           14
Restricted (persons under 18 not admitted unless accom-      15
    panied by parents or adult guardian) (movie code) - R    16
retain - ret.; rtn.                                          17
retained - retd.                                             18
retainer - ret; retnr.                                       19
Reticulum (the Net) - Ret                                    20
retire - ret.                                                21
retired - ret.; retd.                                        22
retroactive - retro                                          23
retrogressive - retrog.                                      24
retro-rocket - retro                                         25
return - ret.                                                26
return air - R.A.                                            27
return loss - RL                                             28
return on investment - ROI                                   29
return to author - r/a                                       30
returned - ret.; retd.; rtd.                                 31
returns - rets.                                              32
return-to-zero - RZ                                          33
Revelation - Rev.                                            34
Revelations - Rev.                                           35
revenue - rev.                                               36
Reverend - Rev.                                              37
reverse - R; rev.; rx                                        38
reverse free - RF                                            39
reverse gate - RG                                            40
reversed - rev.                                              41
review - R.; rev.                                            42
revise - rev.                                                43
revised - rev.                                               44
Revised Standard Version - RSV                               45
Revised Statutes - Rev. Stat.                                46
Revised Version (of the Bible) - RV; Rev. Ver.               47
revision - rev.                                              48
revolution - rev.; revol.                                    49
revolutions - revs.                                          50
revolutions per minute - r.p.m.                              51
revolutions—per-minute indicator - RPMI                      52
revolutions per second - r.p.s.                              53
revolving - rev.                                             54
Revue - R.; Rev.                                             55
reward - rew                                                 56
```

```
rewind - REW                                                    1
rework - rwk                                                    2
Rex - R.                                                        3
rhapsody - rhap                                                 4
Rhenium - Re                                                    5
rheostat(s) - rheo.                                             6
Rhesus Factor - Rh factor                                       7
Rhetoric - Rhet.; rhet.                                         8
rhetorical - rhet.                                              9
rheumatic fever - RF; RAF                                      10
rheumatoid factor - RF                                         11
Rhode Island - R.I.                                            12
Rhodesia - Rho.; Rhod.                                         13
Rhodesia and Nyasaland - Rh. & Nya.                            14
Rhodium - Rh                                                   15
rhombic - rhom                                                 16
ribonucleic acid - RNA                                         17
Richard - Rich                                                 18
Richard M. Nixon - RMN                                         19
Richmond, Fredericksburg & Potomac (RR) - RF&P                 20
Richmond Stock Exchange - RSE; Ri                              21
rifle - R.                                                     22
right (L, dexter) - (d.); R; rt.                               23
Right (stage direction) - R.                                   24
right ascension - R.A.; RA                                     25
right defense (ice hockey) - RD                                26
right end (football) - RE                                      27
Right Excellent - R.E.                                         28
right eye - O.D.                                               29
right field (baseball) - rf.                                   30
right fielder - 9                                              31
right foot (figure skating) - R                                32
right forward (basketball) - rf.                               33
right fullback (field hockey) - RB; RFB                        34
right fullback (soccer) - RB                                   35
right guard (basketball) - rg.                                 36
right guard (football) - rg.                                   37
right halfback (field hockey) - RH; RHB                        38
right halfback (football) - RH; RHB                            39
right halfback (soccer) - RH; RHB                              40
right hand - r.h.                                              41
Right Honorable - Rt. Hon.                                     42
right inside backward edge (figure skating) - RIB             43
right inside forward (field hockey) - RI                      44
right inside forward edge (figure skating) - RIF             45
right outside backward edge (figure skating) - ROB           46
right outside forward edge (figure skating) - ROF            47
Right Reverend - R.R.; Rt. Rev.                                48
right side - r.s.                                              49
right side up with care - r.s.w.c.                             50
right tackle (football) - RT                                   51
right wing (field hockey) - RW                                 52
right wing (ice hockey) - RW                                   53
Right Worshipful - R.W.                                        54
Right Worthy - R.W.                                            55
right-handed page (L, folio recto) - f.r.                      56
```

```
right-handed page (L, recto) - R.                              1
right-of-way - r/w                                             2
rights - rts.                                                  3
rigling (horse racing) - rig.                                  4
ring and ball method - R & B                                   5
Rio Grand Southern (RR) - RGS                                  6
riser - r.                                                     7
rises - r.                                                     8
ritardando (music) - rit.; ritard.                             9
River - R.; riv.                                              10
river water (L, aqua fluvialis) - aq. fluv.                   11
rivet - riv.                                                  12
Rivista - Riv.                                                13
Road - R.; Rd.; rd.                                           14
roan - r.; ro.                                                15
Robert - Robt.                                                16
Robert Francis Kennedy - R.F.K.                               17
rock - rk.                                                    18
Rock Island Southern (RR) - RIS                               19
rocket - rkt                                                  20
rocket-assisted takeoff - rato                                21
Rockwell hardness (C-scale) - Rc                              22
rocky - rky.                                                  23
rod - r.                                                      24
rod(s) - rd.                                                  25
rod memory computer - RMC                                     26
rods - rds.                                                   27
roentgen(s) - r                                               28
roentgen equivalent physical - rep; r.e.p.                    29
Roger - Rog.                                                  30
Roland - Rol.                                                 31
rolled - rld                                                  32
rolling steel curtain - R.S.C.                                33
Rolls-Royce - Rolls                                           34
Roman - Rom.                                                  35
Roman Catholic - RC                                           36
Roman Catholic Church - Rom. Cath. Ch.·                       37
roman type - rom.                                             38
Romance - Rom.                                                39
Romania - Rom.                                                40
Romanic - Rom.                                                41
Romans - Rom.                                                 42
Romans (New Testament) - Rom.                                 43
Ronald - Ron                                                  44
roof conductor - R.C.                                         45
roof drain - R.D.                                             46
roof sump - R.S.                                              47
roofing - rfg.                                                48
room - rm.                                                    49
room temperature - r.t.                                       50
rooms - rms.                                                  51
root mean square - RMS; R.M.S.; r.m.s.                        52
root-mean-square error - RMSE                                 53
Rosaceus (Rose; a Liturgical Color) - Rosac.                  54
rotary - rot.                                                 55
rotate - rot.                                                 56
```

```
rotating - rot.                                                      1
rotation - rotn.                                                     2
rotations per minute - rpm                                           3
rotor - rot.                                                         4
rotten - rot.                                                        5
rough - rgh                                                          6
rough wire glass - RWGL                                              7
round - rd.; rnd.                                                    8
round head - rd. hd.                                                 9
round trip - r.t.                                                   10
roundheaded screw - RHS                                            11
route - rte.                                                        12
routine - rout.                                                     13
Royal - R.; Roy.                                                    14
Royal Academician - R.A.                                           15
Royal Academy - R.A.                                               16
Royal Academy of Music - R.A.M.                                    17
Royal Air Force - RAF                                              18
Royal Architectural Institute of Canada - R.A.I.C.                 19
Royal Dutch Airlines - KLM                                         20
Royal Highness - R.H.                                              21
Royal Mail Service - R.M.S.                                        22
Royal Mail Steamship - R.M.S.                                      23
Royal Naval Reserve - R.N.R.                                       24
Royal Navy - R.N.                                                  25
rubber - rub.                                                      26
Rubber Mat - Rub. Mat.                                             27
rubber tile - R.T.                                                 28
Ruben (Red; a Liturgical Color) - Rub.                             29
Rubidium - Rb                                                      30
ruble - r                                                          31
Rudolf - Rud.                                                      32
rule - r.                                                          33
rules, standards, and instructions - RS&I                          34
ruling class - Rc                                                  35
Rumania - Rum.                                                     36
Rumanian - Rum.                                                    37
run of paper - ROP                                                 38
running reverse - RR                                               39
runs (baseball) - r.                                               40
runs batted in (baseball) - RBI                                    41
runway - rwy                                                       42
rupee - R; r.; Re.; re                                             43
rupees - rs.                                                       44
Rural Delivery - R.D.                                              45
Rural Electrification Administration - REA                         46
rural free delivery - RFD; R.F.D.                                  47
rural route - R.R.                                                 48
rural/urban - Ru/Ur                                                49
Russia - Russ.                                                     50
Russian - Russ.                                                    51
Russian Orthodox - Russ. Orth.                                     52
Russian Secret Police (Narodnyi Kommissariat Vnutrennikh.         53
    Del) - NKVD                                                    54
Russian Secret Service - GPU                                       55
Russian Soviet Federated Socialist Republic - RSFSR               56
```

205

```
Scandinavia - Scan.; Scand.                                          1
Scandinavian - Scand.                                                2
Scandinavian Airlines System - SAS                                   3
Scandium - Sc                                                        4
scanning control register - SCR                                      5
scanning gate - SG                                                   6
scene - sc.                                                          7
schedule - sch.; sched.; SKED                                        8
scheduled - scd.                                                     9
schematic - schem                                                   10
schizophrenia - schizo                                              11
schizophrenic - schizo                                              12
scholar - schl.                                                     13
scholastic - schol.                                                 14
Scholastic Aptitude Test - SAT                                      15
School - S.; sch.; Schl.                                            16
School Library Journal - SLJ                                        17
School Superintendent - School Supt.                                18
schooner - schr.                                                    19
Schopper-Riegler - S-R                                              20
the Schutzstaffel - SS Troops                                       21
science - sc.; sci.                                                 22
science fiction - sf                                                23
Science Fiction Writers of America - SFWA                           24
scientific - sc.; sci.; scient.                                     25
Scientific Equipment bay - SEQ                                      26
scienze - Sci.                                                      27
scilicet (namely) - sc.; scil.; ss                                  28
Scorpio - Scor                                                      29
Scorpius (the Scorpion) - Sco                                       30
Scotch - Sc.; Scot.                                                 31
Scotland - Sc.; Scot.; Scotl.                                       32
Scots - Sc.                                                         33
Scottish - Sc.; Scot.                                               34
scout - sct.                                                        35
screen grid - SG                                                    36
screen-grid input - SI                                              37
screw - sc.; scr.                                                   38
screw and washer assemblies - sems                                  39
screwed - scd.                                                      40
scribe - s.                                                         41
script - scr.                                                       42
Scriptural - Script.                                                43
Scripture - Script.                                                 44
scruple - sc.; scr.                                                 45
scruple, apothecaries' - s.ap.                                      46
sculpsit (he or she carved or engraved it) - sc.                    47
sculptor - sculpt.                                                  48
Sculptor (constellation) - Scl                                      49
scupper - SCUP                                                      50
Scutum (Sobieski's Shield) - Sct                                    51
Sea - S.                                                            52
sea level - s.l.                                                    53
sea water (L, aqua marina) - (aq. mar.); s.w.                       54
Seaboard Airline (RR) - SAL                                         55
Seafarers Political Activity Donation - SPAD                        56
```

```
sealed - sld.                                                        1
sealed with a kiss - s.w.a.k.                                        2
seaman, first class - Slc.                                           3
seamless - smls                                                      4
seamless steel tubing - sstu                                         5
seamstress - smstrs.                                                 6
seaport - spt.                                                       7
search - SRCH                                                        8
Seattle - Seatl                                                      9
secant - sec                                                         10
secants - secs                                                       11
second - s.; 2d; 2nd                                                 12
second - sec.                                                        13
Second Adventist - Second Advent.                                    14
second attack (lacrosse) - SA; 2A                                    15
second base (baseball) - 2b                                          16
second baseman - 4                                                   17
second defense (lacrosse) - SD; 2D                                   18
second lieutenant - 2d Lt.; 2nd Lt.                                  19
second postscript (L, post postscriptum) - P.P.S.                    20
secondary - sec.                                                     21
second-foot - sec.-ft.                                               22
seconds - secs.                                                      23
secret - S; secr                                                     24
Secret Police in the Field (Geheime Feld-Polizei) - G.F.P.           25
Secret Service - SS                                                  26
Secret State Police (Geheime Staatspolizei) - GESTAPO                27
secretary - sec.; secy.; sec'y.; sect'y                              28
section - s.; sect.; sx                                              29
section(s) - sec.; ss.                                               30
sector - sec.; sect.                                                 31
secundum (according to) - sec.                                       32
secundum artem (according to art) - s.a.                             33
secundum legem (according to law) - sec. leg.                        34
secundum naturam (according to nature) - sec. nat.                   35
secundum regulam (according to rule) - sec. reg.                     36
secured - sec.                                                       37
Securities and Exchange Commission - SEC                             38
security - scty.; sec.                                               39
Security Police (Sicherheitspolizei) - SIPO                          40
Security Service of the Chief of the S.S. in the Reich               41
    (Sisherheitsdienst des Reichsfuehrers S.S.) - S.D.               42
security time control - s.t.c.                                       43
sedative - sed                                                       44
see - cf.                                                            45
see (L, vide) - v.; vid.                                             46
see above (L, vide supra) - v.s.                                     47
see also - sa.                                                       48
see below (L, vide infra) - v.i.                                     49
see you - c-u                                                        50
segment(s) - seg                                                     51
segregate - seg                                                      52
seismological - seismol.                                             53
seismology - seismol.                                                54
select - sel                                                         55
select address and contract operate - SACO                          56
```

```
select read numerically - SLRN                                   1
selected - sel.                                                  2
selection(s) - sel.                                              3
selective - sel.                                                 4
Selective Service System - SSS                                   5
selectivity clear accumulator - SCA                              6
Selenium - Se                                                    7
self-addressed envelope - s.a.e.                                 8
self-closing - SC                                                9
self-contained underwater breathing apparatus - scuba          10
Self-Realization Fellowship - SRF                               11
seller's option - s.o.                                          12
seller's option to double - s.o.d.                              13
semi (half) - s.                                                14
semiannual - s.a.                                               15
semiautomatic ground environment - SAGE                         16
semicolon - sem.; smcln.                                        17
semiconductor integrated circuits - SIC                         18
semifinished - SF                                               19
Seminary - Sem.                                                 20
Semitic - Sem.                                                  21
Senate - S.; Sen.; sen.                                         22
the Senate and People of Rome (L, Senatus Populusque           23
    Romanus) - S.P.Q.R.                                         24
Senate bill - S.                                                25
Senate concurrent resolution - S.Con.Res.                      26
Senate document - S.Doc.                                        27
Senate joint resolution - S.J.Res.                             28
Senate report - S.Rept.                                        29
Senate resolution - S.Res.                                     30
Senator - Sen.                                                 31
sends greetings (L, salutem dicit) - S.D.                      32
Senegal - Sen.                                                 33
Senior - Sen.; Sr.                                             34
senior clerk - sen. clk.                                       35
senior master sergeant - Sr.M.Sgt.                             36
Señor (Spanish) - Sr.                                          37
Señora - Sra.                                                  38
Señores - Sres.                                                39
Señorita - Srta.                                               40
sentence - sent.                                               41
sentence sense - ss                                            42
sentenced - sentd.                                             43
Seoul - Seo                                                    44
separate - sep.                                                45
separate cover - s.c.                                          46
separated - sep.                                               47
September - S.; Sept.; 7ber                                    48
Septuagint - Sept.; LXX                                        49
sepultus (buried) - s.                                         50
sequel - seq.                                                  51
sequence - sq.                                                 52
sequence number indicator - SNI                                53
sequens (the following) - seq.; (pl., seqq.)                   54
Serbia - Serb.                                                 55
Serbian - Serb.                                                56
```

```
signature - sg.; sig.; sngr.                                          1
signature missing - sig. mis.                                         2
signature unknown - sig. unk.                                         3
signed - sgd.                                                         4
signifies - sig.                                                      5
signify - sig.                                                        6
signifying - sig.                                                     7
Signor (Ital.) - S.; sig.                                             8
Silas - Si                                                            9
Silicon - Si                                                         10
silicon precision alloy transistor (PHILCO) - SPAT                   11
Silver - Ag; s.                                                      12
Simeon - Sim.                                                        13
similar - sim.                                                       14
similarly - sim.                                                     15
simile - sim.                                                        16
Simon - Si; Sim.                                                     17
Simplified Practice Recommendations - SPR                            18
simulate - sml                                                       19
sine - s.; sin                                                       20
sine anno (without date) - s.a.                                      21
sine die (indefinitely) - s.d.                                       22
sine legitima prole (without lawful issue) - s.l.p.                  23
sine loco, anno, vel nomine (without place, date, or name)           24
     s.l.a.n.                                                        25
sine mascula prole (without male issue) - s.m.p.                     26
sine nomine (without name) - s.n.                                    27
sine prole (without issue) - s.p.                                    28
sine prole superstite (without surviving issue) - s.p.s.             29
sine-cosine - SC                                                     30
Singhalese - Singh.                                                  31
single - s.; sing.                                                   32
single cycle execute - SCE                                           33
single entry - s.e.                                                  34
single pole double throw - SPDT; S.P.D.T.                            35
single pole single throw - SPST; S.P.S.T.                            36
single-actuated voice recorder - SAVOR                               37
single-pole, double-throw - SPDT                                     38
single-pole, single-throw - SPST                                     39
singular - s.; sing.                                                 40
sink - sk                                                            41
sink and laundry tray - S&T                                          42
Sinking Fund - SF; s.f.                                              43
Sir - Sr.                                                            44
Sirach (Ecclesiasticus) - Sir                                        45
sister - S.; sist.; Sr.                                              46
situation report - SIT-REP                                           47
sitz bath - SB                                                       48
Six - VI                                                             49
six hundred - DC                                                     50
sixteen - XVI                                                        51
six-three-two defense (football) - 6-3-2                             52
six-two-two-one defense (football) - 6-2-2-1                         53
sixty - LX                                                           54
sixty-four-mo - 64mo                                                 55
size - sz                                                            56
```

```
Society of St. Vincent De Paul - S.V.P.                          1
Society of the African Missions - S.M.A.                         2
Society of the Catholic Apostolate (Pallottine Fathers) -        3
   S.C.A.                                                         4
Society of the Divine Word - S.V.D.                              5
Society of the Fathers of Mercy - S.P.M.                         6
Society of the Holy Cross (L, Societas Sanctae Crucis) -         7
   S.S.C.                                                         8
Society of the Precious Blood - C.P.P.S.                         9
Society of the Priests of the Sacred Heart - S.C.J.             10
socio-cultural - S-cul                                          11
socio-economic - SE                                             12
socio-economic-status - SES                                     13
sociological - sociol.                                          14
Sociological Abstracts - SA                                     15
sociology - sociol.                                             16
socio-political - SP                                            17
socius or sodalis (fellow) - S.                                 18
socket - soc                                                    19
socks - sox                                                     20
Socrates - Soc.                                                 21
sodium (L, natrium) - Na                                        22
soft - sft                                                      23
soft pedal (music) - u.c.                                       24
softly (It, mezza voce, music) - m.v.                           25
softly (It, piano) - p.                                         26
software - sftwr                                                27
softwood - sftwd                                                28
soil pipe - SP                                                  29
Solar Wind Composition - SWC                                    30
sold - sld.                                                     31
solder - sld                                                    32
soldier - Sol                                                   33
solicitor - sol.; solr.                                         34
solid - SLD                                                     35
solid logical technology - SLT                                  36
solid oxygen - sox                                              37
solid state - ss                                                38
solids content index - SCI; S.C.I.                             39
solidus (shilling) - s.                                         40
solo - s                                                        41
Solomon Islands - Sol. Is.                                      42
soluble - sol.                                                  43
solution - sol.; SOLN                                           44
a solution (medical) - solutio                                  45
solvent - solv                                                  46
Somalia - Som.                                                  47
Somersetshire - Som.                                            48
son (L, filius) - (f.); s.                                      49
son of a bitch - s.o.b.                                         50
sonata - son.                                                   51
Song of Solomon - S. of Sol.                                    52
Sons of Confederate Veterans - S.C.V.                          53
Sons of Divine Providence - F.D.P.                             54
Sons of the American Revolution - S.A.R.                       55
Sons of the Holy Family - S.F.                                 56
```

sized and supercalendered - s. and s.c.   1
skates crossed (figure skating) - X   2
skates crossed, backward (figure skating) - XB   3
skates crossed, forward (figure skating) - XF   4
sketch - sk   5
skewbald - sk.   6
skilled - skd   7
slate - sl   8
Slavic - Slav.   9
Slavonian - Slav.   10
Slavonic - Slav.   11
sleeve - slv.   12
sloppy (horse racing, condition of the track) - Sly.   13
slow - s   14
slow (horse racing, condition of the track) - Sl.   15
slug feet - SF; S.F.   16
slugging percentage (baseball) - SLG PC   17
small - s; sm.   18
Small Business Administration - SBA   19
small calorie - cal.   20
small capitals - S.C.; s.caps.   21
small profits and quick returns - s.p.q.r.   22
smoke - smk   23
Smoky Mountain (Tenn.) (RR) - SM   24
Smyth sewn - Sm   25
Snatch (weight lifting) - S   26
snow water (L, aqua nivialis) - aq. niv.   27
so as to make (Latin) - ad   28
so as to make two drams - ad℈ij   29
social distance - SD   30
social level - SL   31
social science - soc sci   32
Social Security Act - S.S.A.   33
Social Security Administration - SSA   34
Socialist - Soc.   35
Socialist Soviet Republic - SSR; S.S.R.   36
Societatis Antiquariorum Socius (Fellow of the Society   37
    of Antiquaries) - S.A.S.   38
Societatis Historiae Socius (Fellow of the Historical   39
    Society) - S.H.S.   40
Societatis Philosophiae Americanae Socius (Fellow of the   41
    American Philosophical Society) - S.P.A.S.   42
Societatis Regiae Socius or Sodalis (Fellow of the Royal   43
    Society) - S.R.S.   44
Societas Sanctae Crucis (Society of the Holy Cross) - S.S.C.   45
society - soc.   46
Society for Individual Rights - SIR   47
Society for the Preservation and Encouragement of Barber   48
    Shop Quartet Singing in America Inc. - SPEBSQSA   49
Society for the Prevention of Cruelty to Animals - S.P.C.A.   50
Society for the Prevention of Cruelty to Children - S.P.C.C.   51
Society of Automotive Engineers - SAE; S.A.E.   52
Society of Jesus - S.J.   53
society of knowledge - S of K   54
Society of Priests of St. Suplice - S.S.   55
Society of Saint Edmond - S.S.E.   56

```
Sons of the American Revolution - S.A.R.            1
Sons of the Holy Family    S.F.                     2
Sons of the Revolution - S.R.                       3
soon as possible - s.a.p.                           4
Sophocles - Soph.                                   5
sophomore - soph                                    6
soprano - sop.                                      7
sorority - sor                                      8
sound - sd.                                         9
sound (preferred stock rating) - A                 10
sound fixing and ranging - sofar                   11
sound, navigation, and ranging - sonar             12
sound pressure level - spl                         13
sound-detecting and ranging - sodar                14
south - S.; s.; So.                                15
South Africa - S.A.; S.Afr.; U.S.Afr.;             16
South African - S.Afr.                             17
South African Dutch (Afrikaans) - S.Afr.D.         18
South America - S.A.; S.Am.; S.Amer.               19
South American - S.Am.; S.Amer.                    20
South Australia - S.A.                             21
South Britain (England and Wales) - S.B.           22
South by West - SbW                                23
South Carolina - S.C.                              24
South Dakota - S.D.; S.Dak.                        25
South Georgia (RR) - SG                            26
South latitude - s.l.                              27
South Wales - S.W.                                 28
southbound - SB                                    29
Southeast - SE; S.E.                               30
Southeast Asia Treaty Organization - SEATO         31
Southeastern - SE; S.E.                            32
southerly - Sly                                    33
Southern - S.; s.; So.; sou.                       34
Southern (RR) - SOU                                35
Southern Airways    SO                             36
Southern Christian Leadership Conference - SCLC    37
Southern Pacific (RR) - SP                         38
south-southeast - SSE; S.S.E.                      39
south-southwest - SSW; S.S.W.                      40
southwest - SW; S.W.                               41
South-West Africa - S.W.Afr.                       42
south-westerly - SWly                              43
southwestern - SW; S.W.                            44
sovereign - sov.                                   45
sovereigns - sovs.                                 46
Soviet Union - Sov. Un.                            47
space - sp.                                        48
space available mail - S.A.M.                      49
Spain - Sp.                                        50
spandrel - Sp                                      51
Spaniard - Sp.                                     52
Spanish - Sp.; Span.                               53
spare - sp                                         54
spare (scoring) - /                                55
speaker - spkr.                                    56
```

special – sp.; spec.; spl.   1
special delivery – sp. del.   2
special duty – s.d.   3
special finish – sf   4
special handling – sp hdlg   5
Special Libraries Association – S.L.A.   6
Special United Nations Fund for Economic Development –   7
  SUNFED   8
special weights (horse racing) – SplW   9
specialist – specl   10
specialist, third class – Sp3c   11
specially – spec.   12
specialty – spec.   13
species – sp.; spp.   14
specific – sp.; spec.; specif.   15
Specific Gravity – G.; s.g.; SP/GR; sp.gr.   16
specific heat – sp.ht.   17
specific volume – sp.vol.   18
specifically – spec.; specif.   19
specification – SPEC   20
specifications – specs.   21
specimen – sp.   22
spectacles – specs   23
spectrum – sptr   24
speculative (preferred stock rating) – B   25
speech auto instruction device – SAID   26
speech interference level – SIL   27
speed – s   28
speed regulator – SR   29
speeds of surface wind – ff   30
spelling – sp.   31
Spenser – Spens.   32
Sperry & Hutchinson (green stamps) – S&H   33
sphere – sph.   34
spherical – sph.; spher.   35
spirit – sp.   36
spirit(s) – spir.   37
spiritual – spir.   38
spiritualism – spirit.   39
Spiro Agnew Fans and Rooters Inc. – SAFARI   40
split (bowling) – o   41
Spokane International (RR) – SI   42
Spokane, Portland & Seattle (RR) – SP&S   43
Spokane Stock Exchange – STS; Sp   44
sponsor – spn   45
spontaneous polarization – Ps   46
spool – S   47
a spoon, a spoonful (L, cochlear) – coch.   48
Sprayed on Mineral Fiber – Sp.M.Fib.   49
Spring – Sp.   50
spring – spg.   51
spring water (L, aqua fontana) – aq. font.   52
springs – spgs.   53
sprinkler – spkr.; spr.   54
spurs – s.   55
squad – sqd.   56

Squadron - Sq.; sqn.   1
squadron leader - Sqn. Ldr.   2
square - sq.   3
square centimeter - cm^2; sq. cm.   4
square chain - sq. ch.   5
square decimeter - $dm.^2$; sq. dm.   6
square dekameter - $dkm.^2$; sq. dkm.   7
square edge - Sq.E   8
square foot - sq. ft.   9
square feet - sq. ft.   10
square hectometer - $hm.^2$; sq. hm.   11
square inch - $in.^2$; sq. in.   12
square inches - sq. $in.$ 13
square kilometer - $km.^2$; sq. km.   14
square meter - $m.^2$; sq. m.   15
square micron - mu^2 16
square mile(s) - sq. mi.   17
square millimeter - $mm.^2$; sq. mm.   18
square punch - SP   19
square rod - sq. r.   20
square yard(s) - sq. yd.   21
square-root-of-mean-square - r.m.s.   22
stabilizer - stab.   23
stable - stab.   24
staccato - stac.   25
staff - stf.   26
Staff Corps - S.C.   27
Staff sergeant - S.Sgt.   28
Staffordshire - Staffs.   29
stagger - stag.   30
staggered - stagg.   31
stained - STN; stnd   32
stained-waxed - SW   33
stainless steel - SS; St.St.; Stn.St.   34
stairs - ST   35
Stairs & Enclosures - St.Encl.   36
stairway - stwy   37
stallion - s.   38
stamped - sta.; stp.   39
stanchion - stan   40
stand - st.   41
standard - std.   42
Standard & Poor's - S&P   43
Standard Book Number - SNB   44
standard cubic feet - s.c.f.   45
standard cubic feet per minute - s.c.f.m.   46
standard cubic foot - std.c.f.   47
standard deviation - s.d.; std.dev.   48
standard metropolitan area - SMA   49
standard operating procedure - SOP   50
standard processing languages internally translated -   51
    SPLIT   52
standard Saybolt furol - S.S.F.   53
standard Saybolt universal - S.S.U.   54
standard temperature and pressure - STP   55
standard wave ratio - SWR   56

standard wire gauge - SWG; S.W.G.   1
standby - sby   2
standing order - so   3
standing room only - SRO   4
standpipe - SP   5
Stanford Research Institute - SRI   6
stanza - st.   7
Staphylococcus - Staph.   8
starboard - stbd.   9
start - st.   10
start of message - SOM   11
state - St.   12
state of the ground - E   13
Staten Island - S.I.   14
Staten Island Rapid Transit (RR) - SIRT   15
Statesman - Stsm.   16
static - stat.   17
static pressure - SP   18
static test stand - STS   19
statim (immediately) - stat.   20
station - sta.   21
Station (Bell Telephone) - S   22
station open to official correspondence only - CO   23
station to station - S. to S.   24
stationary - sta.   25
stationery - sta.   26
statistic - stat.   27
statistical quality control - SQC   28
statistical standards - SS   29
statistics - stats.   30
statuary - stat.   31
statue - stat.   32
statute - St.   33
statute(s) - stat.   34
statute (miles) - stat.   35
Statutes at Large - Stat.   36
steam working pressure - ST WP   37
steamer - str.   38
steamfitter - stmftr.   39
steamship - S.S.   40
steel - s.; st.; stl.   41
Steel-Painted - St.Pt.   42
steel partition - ST PART   43
steel saddle - ST S   44
Steel Sash-Painted - St.Sash/Pt.   45
steel steeple tips - SST   46
stem - s.   47
stem of - s.   48
stencil - sten.   49
stenographer - sten.; steno.   50
stenography - stenog.   51
Stephen - Steph.   52
stere - s.   53
stereo - ST   54
stereophonic - stereo   55
stereotype - stereo.   56

218

```
suggest - sug.                                                          1
suggested - sug.                                                        2
suggestion - sug.                                                       3
sulphur - S                                                             4
Sultan - Sult.                                                          5
Summer - Su.                                                            6
sump pit - SP                                                           7
Sumter & Choctaw (RR) - S&C                                             8
Sun Oil Company - Sunoco                                                9
Sunday - S.; Sun.; Sund.                                               10
Sunday School - S.S.                                                   11
sundries - sund.                                                       12
Sunset (RR) - SUN                                                      13
supercalendered - s.c.                                                 14
super-high frequency - SHF; s.h.f.; shf                                15
superintendent - Supt.; supt.                                          16
superior - sup.; super.                                                17
superlative - sup.; superl.                                            18
supersede - supsd                                                      19
Supersonic Transport - SST                                             20
superstructure - superstr                                              21
supervisor - supvr.                                                    22
supervisory - supvry.                                                  23
supervisory control - SC                                               24
supine - sup.                                                          25
supplement - sup.; supp.; suppl.                                       26
Supplement to the Revised Statutes - Supp.Rev.Stat.                    27
Supplemental Unemployment Benefit - SUB                                28
supplementary - sup.; suppl.; suppy.                                   29
supplements - supps.                                                   30
supply - sup.                                                          31
supply and demand - s.&d.                                              32
support - spt; supt                                                    33
supra (above) - sup.                                                   34
supreme - supr.                                                        35
Supreme Allied Commander Europe - SACEUR                               36
Supreme Commander for the Allied Powers (Japan) - SCAP                 37
Supreme Court - S.C.; Sup.Ct.                                          38
Supreme Court Reporter - Sup.Ct.                                       39
Supreme Head of the S.A. (Oberster S.A. Fuehrer) - O.S.A.F.            40
Supreme Headquarters Allied Expeditionary Force - SHAEF                41
Supreme Headquarters Allied Powers (Europe) - SHAPE                    42
surface - s; sur                                                       43
surface area - A; S                                                    44
surface barrier transistor - SBT                                       45
surface feet per minute - s.f.m.; s.f.p.m.                             46
surface foot - SF                                                      47
surface measure - SM                                                   48
surfaced and matched - S&M                                             49
surfaced four sides - S4S                                              50
surfaced one side and one edge - S1S1E                                 51
surgeon - surg.                                                        52
Surgeon General - Surg. Gen.                                           53
surgery - surg.                                                        54
surgical - surg.                                                       55
Surinam - Sur.                                                         56
```

220

```
surplus - sur.                                                      1
surrender - surr.                                                   2
surrendered - surr.                                                 3
surrey - sur.                                                       4
surrogate - surr.                                                   5
Surveillance and Missile Observation Satellite - SAMOS             6
survey - surv.                                                      7
surveying - surv.; survey.                                          8
surveyor - surv.                                                    9
surviving - surv.                                                  10
Susan - Su.                                                        11
suspend - susp.                                                    12
suspended - susp.                                                  13
Suspended Aluminum Grid - Sus.Al.G.                                14
suspended ceiling - susp ceil                                      15
Suspended Metal Grid - Susp.Met.G.                                 16
Suspended Plastic Grid - Susp.Pl.G.                                17
suspension - susp.                                                 18
Sussex - Sus.                                                      19
Svedberg flotation - Sf                                            20
Swahili - Swa                                                      21
Swaziland - Swaz.                                                  22
Sweden - Sw.; Swe.; Swed.                                          23
Swedish - Sw.; Swed.                                               24
sweep - swp                                                        25
swell - sw.                                                        26
Swiss - Sw.                                                        27
Swiss francs - FS                                                  28
Swissair - SR                                                      29
switch - sw.                                                       30
switch, key operated - SK                                          31
switchboard - swbd.                                                32
switching - swtg.                                                  33
switchman - swchmn.                                                34
Switzerland - Swit.; Switz.; Swtz.                                 35
Sydney - Sid                                                       36
Sydney and Louisburg (Mar.-Prov.)(RR) - S&L                        37
syllable - syll.                                                   38
syllabus - syll.                                                   39
Sylvestrine Benedictians - S.O.S.B.                                40
symbol - s; sym.                                                   41
symbol generator - SG                                              42
symbolic machine language - SML                                    43
Symbolic Programming System - SPS                                  44
symmetrical - sym.                                                 45
symphony - sym.                                                    46
symposium - symp                                                   47
symptom - sym.                                                     48
sync - S                                                           49
synchronize - sync.; synch.                                        50
synchronized - SY; synch.                                          51
synchronizing - synch.                                             52
syncopated - synco                                                 53
syndicate - synd.                                                  54
synod - syn.                                                       55
synonym - syn.                                                     56
```

```
synonymous - syn.                                              1
synonymy - syn.                                                2
synopsis - synop.                                              3
syntax - synt                                                  4
synthesis - synth                                              5
syphilis - syph                                                6
Syria - Syr.                                                   7
Syriac - Syr.                                                  8
Syriac Apocalypse of Baruch - S Baruch                         9
Syrian - Syr.                                                 10
syringe - syrg                                                11
syrup - syr.                                                  12
system - sys.; Syst.                                          13
system advisory board - SAB                                   14
systemic lupus erythematosus - S.L.E.                         15
systems and procedures - S-P                                  16
tab card puncher control - TCPC                               17
table(s) - tab.                                               18
tablespoon - T.; tablesp.; tbs.; tbsp.                        19
a tablespoonful (L, cochlear amplum) - coch. amp.             20
tablespoons - tbs.; tbsp.                                     21
tablet - tab.                                                 22
tabulate - tab.                                               23
tabulate switch - TAB                                         24
TACA International Airlines - TACA                            25
tachometer - tach                                             26
Tacitus - Tac                                                 27
tack board - T. Bd.                                           28
tackle (football) - T                                         29
tactic(s) - tac.                                              30
tactical - tac.                                               31
Tactical Mobile Unit (police) - TMU                           32
Tagalog - Tag.                                                33
take (L, recipe) - Rx                                         34
take off pounds sensibly - TOPS                               35
taken from - t.                                               36
talis qualis (just as they come; average quality) -          37
    tal. qual.                                                38
Tallulah Falls (RR) - TF                                      39
tambourine - tam                                              40
Tan Airlines - TAN                                            41
Tanganyika - Tan.                                             42
tangent - tg; tan                                             43
tank - tk.                                                    44
tanker - tkr.                                                 45
Tantalum - Ta                                                 46
tap water (L, aqua communis) - aq. com.                       47
tape mark record - TM                                         48
tape preventive maintenance - TPM                             49
tape unit - TU                                                50
tare - t.                                                     51
target - t; targ.; tgt.                                       52
tariff - tar.; trf.                                           53
tariffs - tar.                                                54
tarpaulin - tarp                                              55
Tartar - Tart.                                                56
```

223

```
temperature - t.; temp.                                        1
Temperature of sea - $T_wT_w$                                   2
temperature, pulse, respiration - t.p.r.                       3
template - temp                                                4
template-machine screws - TMS                                  5
tempo - t.                                                     6
temporal - tem.; temp.                                         7
temporarily (L, pro tempore) - pro tem.                        8
temporarily out of print - t.o.p.                              9
temporary - temp.; tmpry.                                     10
tempore (in the time of) - t.; temp.                          11
ten - X                                                       12
tenant - ten.                                                 13
tender love and care - tlc                                    14
tender loving care - tlc                                      15
ten-dollar bill (U.S.) - X                                    16
tenement - ten.                                               17
Tennessee - Tenn.                                             18
Tennessee (RR) - TENN                                         19
Tennessee, Alabama & Georgia (RR) - TA&G                      20
Tennessee & North Carolina (RR) - T&NC                        21
Tennessee Central (RR) - TC                                   22
Tennessee Valley Authority - TVA                              23
tennis shoes - tens                                           24
Tennyson - Tenn.                                              25
tenor - t.; ten.                                              26
tense - t.                                                    27
tensile - tens                                                28
tensile strength - TS; T.S.; t.s.                             29
tensile yield strength - TYS; T.Y.S.                          30
tension (surface) - T                                         31
tension - tens                                                32
tentative - tent.                                             33
tenth - X                                                     34
tenuto (music) - ten.                                         35
tepid water (L, aqua tepida) - aq. tep.                       36
teracycle - TC                                                37
Terbium - Tb                                                  38
term of enlistment - t.o.e.                                   39
terminal - term.                                              40
terminal address selector - TAS                               41
terminal area sequence and control - TASC                     42
terminals per station - TPS                                   43
terminal-to-computer-multiplexer - TCM                        44
termination - term.                                           45
terminology - term.                                           46
Termont & Gulf (La.)(RR) - T&G                                47
terra cotta - t.c.                                            48
terrace - Ter.; ter.; terr.                                   49
terrazzo - Terr.                                              50
Terrazzo Treads & Landing - Terr.Tr.&La.                      51
territorial - ter.; terr.                                     52
territory - T.; t.; ter.; terr.; Ty.                          53
Territory of Hawaii - T.H.                                    54
Testament - Test.                                             55
Tetragrammaton - YHVH; YHWH                                   56
```

tetrahydrocannabinol (the active principle of marijuana) -   1
   THC   2
Tetrethyl Pyrophosphate - TEPP   3
Teuton - Teut.   4
Teutonic - Teut.   5
Texan - Tex.   6
Texas - Tex.   7
Texas and Pacific (RR) - T&P   8
Texas Christian University - TCU   9
Texas Mexican (RR) - TM   10
Texas New-Mexico (RR) - TNM   11
Texas, Oklahoma & Eastern (RR) - TO&E   12
Thaddeus - Tad; Thad   13
Thailand - Thai.   14
Thallium - Tl   15
thank God it's Friday - tgif   16
thanks to God (L, Deo gratias) - D.G.   17
that (L, id) - i.   18
that is (L, hoc est) - h.e.   19
that is (L, id est) - i.e.   20
theater - theat.   21
Theatine Fathers - C.R.   22
theatrical - theat.   23
Thematic Appreciation Test - TAT   24
Theobald - Thbd.   25
Theodore - Theo.   26
Theodosius - Theo.   27
theologian - theol.   28
theological - theol.   29
theology - theol.   30
theorem - theor.   31
theosophical - theos.   32
theosophist - theos.   33
theosophy - theos.   34
therapeutic - therapeut.; therap.   35
therapeutics - therapeut.; therap.   36
Therapy Group - T-Group   37
thermal conductance - C   38
thermal conductivity - k   39
thermal megawatt - t.m.w.   40
thermochemistry - thermochem.   41
thermodynamics - thermodyn.   42
thermometer - therm.   43
thermostat - thermo   44
1 Thessalonians - 1 Thes   45
2 Thessalonians - 2 Thes   46
thick - thk.   47
thickness - thk.   48
thin-film technology - TFT   49
thin-film transistor - TFT   50
third - 3d; 3rd   51
third base (baseball) - 3b   52
third baseman (on a scorecard) - 3; 5   53
Third Order Regular of Saint Francis - T.O.R.   54
thirteen - XIII   55
thirty - XXX   56

thirty-six-mo - 36 mo.   1
thirty-two mo - 32 mo; 32°   ,   2
this is (L, hic est) - h.e.   3
this month's (huius mensis) - h.m.   4
this side up - t.s.u.   5
this year (L, hoc anno) - h.a.   6
this year's (L, hujus anni) - h.a.   7
Thomas - Thos.; Tom   8
Thorium - Tn   9
thoroughbred (horse racing) - th.   10
thousand - M   11
thousand calories - kcal.   12
thousand (feet) board measure - M b.m.   13
thousand cubic feet - M c.f.   14
thousand pounds per square inch - K s.i.   15
thousand standard cubic feet - M.s.c.f.   16
thousands (L, millia) - mm.   17
thread(s) - thd   18
threaded - thd; thr   19
threads per inch - tpi   20
three - III   21
three base hit (scoring) - ≡   22
three hundred - CCC   23
three thousand - MMM   24
three times a day - t.i.d.   25
three times daily (L, ter(in) die) - t.(i.)d.   26
three-base hit (baseball) - 3B   27
three-dimensional - 3-D   28
three-year-old horse - 3YO   29
threshold - thresh.   30
Thulium - Tm   31
Thunderbird - T-bird   32
Thursday - Th.; Thurs.   33
thus - sic   34
Tiberius - Ti.; Tib.   35
Tibetan - Tibet.   36
ticket - tkt   37
Tidewater Southern (Calif.)(RR) - TS   38
tied (games) - T   39
Tijuana and Tecate (Mexico) (RR) - T&T   40
Tile Window Stools - T.W.Stl.   41
till counter balanced - t/c   42
till forbidden - t.f.   43
time - t.   44
time and materials - T-M   45
time at which precipitation began or ended - R_t 46
time code word - TCW   47
time delay - TD   48
time deposit - T.D.; t/d   49
time during missile countdown (launch time is T) - T   50
time limit - TL   51
time modulation - TM; T.M.   52
the time set for an attack - H-hour   53
time to computation - TC   54
time-division switching - TDS   55
time-division multiplex - TDM   56

```
topographical - topog.                                              1
topography - topog.                                                 2
Toronto Stock Exchange - TOR; TS                                    3
total - tot                                                         4
total bases (baseball) - TB                                         5
total chances (baseball) - TC                                       6
total composite error - TCE                                         7
total digestible nutrients - TDN                                    8
total loss - t.l.                                                   9
total loss only - t.l.o.                                           10
total operating expense - TOE                                      11
total points - TP                                                  12
total response index - TRI                                         13
touchdown (footfall) - TD                                          14
tournament - tourn                                                 15
toward the lee side of a ship - alee                               16
toward the port side (nautical) - aport                            17
toward the rear - aft                                              18
toward the stern - aft                                             19
town - t.; tn.                                                     20
township - T.; Tp.; twp.                                           21
townships - tps.                                                   22
toxic - tox.                                                       23
toxicology - toxicol.                                              24
trace - tr.                                                        25
tractor - trac.                                                    26
trade union - t.u.                                                 27
tradition - trad.                                                  28
traditional - trad.                                                29
trademark - tm                                                     30
traffic - traf.                                                    31
traffic data processor - TDP                                       32
traffic manager - T.M.                                             33
tragedy - trag.                                                    34
tragic - trag.                                                     35
trailer - tlr.                                                     36
train - tn.                                                        37
training - tng.                                                    38
Trans Caribbean Airways - TRC                                      39
Trans Lunar Injection - TLI                                        40
Trans World Airlines - TWA                                         41
transaction(s) - trans.                                            42
Transair, Ltd. - TAL                                               43
transceiver - xcvr                                                 44
transconductance - gm                                              45
transducer - xdcr                                                  46
Transearth Injection - TEI                                         47
transfer - trf.; trfr.; xfer                                       48
transfer less than zero - TLZ                                      49
transfer no overflow - TNF                                         50
transfer no zero - TNZ                                             51
transference - transf.                                             52
transferred - tranf.; trans.; transf.; transfd.; trfd.            53
transformer - trans.; xfmr                                         54
transient - tran                                                   55
transistorized automatic control - TAC                            56
```

```
transistorized carrier - TC                                          1
transistor-transistor logic - TTL                                    2
transitive - t.; tr.; trans.                                         3
translate - trans.                                                   4
translated - tr.; trans.; transl.                                    5
translation - tr.; trans.; transl.                                   6
translator - tr.; trans.                                             7
transliteration - translit.                                          8
transmission - xmsn                                                  9
transmission adapter - XA                                           10
transmission and distribution - T&D                                 11
transmission controller - TC                                        12
transmission interface converter - XIC                              13
transmission level - TL                                             14
transmission line - TL                                              15
transmission unit - TU                                              16
transmit - xmit; XMT                                                17
transmit & receive - TR                                             18
transmit-receiver tube - TR; T-R tube; T.-R.; T.R.                  19
transmitter - TR; xmtr                                              20
transmitter distributor - TD                                        21
transmitting - xmtg                                                 22
transparency - transp.                                              23
transparent - transp.                                               24
transportation - trans.                                             25
transpose - tr.; trans.                                             26
Trans-Texas Airways - TT                                            27
transverse - trans.                                                 28
transverse direction - TD; T.D.                                     29
transverse magnetic - TM                                            30
travel - trav.                                                      31
traveler - trav.                                                    32
traveling wave tube - T.W.T.                                        33
travels - trav.                                                     34
Travertine - Trav.                                                  35
tread - T.; tr.                                                     36
tread (in notes) - trd.                                             37
treasurer - tr.; Treas.; treas.; treasr.                            38
Treasury - Treas.                                                   39
treasury - treas.                                                   40
Treasury Decisions - T.D.                                           41
treponemal immobilizing (antibody test for syphilis) - TPI          42
trial balance - T.B.; t.b.                                          43
triangle - T; trian.                                                44
Triangulum (the Southern Triangle) - TrA                            45
Triangulum (the Triangle) - Tri                                     46
tricycle - trike                                                    47
trigonometric - trig.; trigon.                                      48
trigonometry - trig.; trigon.                                       49
trill (music) - tr.                                                 50
trimmed opening - TO                                                51
Trinidad and Tobago - Trin.                                         52
trinitrotoluene - TNT                                               53
Trinity - Trin.                                                     54
triple - trip.                                                      55
triplicate - trip.; tripl.                                          56
```

229

```
trombone - trom                                               1
troop - tr.                                                   2
trooper - tpr.                                                3
troops - trs.                                                 4
tropic - trop.                                                5
tropical - trop.                                              6
tropics - trop.                                               7
troy - t.                                                     8
truck - trk.                                                  9
truck load - T.L.; t.l.                                      10
true mean - t.m.                                             11
true mean value - t.m.v.                                     12
true north - TN                                              13
trumpet - trump.                                             14
trust - tr.                                                  15
trustee - tr.                                                16
trusteeship - trust.                                         17
tube counter (Geiger-Muller) - G-M; G.-M.                    18
tuberculin unit(s) - T.U.                                    19
tuberculosis - TB; T.B.; t.b.                                20
tubular - tub.                                               21
Tucana (the Toucan) - Tuc                                    22
Tucson, Cornelia & Gila Bena (RR) - TC&GB                    23
Tuesday - T.; Tu.; Tues.                                     24
tuned radiofrequency - TRF; T.R.F.                           25
Tungsten - W                                                 26
Tunisia - Tun.                                               27
tunnel diode - TD                                            28
tunnel diode transistor logic - TDTL                         29
turbine - tb; turb                                           30
Turkey - Tur.                                                31
Turkish - Turk.                                              32
turn over - t.o.                                             33
turnbuckle - trnbkl                                          34
turnover - to.                                               35
Turnpike - Tnpk                                              36
turns per inch - t.p.i.                                      37
turpentine - turp                                            38
tuxedo - tux                                                 39
Twaddell - Twad.                                             40
twelve - XII                                                 41
twenty - XX                                                  42
twenty-four mo - 24 mo; 24°                                  43
twice a day - b.i.d.                                         44
twice a week - t.a.w.                                        45
twice daily (L, bis(in) die) - b.(i.)d.                      46
two - II                                                     47
two base hit (scoring) - ═                                   48
two degrees of freedom - TDF                                 49
2,4,5-Trichlorophenoxyacetic Acid - 2,4,5T                   50
two hands (weight lifting) - T.H.                            51
two hundred - cc                                             52
two hundred and twenty yard race (1 furlong) - 220           53
two thousand - MM                                            54
two-base hit (baseball) - 2B                                 55
two-seater canoe - c.2                                       56
```

two-seater kayak - K.2   1
two-twenty - 1 furlong   2
two-year-old horse - 2YO   3
type - ty.   4
types of cloud - $C_L.C_M.C_H$ 5
typewriter - typw   6
typewriter output routine - TYPOUT   7
typewritten - typw.   8
typical - typ.   9
typist - typ.   10
typographer - typog.   11
typography - typog.   12
ubi supra (in the place above mentioned) - u.s.   13
Uganda - Ug.   14
Ukraine - Ukr.   15
ukulele - uke   16
ultimate - ult.   17
ultimate tensile strength - uts   18
ultimately - ult.   19
ultimo - ult.; ulto.   20
ultra high frequency - UHF   21
ultra violet - U.V.   22
ultraviolet - uv   23
umbilical - umbl   24
umpire - ump   25
unabridged - unabr.   26
unacceptable person (L, persona non grata) - p.n.g.   27
unaccompanied - unacc.   28
Unadilla Valley (RR) - UV   29
unanimous - unan   30
unassigned - unasgd   31
unattached - unatt   32
unauthorized - unauthd   33
unbound - unbd.   34
uncertain - unc.; uncert.   35
uncirculated - uncir   36
unclassified - u; unclas   37
Uncle - U.; u.   38
unconditioned response - ucr   39
unconditioned stimulus - ucs   40
uncorrected - uncor   41
uncover - uncov   42
uncovered - uncov   43
und - u.   44
und so weiter (German) - usw; u.s.w.   45
under - und   46
under consideration (L, sub judice) - s.j.   47
under deck - und. dk.   48
Under Secretary of the Navy - Under Sec Nav   49
under separate cover - usc   50
under the entry (L, sub verbo) - s.v.   51
under this word (L, sub hac voce or sub hoc verbo) - s.h.v.   52
undercharge - u/c; u.c.   53
underdeck tonnage - udt   54
Underdeveloped Countries - UDCs   55
undergraduate - undergrad.   56

```
underground - ug                                              1
undersea boat - U-boat                                        2
undersigned - undsgd.                                         3
undersize - us.                                               4
understand, supply (L, subaudi) - sub.                        5
undertaker - undtkr.                                          6
underwater - undw; uwtr.                                      7
underwriter - U/w                                             8
Underwriters Laboratories - UL                                9
undistorted power output - u.p.o.                            10
unexploded bomb - UXB                                        11
unexpurgated - unexpur                                       12
unfavorable - unfav                                          13
unfinished - unfin                                           14
unfurnished - unfd                                           15
unguentum (ointment) - ung.                                  16
Unidentified Flying Object - UFO; ufo                        17
unidentified flying objects - ufo's                          18
unified - un.                                                19
unified course thread - unc                                  20
unified fine thread - unf                                    21
uniform - unif.                                              22
uniform allowance - ua                                       23
Uniform Regulations - U.R.                                   24
uniform reporting system - URS                               25
uniform system - u.s.                                        26
uniform thread standard - UTS                                27
uniformity - unif.                                           28
unincorporated - uninc.                                      29
uninterrupted power supply - UPS                             30
Union de Transports Aeriens - UTA                            31
Union of South Africa - U. of S. Afr.                        32
Union of Soviet Socialist Republics - USSR                   33
Union Pacific (RR) - UP                                      34
unison - unis.                                               35
unit(s) - u.                                                 36
unit heater - UH                                             37
unit junction transistor - UJT; U.J.T.                       38
unit of measure - u/m                                        39
unit of resistance - ohm                                     40
unit under test - uut                                        41
Unitarian - Unit.                                            42
United Air Lines - UA                                        43
United Arab Republic - UAR                                   44
United Artists - UA                                          45
United Automobile Workers - UAW                              46
United Brethren - U.B.                                        47
United Community Services - UCS                              48
United Farm Workers - UFW                                    49
United Farm Workers Organizing Committee - UFWOC             50
United Federation of Teachers - UFT                          51
United Jewish Appeal - U.J.A.                                52
United Kingdom - U.K.                                        53
United Kingdom of Great Britain and Northern Ireland - UK    54
United Lutheran - UL                                         55
United Mine Workers - UMW                                    56
```

United Nations - U.N.   1
United Nations Association - UNA   2
United Nations Educational, Scientific, and Cultural   3
  Organization - UNESCO   4
United Nations International Children's Emergency Fund -   5
  UNICEF   6
United Nations Relief and Rehabilitation Administration -   7
  UNRRA   8
United Nations Security Council - UNSC   9
United Parcel Service - UPS   10
United Press Associations - UP; U.P.   11
United Press International - UPI   12
United Service Organizations - USO   13
United States - U.S.   14
U.S. Air Force - USAF   15
United States Army - USA   16
U.S. Army, Europe - USAREUR   17
U.S. Army Training Center Armor - USATCA   18
United States Auto Club - USAC   19
United States Code - U.S.C.   20
United States Code Annotated - U.S.C.A.   21
United States Code Supplement - U.S.C.Supp.   22
United States Coast Guard - USCG   23
United States Department of Agriculture - USDA   24
United States Employment Service - USES   25
United States Golf Association - USGA   26
United States Government (RR) - USG   27
United States Government Printing Office - USGPO   28
U.S. Highway No. 40 - U.S.40   29
United States Housing Authority - USHA   30
U.S. Information Agency - USIA   31
United States Information Service - USIA   32
United States Mail - U.S.M.   33
United States Marine(s) - U.S.M.   34
United States Marine Corps - USMC   35
United States Merchant Marine - USMM   36
United States Military Academy - U.S.M.A.   37
United States Mint - U.S.M.   38
United States National Army - U.S.N.A.   39
United States National Guard - U.S.N.G.   40
United States Naval Academy - U.S.N.A.   41
United States Naval Reserve - U.S.N.R.; USNR   42
United States Navy - USN   43
United States of America - U.S.A.   44
United States Pharmacopoeia - U.S.P.   45
United States Public Health Service - U.S.P.H.S.   46
U.S. Senate - U.S.S.   47
United States Service - U.S.S.   48
United States Ship - U.S.S.   49
United States Shipping Board - U.S.S.B.   50
United States Standard - USS   51
U.S. Standard Gauge - USSG   52
United States Steamer - U.S.S.   53
United States Steamship - U.S.S.   54
United States Steel - USS   55
U.S. Supreme Court Reports - U.S.   56

```
United Steel Workers - USW                                          1
units of variance - uov                                             2
units per milligram - u./mg.                                        3
unity - u                                                           4
universal - univ.                                                   5
universal buffer-controller - UBC                                   6
universal communication - unicom                                    7
universal decimal classification - UDC; udc                         8
universal extra fine thread - uef                                   9
Universal Military Training - UMT                                  10
Universal Military Training Service - UMTS                         11
Universal Postal Union - U.P.U.                                    12
Universal Service - US                                             13
Universal Time - U.T.; u.t.                                        14
Universalist - Univ.                                               15
universally - univ.                                                16
Universities National Anti-War Fund - UNAF                         17
University - U.; u.; Univ.                                         18
University of Alabama - U of A                                     19
University of Arizona - U of A                                     20
University of Arkansas - U of A                                    21
University of California - UC; U of C                              22
University of California in Los Angeles - U.C.L.A.; UCLA           23
University of Chicago - U of C                                     24
University of Colorado - UC; U of C                                25
University of Connecticut - UC; U of C                             26
University of Delaware - U of D                                    27
University of Detroit - UD; U of D                                 28
University of Detroit High School - UDHi.Schl.                     29
University of Florida - U of F                                     30
University of Georgia - U of G                                     31
University of Hawaii - U of H                                      32
University of Idaho - U of I                                       33
University of Illinois - U of I                                    34
University of Iowa - U of I                                        35
University of Kansas - U of K                                      36
University of Kentucky - U of K                                    37
University of Maine - U of M                                       38
University of Maryland - U of M                                    39
University of Massachusetts - U of M                               40
University of Michigan - U of M                                    41
University of Minnesota - U of M                                   42
University of Mississippi - U of M                                 43
University of Missouri - U of M                                    44
University of Nebraska - U of N                                    45
University of Nevada - U of N                                      46
University of New Hampshire - U of NH                              47
U. of New Hampshire Improve the Environment! - UNHITE!             48
University of North Carolina - U of NC                             49
University of North Dakota - U of ND                               50
University of Notre Dame - U of ND                                 51
University of Ohio - U of O                                        52
University of Oklahoma - U of O                                    53
University of Oregon - U of O                                      54
University of Pennsylvania - U of P                                55
University of Rhode Island - U of RI                               56
```

```
University of South Carolina - USC                                        1
University of Southern California - USC                                   2
University of Tennessee - U of T                                          3
University of Texas - U of T                                              4
University of Utah - U of U                                               5
University of Vermont - U of V                                            6
University of Virginia - U of V                                           7
University of Washington - U of W                                         8
University of Wisconsin - U of W                                          9
University of Wyoming - U of W                                           10
University Without Walls - UWW                                           11
unknown - unkn.                                                          12
an unknown quantity - X; Y; Z                                            13
unless before (L, nisi prius) - ni. pri.                                 14
unless caused by - ucb                                                   15
unlimited - unl.                                                         16
unlock - unlk.                                                           17
unmarried - um.; unm.                                                    18
unnecessary - unnec.                                                     19
unofficial - unof.                                                       20
unofficial withdrawal (grading) - UW                                     21
unpaged - unp.                                                           22
unpaid - unpd.                                                           23
unpublished - unpub.                                                     24
unsatisfactory - unsat; unsatfy                                          25
unserviceable - unsev                                                    26
unsigned - unsgd.                                                        27
unsymmetrical diamethyl hydrazine (rocket fuel) - UDMH                   28
unthreaded - unthd.                                                      29
until further notice - ufn                                               30
unwatermarked - unwmkd.                                                  31
up - U                                                                   32
upholsterer - uphol.                                                     33
upholstering - uphol.                                                    34
upholstery - uphol.                                                      35
upper - u.; up.; upr.                                                    36
upper and lower case - u & lc                                            37
Upper Bench - U.B.                                                       38
upper case - u.c.                                                        39
upper class - Uc                                                         40
upper deck - ud; u.dk.                                                   41
upper half - uh                                                          42
upper left - ul                                                          43
upper middle status - UMs                                                44
upper peninsula - U.P.                                                   45
upper respiratory infection - U.R.I.                                     46
upper upper class - UUc                                                  47
upper status - Us                                                        48
upper statuses - Us's                                                    49
uppercase - uc.                                                          50
Uranium - U                                                              51
urban - Ur; urb                                                          52
Urban Police (Schutzpolizei) - SCHUPO                                    53
Urban Renewal Administration - URA                                       54
urgent - UGT; ugt                                                        55
urinal - urin.                                                           56
```

```
urinary tract - ut                                                        1
urine - ur.                                                               2
urological - urol.                                                        3
urology - urol.                                                           4
Ursa Major (the Greater Bear) - UMa                                       5
Ursa Minor (the Lesser Bear) - UMi                                        6
Uruguay - Ur.; Uru.                                                       7
use & occupancy - u. & o.                                                 8
use until exhausted - uue                                                 9
U-shaped beam - U-beam                                                   10
U-shaped channel - U-channel                                            11
usher - ush                                                              12
usual - usu.                                                             13
usually - usu.                                                           14
ut dictum (as directed) - ut dict.                                      15
ut supra (as above) - ut sup.                                           16
Utah State University - USU                                             17
utensil - uten                                                          18
utility - u; ut.; util.                                                 19
utility room - UR                                                       20
utilization - util.                                                     21
utriusque juris doctor (doctor of both civil and canon law)             22
      U.J.D.                                                            23
uxor (wife) - ux.                                                       24
vacant - vac                                                            25
vacation - vac                                                          26
vaccination - vacc                                                      27
vaccine - vacc                                                          28
vacuum - v; vac.                                                        29
vacuum-tube voltmeter - VTVM; vtvm                                      30
vagabond - vag                                                          31
vagina - vag                                                            32
vagrant - vag                                                           33
valence - val                                                           34
valentine - val.                                                        35
valley - val.                                                           36
Valley & Siletz (RR) - V&S                                              37
valuation - val.                                                        38
value - v.; val.                                                        39
valve - v.; val.                                                        40
valve box - VB                                                          41
Vanadium - V                                                            42
Vancouver Island - V.I.                                                 43
Vancouver Stock Exchange - VAN; VS                                      44
vanishing point - VP                                                    45
vapor proof - vap prf                                                   46
varia lectio - v.l.                                                     47
variable - v; va; var; X                                                48
variable frequency oscillator - VFO                                     49
variable pressure - VP; V.P.                                            50
variable-capacitance diode - VCD                                        51
variable-gain amplifier - VGA                                           52
variable-speed constant frequency - VSCF                                53
variae lectiones - vv.ll.                                               54
variant - var.                                                          55
variation - var.                                                        56
```

```
varieties - vars                                                 1
variety - var                                                    2
Varig Air Lines - VARIG                                          3
various - var.                                                   4
various dates - v.d.                                             5
varnish - varn                                                   6
vascular - vasc                                                  7
Vatican - Vat.                                                   8
vector - V; v.                                                   9
Vedic - Ved.                                                    10
vegetable - veg                                                 11
vehicle - vehic.                                                12
Vela (the Sail [of Argo]) - Vel                                 13
vellum - vel.                                                   14
velocity - V; vel                                               15
vending - vend                                                  16
vending machine - vend                                          17
vendor(s) - vend                                                18
veneer - ven                                                    19
venerable - V.; Ven.                                            20
Venereal Disease - V.D.                                         21
Venereal Disease Research Laboratories - VDRL                   22
Venetian - Venet.                                               23
Venetian Blinds - Ven.Blds.                                     24
Venezolana International de Aviacion - VIASA                    25
Venezuela - Ven.; Venez.                                        26
Venice - Ven.                                                   27
vent - v                                                        28
vent duct - VD                                                  29
vent pipe - VP                                                  30
vent shaft - VS                                                 31
vent stack - VS                                                 32
ventilate - vent.                                               32
ventilating - vent.                                             33
ventilation - vent.                                             34
ventilator - v; vent.                                           35
Venus - Ven.                                                    36
verb - v.; vb.                                                  37
verb active - v.a.                                              38
verb auxiliary - v.aux.                                         39
verb impersonal - v.imp.                                        40
verb intransitive - v.i.                                        41
verb neuter - v.n.                                              42
verb passive - v.p.                                             43
verb reflexive - v.r.                                           44
verb transitive - v.t.                                          45
verbal - vb.                                                    46
verbal order - VO                                               47
verbi gratia (for example) - v.g.                               48
verbs - vv.                                                     49
verbum sapienti sat est - verbum sap.                           50
Verhandlunger - Verhandl.                                       51
verify - vfy                                                    52
Vermont - Vt.                                                   53
verse - v.; ver.; vs.                                           54
verses - ver.; vv.                                              55
versicle - V                                                    56
```

```
version - v.; ver.                                            1
versions - vss.                                               2
verso - vo.                                                   3
versus (against) - v.; vs.                                    4
vertebra - vert.                                              5
vertebrata - vert.                                            6
vertebrate - vert.                                            7
vertical - vert.                                              8
Vertical Assembly Building - VAB                              9
vertical file - vf                                           10
vertical grain - VG                                          11
vertical take-off - VTO; V.T.O.                              12
vertical take-off and landing - VTOL; V.T.O.L.               13
vertigo - vert                                               14
very - vy.                                                   15
very good - XXX                                              16
very high frequency - VHF; V.H.F.                            17
very high output - VHO                                       18
very high performance - VHP                                  19
very important person - VIP                                  20
very low frequency - VLF; V.L.F.                             21
very rarely (L, rarissime) - rr.                             22
Very Reverend - V.Rev.                                       23
vessel - ves.                                                24
vestibule - vest.                                            25
vestry - ves.                                                26
veteran - vet                                                27
veterans - vets                                              28
Veterans' Administration - VA; V.A.                          29
Veterans of Foreign Wars - V.F.W.                            30
veterinarian - vet.                                          31
veterinary - vet.; veter.                                    32
Veterinary Corps - V.C.                                      33
veterinary science - vet. sci.                               34
Veterinary Surgeon - V.S.                                    35
viaduct - viad                                               36
vibration - vib.                                             37
vibration velocity per hour - v./v./hr.                      38
vibrations - vibs.                                           39
vibrations per second - vps                                  40
vicar - vic.                                                 41
Vicar Apostolic - V.A.; Vic. Ap.                             42
Vicar General - V.G.                                         43
Vicarage - vic.                                              44
Vicar-General - V.G.                                         45
vice- - v.                                                   46
vice admiral - Vice Adm.                                     47
vice versa - v.v.                                            48
Vice-Admiral - V.A.                                          49
Vice-Chairman - V.C.                                         50
Vice-Chamberlain - V.C.                                      51
Vice-Chancellor - V.C.                                       52
Vice-Consul - V.C.                                           53
Vice-President - V.P.; V.Pres.                               54
vicinity - vcnty; vic                                        55
Vickers hardness number - VHN; V.H.N.                        56
```

Vickers pyramid number - VPN; V.P.N.   1
Vicomte - Vte.   2
Vicomtesse - Vtesse.   3
Victor - Vic   4
victor analog computer - VAC   5
victor impedance locus plotter - VILP   6
Victoria - Vict.   7
Victoria and Albert (Order of) - V.A.   8
Victorian - Vict.   9
Victoria Cross - V.C.   10
victory - V; vic   11
vide (see) - v.; vid.   12
vide infra (see below) - v.i.   13
vice supra (see above) - v.s.   14
videlicet (namely) - viz.   15
video amplifier - VA   16
video amplifier chain - VAC   17
video correlator - VC   18
video frequency - VF; vf   19
video integrating group - VIG   20
video tape recorder - VTR   21
Viet Cong - V.C.   22
Viet Nam - Nam.   23
Vietnam - Viet.   24
Vigil - Vig.   25
village - vil.   26
Vincent - Vin.   27
vinegar - vin   28
vinyl asbestos tile - V.A.T.   29
vinyl tile - Vin.T.   30
Viola - Va.   31
Violaceus (purple; liturgical color) - Viol.   32
violins - vv.   33
Virgil - Vir.; Virg.   34
Virgin - Virg.   35
Virgin Islands - V.I.; Vir.Is.   36
Virginia - Va.   37
Virginia & Carolina Southern (RR) - V&CS   38
Virginian (RR) - VIR   39
Virgo (the Virgin) - Vir   40
Viridis (green; a liturgical color) - Vir.; Virid.   41
viscosity - visc.   42
viscosity gravity constant - VGC; V.G.C.   43
viscosity index - VI; V.I.   44
Viscount - V.; Vis.; Visc.; Visct.   45
Viscountess - Vis.; Visc.; Visct.   46
visibility - vis.; VV   47
visible - vis.   48
vision - v.   49
Visiting Nurse Association - VNA   50
visitor's card (Fr, carte de visite) - c.d.v.   51
visual - vis.   52
visual data acquisition - VIDAT   53
visual field - vf   54
visual instrumentation subsystem - VIS   55
visual radio range - VRR   56

```
visual-aural range - VAR                                          1
vital records - vit rec                                           2
vital statistics - vit stat                                       3
vitreous - vit                                                    4
vocabulary --vocab.                                               5
vocal - voc.                                                      6
vocation - voc.                                                   7
vocational - voctl.                                               8
vocative - v.; voc.; vocat.                                       9
voce (voice) - v.                                                10
voice - v.                                                       11
voice answer back - VAB                                          12
voice data communications - VODACOM                             13
voice frequency - VF; vf                                        14
voice interruption priority system - VIPS                       15
the voice of the people (L, vox populi) - vox pop.              16
voice operation demonstrator - VOPER                            17
voice-frequency carrier telegraph terminal - VFT               18
voices - vcs                                                    19
Volans (the Flying Fish) - Vol                                  20
volcanic - volc.                                                21
volcano - vol.; volc.                                           22
Volkswagen - VW                                                 23
volt - V; v.                                                    24
Voltage - E; e; V; v                                            25
voltage regulator - VR                                          26
voltage standing-wave ratio - VSWR                              27
volt-ampere - VA; va                                            28
volt-ampere-reactive unit - VAR                                 29
voltmeter - vm.                                                 30
volume - V.; vol.                                               31
volume index - V.I.                                             32
volume percent - v/o                                            33
volume unit - VU                                                34
volumes - vols.                                                 35
volunteer - vol.                                                36
volunteers - vols.                                              37
Volunteers in Service to America - VISTA                        38
Von - V.                                                        39
vote - vt.                                                      40
Vote Profile Analysis - V.P.A.                                  41
voting - vtg.                                                   42
Voting Trust Certificates - vtc                                 43
voucher - vou.                                                  44
voussoir - V                                                    45
vox populi - vox pop.                                           46
voyage - voy.                                                   47
vulgar -- vulg.                                                 48
Vulgar Latin - VL                                               49
vulgarism - vulg.                                               50
vulgarity - vulg.                                               51
vulgarly - vulg.                                                52
Vulgate - Vul.; Vulg.                                           53
Vulpecula (the Fox) - Vul                                       54
Wabash (RR) - WAB                                               55
wagon - wag.                                                    56
```

```
wainscot - wains.                                             1
waived - wvd                                                  2
Wales - W.                                                    3
wall cabinet - WCAB                                           4
wall paint flat - WF                                          5
wall paint gloss - WG                                         6
wall paint semi gloss - WSG                                   7
wall vent - WV                                                8
Wallace - Wall.                                               9
Wallachian - Wal.                                            10
Walloon - Wal.                                               11
wall-to-wall - w/w                                           12
Walnut - Wal.                                                13
Walter - Wa.; Walt                                           14
Walton - Walt                                                15
waltz - wlz                                                  16
War Department - W.D.                                        17
War Labor Board - WLB                                        18
War Manpower Commission - WMC                                19
War Production Board - WPB                                   20
War Relocation Authority - WRA                               21
War Shipping Administration - WSA                            22
ward - wd.                                                   23
warden - w.                                                  24
ward room - wrm.                                             25
warehouse - whs.; whse.                                      26
warehouse book - w.b.                                        27
warehouse receipt - W.R.; w.r.; whs.rec.                     28
warehouse stock - whs. stk.                                  29
warehouse warrant - W.W.; w.w.                               30
warehouseman - whsmn.                                        31
Warner & Swasey Company - WS                                 32
warrant - war.; wrnt.                                        33
Warrant Officer - WO; W.O.                                   34
warrant officer (junior grade) - WO(jg.)                     35
warranted - warrtd.; wrtd.                                   36
warranty - warrty.                                           37
Warwickshire - War.                                          38
Washburn and Moen gauge - W&MGA                              39
washing machine - WM                                         40
Washington - Wash.                                           41
Washington Free Clinic - WFC                                 42
Washington, Idaho & Montana (RR) - WI&M                      43
washroom - WR                                                44
Wassermann reaction - W.r.                                   45
water (L, aqua) - (aq.); H₂O; W                              46
water closet - w.c.                                          47
water cooler - WCR                                           48
water energy - pF                                            49
water heater - WH                                            50
water in oil - WIO                                           51
water line - WL                                              52
water quench - wq                                            53
water tight - w.t.                                           54
water tight door - WTD                                       55
water vapor transmission - WVT; W.V.T.                       56
```

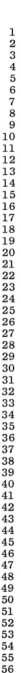

```
waterline - wl                                                    1
watermark - wmk.                                                  2
watermarked - wmkd.                                               3
waterproof - WP                                                   4
waterproofing - WP                                                5
watertank - w.tk.                                                 6
watertight - wt                                                   7
Watson characterization factor - WCF; W.C.F.                      8
watt(s) - W                                                       9
watt hour - wh; whr                                              10
watt-hour - w.-hr.                                               11
watt-hours - watt hr.                                            12
wattmeter - wm                                                   13
watts per candle - wpc; w/c                                      14
watts per candle power - watts per c.p.                          15
wave length - w.l.                                               16
waybill - W/B; W.B.; WB; w/b; w.b.                               17
Wayne State University - WSU                                     18
weak - wk.                                                       19
weapon(s) - wpn.                                                 20
weather - w; wea; wthr                                           21
weather bureau - WB                                              22
weather permitting - w.p.                                        23
weather stripping - ws                                           24
weatherproof - WP                                                25
Webster's New International Dictionary (Abridged;                26
    Unabridged) - Webster                                        27
Wednesday - W.; Wed.                                             28
week - w.; wk.                                                   29
weekly - wkly.                                                   30
weeks - w.; wks.                                                 31
weephole - WH                                                    32
weight - w.; wt.                                                 33
weight for weight - w/w                                          34
weight hourly space velocity - WHSV; W.H.S.V.                    35
weight in volume - w/v                                           36
weight-for-age (horse racing) - Wfa.                             37
weight-for-age stake (horse racing) - Wfa-S.                     38
weights - wts.                                                   39
welded wire fabric - W.W.F.                                      40
welder - wldr.                                                   41
Welsh - W.                                                       42
west - W.; w.                                                    43
West Africa - W.A.                                               44
West African - W.Afr.                                            45
West Central (postal district, London) - W.C.                    46
West Flemish - W.Fl.                                             47
West Germanic - W.Ger.; W.Gmc.                                   48
West Indian - W.I.; W.Ind.                                       49
West Indies - W.I.                                               50
West Indies Federation - W.I.Fed.                                51
West Saxon - W.S.                                                52
West Virginia - W.Va.                                            53
westbound - WB; w.b.                                             54
westerly - Wly                                                   55
western - W.; w.                                                 56
```

Western Air Lines - WA	1
Western Allegheny (RR) - WA	2
Western Australia - W.A.	3
Western Interstate Commission for High Education - WICHE	4
Western Maryland (RR) - WM	5
Western Pacific (RR) - WP	6
Western Ry. of Alabama (RR) - WRA	7
Western Union - WU	8
Western Union telegram - WUX	9
Westminster - Westm.	10
west-northwest - WNW; W.N.W.	11
west-southwest - WSW; W.S.W.	12
wharf - whf.	13
wharfage - whfg.; whge.	14
what was to be proved (L, in quod erat demonstrandum) -	15
i.q.e.d.	16
Wheaton - Wheat.	17
when actually employed - w.a.e.	18
when issued - w.i.	19
which - wh	20
which is (L, quod est) - q.e.	21
which see (L, quod vide) q.v.	22
which see (L, quae vide) (plural) - qq.v.	23
which was to be demonstrated (L, quod erat demonstrandum) -	24
Q.E.D.	25
which was to be done (L, quod erat faciendum) - Q.E.F.	26
which was to be found out (L, quod erat inveniendum) -	27
Q.E.I.	28
white - w; wh	29
white blood cell(s) - w.b.c.	30
white blood cell count - W.B.C.	31
white blood count - W.B.C.	32
white cathode follower - WCF	33
White Fathers - W.F.	34
White Panther Party - WPP	35
wholesale - whsle.	36
Wichita Falls & Southern (RR) - WF&S	37
wide - w	38
wide-area data service - WADS	39
wide-area telephone service - WATS	40
wide flange - WF	41
widow - W	42
widower - wid.	43
width - w.; wth.	44
Wien Air Alaska - WEN	45
wife - w.	46
wife (L, conjunx) - con.	47
wife (L, uxor) - ux.	48
wild pitch (baseball) - WP	49
wild throw (baseball) - W	50
will advise - wa	51
will call - w/c	52
will comply - wilco	53
will not prosecute (L, nolle prosequi) - nol. pros.	54
Willard - Will	55
William - Will; Wm.	56

```
Willis - Will                                                    1
Wiltshire - Wilts.                                               2
wind direction - w/d                                             3
wind velocity - wv                                               4
winding - wdg.                                                   5
window - wdw                                                     6
window opening - w.o.                                            7
Windward Islands - Win. Is.                                      8
wing - wg.                                                       9
Winston-Salem Southbound (RR) - WSS                             10
Winter - W.; wntr.                                              11
wire - W                                                        12
wire glass - W.Gl.                                              13
wire gauge - w.g.                                               14
wire payment - W.P.                                             15
wireless distress signal - SOS                                  16
Wisconsin - Wis.; Wisc.                                         17
Wisconsin State University - WSU                                18
wisdom - wis.; wisd.                                            19
Wisdom of Solomon (Apocrypha) - Wisd.                           20
with - w.; w/                                                   21
with (Fr, avec) - av.                                           22
with (Ger, mit) - m.                                            23
with (L, cum) - c.                                              24
with (hardware) - X                                             25
with dividend - cumd.; cum div.                                 26
with illustrations (L, cum figuris) - c.f.                      27
with interest - cum. int.                                       28
with rights - w.r.                                              29
with the necessary changes (L, mutatis mutandis) - m.m.         30
with warrants - W.W.; w.w.                                      31
withdrawal (grading) - W                                        32
withdrawal failing (grading) - WF                               33
withdrawal passing (grading) - WP                               34
withdrawn - wd                                                  35
withholding - wh; w/h                                           36
withholding tax - wt                                            37
without - w/o; w.o.                                             38
without charge - w.c.                                           39
without compensation - w.o.c.                                   40
without date (L, sine anno) - s.a.                              41
without date (L, sine die) - s.d.                               42
without dividend - ex div.; xd.                                 43
without issue (L, sine prole) - s.p.                            44
without lawful issue (L, sine legitima prole) - s.l.p.          45
without male issue (L, sine mascula prole) - s.m.p.             46
without name (L, sine nomine) - s.n.                            47
without place (L, sine loco) - s.l.                             48
without place, date, or name (L, sine loco, anno, vel nomine)   49
    s.l.a.n.                                                    50
without privileges - xpr                                        51
without rights - xrts                                           52
without surviving issue (L, sine prole superstite) - s.p.s.     53
without warrants - xw                                           54
without year or date (L, sine anno) - s.a.                      55
witness - wit.                                                  56
```

witnessed - witned.   1
Witwatersrand - The Rand   2
Woman's Christian Temperance Union - W.C.T.U.   3
Women Accepted for Voluntary Emergency Service - WAVES   4
Women in the Air Force - WAF   5
Women's - Wom.   6
Women's American Organization for Rehabilitation Through   7
    Training - ORT   8
Women's Army Auxiliary Corps - W.A.A.C.   9
Women's Army Corps - WAC   10
Women's Economic Club - WEC   11
Women's Equality Action League - WEAL   12
Women's International Terrorist Conspiracy from Hell -   13
    WITCH   14
Women's Liberation - Women's Lib.   15
women's rest room - WRR   16
women's toilet - WT   17
won (games) - W   18
won - w.   19
the wonderful year (1666) (L, Annus mirabilis) - A.M.   20
wood - wd.   21
wood screw - wd. sc.   22
Wood-Painted - Wd./Pt.   23
wood door - WD   24
wood frame - WF   25
Wood Paneling - Wd. Pan.   26
Worcestershire - Worcs.   27
word - wd.   28
word control register - WCR   29
word terminal synchronous - WTS   30
a word to the wise is sufficient (L, verbum sapienti sat   31
    est) - verbum sap.   32
wordiness - w   33
wording - wdg.   34
words per minute - wpm   35
work - w.; wk.   36
work (L, opus) - op.   37
the work cited (L, opus citatum) - op. cit.   38
work in progress - wip   39
Work Incentive - WIN   40
Work Projects Administration - WPA   41
workbook - wkbk.   42
workhouse - workho.   43
working - wkg.   44
working class - Wc   45
working point - w.p.   46
working pressure - WP   47
workmen's compensation - work. comp.   48
works - wks.   49
works (L, opera) - op.   50
World Health Organization - WHO   51
World Medical Relief - WMR   52
World Meteorological Organization - WMO   53
World War I - WWI   54
World War II - WWII   55
World Weather Watch - WWW   56

```
would - wd.; wld.                                            1
wound - wd.                                                  2
wounded in action - WIA                                      3
wrangler - wrang.                                            4
Wrightsville & Tennille (RR) - W&T                           5
wringer-washing machine - WWM                                6
write (L, signa) - (S; Sig.); wr.                            7
write address counter - WAC                                  8
write and compute - WC                                       9
write check - WR CHK                                        10
write forward - WF                                          11
write out - WO                                              12
writing - wr.                                               13
wrong font - wf; w.f.                                       14
wrought - wrt                                               15
wrought iron - W.I.                                         16
Wyoming - Wy.; Wyo.                                         17
Wyoming (RR) - WYO                                          18
Xaverian Missionary Fathers - S.X.                          19
Xavier University - XU                                      20
Xenon - Xe                                                  21
Xenophon - Xen.                                             22
Xerox - Xrx                                                 23
xylograph(s) - xyl.                                         24
xylophone - xylo.                                           25
yacht - yct                                                 26
Yadkin (RR) - YAD                                           27
Yale Law Journal - Yale L.J.                                28
Yale University - YU                                        29
yard - y.: yd.                                              30
yard drain inlet - YDI                                      31
yards - y.; yd.; yds.                                       32
year - y.; yr.                                              33
yearbook - Y.B.; yearb.                                     34
yearly - yrly.                                              35
years - y.; yr.; yrs.                                       36
years (L, anni) - ann.                                      37
Year-to-Date earnings - YTD earnings                        38
yellow - y; yel                                             39
yellowish - ysh                                             40
yellowish brown - yBr                                       41
yellowish green - yG                                        42
yellowish pink - yPk                                        43
yen - y; yn.                                                44
yeoman - yeom.                                              45
yeomanry - yeom.                                            46
yesterday - yday; yesty.                                    47
Yiddish - Yid.                                              48
yield point - YP; Y.P.                                      49
yield strength - ys                                         50
Yorkshire - Yorks.                                          51
young adult - YA                                            52
Young Men's Christian Association - Y.; YMCA                53
Young Men's Hebrew Association - Y.M.H.A.                   54
Young People's Society of Christian Endeavor - Y.P.S.C.E.   55
Young Women's Christian Association - YWCA                  56
```

Young Women's Hebrew Association - Y.W.H.A.   1
younger - yr.   2
youngest - yst.   3
Youngstown & Southern (RR) - Y&S   4
your - yr.   5
your memorandum - urmen   6
yours - yrs.   7
Youth International Party - YIP   8
Youth Uncovering Krud - YUK   9
Ytterbium - Yb   10
Yttrium - Y   11
Yugoslavia - Yugo.   12
Yukon - Yuk   13
Yukon Territory - Y.T.   14
Yvette - Yv   15
Yvonne - Yv   16
Zachary - Zach   17
Zambia - Zamb   18
Zanzibar - Zan.   19
Zechariah - Zech   20
zed - z   21
Zeitschrift - Ztschr.   22
Zeitung - Ztg.   23
zenith - zen   24
zenith distance - Z; Zd   25
Zentralblatt - Zentralbl.   26
Zephaniah - Zeph   27
zeppelin - zepp   28
zero - 0; z   29
zero and add - ZA   30
zero defects - zd   31
zero hour - z hr   32
Zero Population Growth - ZPG   33
zero-energy - ZOE   34
Zinc - Z; Zn   35
Zirconium - Zr   36
zither - zith   37
zodiac - zod.   38
Zone - Z; z   39
zoölogical - zool.; zoöl.   40
Zoölogie - Zoöl.   41
Zoölogischer - Zoöl.   42
zoölogist - zool.; zoöl.   43
zoölogy - zool.; zoöl.   44

Co p049n17
CO p044n22
  p048n55 p051n24
  p056n28 p062n20
  p217n23
co. p050n23
  p059n43
Co. p052n55
  p059n43
c.o. p039n18
  p039n44 p169n15
C.O. p040n18
  p048n18 p055n37
c/o p039n18
  p039n44 p040n18
C&O p045n26
COA p058n09
coax p049n15
COAX p049n16
COBOL p052n04
coc p049n18
coch. p049n19
  p215n48
coch. amp.. p049n20
  p222n20
coch. mag.. p049n21
  p133n13
coch. med.. p049n22
  p069n48
coch. parv. p049n23
  p223n12
COD p040n16
  p045n17 p048n21
  p049n31 p054n15
cod. p040n16
  p049n30
c.o.d. ... p040n16
  p043n43 p050n02
C.O.D. ... p040n16
  p045n17 p050n02
CODIC p054n04
CODIPHASE . p049n41
CODIT p053n52
CO&DP p048n20
coe p036n22
COED p054n06
coed. p049n32
  p049n33
coef p049n34
C.O.F. ... p041n07
C of C ... p044n12
coff. p049n37
C of G ... p043n07
C. of S. . p045n49
cog. p049n38

COGB p043n46
cogn. p049n38
COGO p057n50
coh p040n22
  p049n40
coho p049n42
coins. cl.. p049n43
Col p050n41
COL p053n56
col. p050n03
  p050n11 p050n25
  p050n26 p050n35
  p050n49
Col. p050n22
  p050n24 p050n37
  p050n40
COLA p059n07
Col.Eng. . p050n14
coll. p049n52
  p049n55 p049n56
  p050n03 p050n04
  p050n08 p050n09
  p050n11 p050n13
  p050n15 p050n17
collab. .. p049n50
  p049n51
coll agc . p050n05
collat. .. p049n52
  p049n54
coll. cl. . p050n16
collect. . p050n09
  p050n10
coll/L ... p050n07
colloq. .. p050n17
  p050n18 p050n19
collr. ... p050n11
coll.tr. . p049n53
Coln. p050n21
COLO p050n32
Colo. p050n31
colog p050n20
colorl. .. p050n30
COLT p054n05
Com p050n50
com. p051n05
  p051n06 p051n07
  p051n30 p051n40
  p051n43 p052n03
  p052n17 p052n15
  p052n20 p052n21
  p052n28
Com. p052n02
  p052n16 p052n44
COMAC p051n48
COMAR p053n48

comb. p050n53
  p051n02 p051n04
Comb. p050n55
comb. form. p051n03
com. carr.. p052n05
comd. p051n09
  p051n42
comdg. ... p051n22
comdr. ... p051n18
Comdr. ... p051n18
comdt. ... p051n17
Comdt. ... p051n17
Com. in Chf.
  p051n19
coml. p051n31
com'l. ppr. p051n34
comm. p051n27
  p051n28 p052n21
  p052n28
Comm. p051n44
  p052n16 p052n18
COMMCEN .. p052n29
commod. .. p051n55
COMMSWITCH. p052n32
commt. ... p051n26
COMMZ p052n40
comp. p052n53
  p053n05 p053n06
  p053n08 p053n13
  p053n14 p053n15
  p053n16 p053n17
  p053n26 p053n27
  p053n28 p053n29
  p053n30 p053n32
  p053n33 p053n39
compar. .. p053n05
  p053n08
Comp. Dec.. p053n43
comp. g. . p053n36
Comp. Gen.. p053n44
compn. ... p052n53
compo p053n24
compo. ... p053n13
  p053n27 p053n28
  p053n29
COMPOOL .. p052n36
compr p053n38
comps p053n34
compt. ... p053n09
  p053n41
COMSAT ... p052n38
  p052n39
Com Sec .. p052n27
comsry. .. p051n39
comsy. ... p051n39

plur. p181n16
  p181n17
Ply p181n19
plywd p181n20
pm p184n50
PM p177n34
  p178n33
p.m. p005n53
  p088n05 p183n02
  p183n25
P.M. p005n49
  p088n05 p175n32
  p176n08 p181n42
  p183n02 p183n03
  p183n23 p183n25
  p185n20 p185n45
  p188n43
p/m p183n45
PMD p183n04
P.M.G. ... p176n09
  p183n24 p188n44
p.m.h. ... p175n33
pmk. p183n21
pmkd. p183n22
PMLA p189n16
P&MP p174n31
pmt. p176n10
pn p174n43
PN p173n10
  p174n43
pn. p175n04
  p182n36
p.n. p181n04
  p187n38
p-n p182n45
p/n p174n43
  p187n38
P/N p187n38
PNdB p177n10
pndg p176n37
pneum. ... p181n21
p.n.g. ... p177n45
  p231n27
pnl. p173n48
p.n.r. ... p186n13
pntr. p173n32
pnxt. p180n11
po p185n32
PO p178n18
  p189n07 p189n56
po. p190n13
p.o. p186n11
P.O. p174n21
  p178n18 p181n55
  p183n05 p183n16

p/o p174n44
p&o p179n43
P.O.A. ... p173n30
POB p183n06
P.O.B. ... p183n06
POC p182n26
  p186n48
POD p183n07
p.o.d. ... p176n03
P.O.D. ... p176n03
  p183n07
Pod.D. ... p075n42
poet. p181n22
  p181n23 p181n26
Poet. p181n24
  p181n25
p.o.f. ... p181n05
POGO p181n37
POL p186n41
pol. p181n47
  p181n48 p181n51
  p182n02
Pol. p181n36
  p181n46
pol. dist.. p181n53
pol. econ.. p181n54
Pol. Econ.. p181n54
Police Supt.
  p181n43
pol ind .. p182n03
poli. sci.. p181n56
polit. ... p181n51
  p182n01 p182n02
poll. p182n04
Poly p182n06
POLY p182n05
poly. p182n07
  p182n08
pom p182n10
Pont p182n12
pont. p182n14
POOFF p185n10
POOL p187n09
pop. p182n16
  p182n18 p182n19
pop. ed. . p182n17
POPS p174n28
p.o.r. ... p176n04
  p176n05
P.O.R. ... p176n04
porc. p182n21
Porc. Enam. p182n22
PORT p179n20
port. p182n27
Port. p182n32

  p182n33
Port. Gui.. p182n34
ports p182n30
Port. Timo. p182n35
pos. p182n36
  p182n40 p182n47
posn. p182n36
pos pron . p182n48
poss. p182n46
  p182n47 p182n49
  p182n50
post. p183n12
poster. .. p183n18
postgrad . p183n19
posth p183n20
post. rcts. p183n17
pot. p183n31
  p183n33 p183n34
potats ... p183n30
poul p183n35
p.o.v. ... p186n25
POW p186n16
pow. p183n54
powd. p183n52
pp p183n11
PP p176n33
  p180n06 p185n24
pp. p173n27
  p175n34 p179n41
  p186n26
PP. p173n22
  p177n16
p.p. p168n35
  p174n18 p174n45
  p175n34 p177n05
  p177n49 p183n26
P.P. p174n18
  p174n33 p184n52
P-P p176n17
p&p p173n53
ppb p175n09
p.p.c. ... p183n51
  p227n20
P.P.C. ... p183n51
  p227n20
PPD p190n05
ppd. p183n26
  p184n52
PPGL p181n49
pph. p173n44
p.p.h.m. . p175n11
PPI p180n39
  p180n42
p.p.i. ... p174n19
  p181n45

```
        p212n49  p214n15
        p214n34  p215n55
        p216n38  p217n41
        p217n47  p217n48
        p217n53  p218n15
        p219n39
S.      ....... p035n51
        p093n23  p132n28
        p204n05  p204n14
        p204n31  p205n24
        p205n25  p205n40
        p206n16  p206n52
        p208n22  p208n25
        p208n48  p211n08
        p211n46  p212n18
        p214n15  p214n34
        p220n10
SA      ....... p207n15
        p209n15  p212n15
sa.     ...... p207n48
Sa.     ...... p204n08
s.a.    ...... p002n29
        p207n33  p208n15
        p209n39  p211n21
        p219n17  p244n41
        p244n55
S.A.    ...... p019n19
        p100n17  p204n55
        p214n16  p214n19
        p214n21
s/a     ...... p219n17
        p218n29
S/A     ...... p210n13
S&A     ...... p205n44
SAB     ....... p204n07
        p222n14
Sab.    ...... p204n05
sabbat. .. p204n06
sac     ...... p204n12
        p204n14
SAC     ...... p218n38
SACEUR  ... p220n36
SACO    ..... p207n56
Sacr    ..... p204n13
SAE     ...... p213n52
s.a.e.  ... p208n08
S.A.E.  ... p213n52
saf     ...... p204n22
SAFARI  ... p215n40
S.Afr.  ... p214n16
        p214n17
S.Afr.D. . p214n18
SAGE    ..... p208n16
Sai     ...... p204n28
SAID    ..... p215n26

SAL     ...... p206n55
Sal.    ..... p081n06
Salop.  ... p210n36
SALT    ..... p218n39
salut   ... p204n50
salv.   .... p204n53
Salv.   .... p204n52
Sam     ...... p205n12
Sam.    ...... p205n01
        p205n05
S.Am.   .... p214n19
        p214n20
S.A.M.  ... p214n49
S.Amer. .. p214n19
        p214n20
Saml    ..... p205n12
SAMOS   .... p221n06
san.    ...... p205n20
        p205n22
s. and s.c. p213n01
sanit.  ... p205n20
        p205n22
Sans.   .... p205n23
Sansk.  ... p205n23
sap     ...... p205n26
s.ap.   .... p206n46
s.a.p.  ... p214n04
Sar.    ..... p205n28
        p205n29  p205n30
S.A.R.  ... p212n55
        p214n01
SAS     ...... p206n03
S.A.S.  ... p093n52
        p213n38
Sask.   .... p205n33
Sat     ...... p205n34
SAT     ...... p206n15
sat.    ...... p205n38
        p205n39
Sat.    ..... p205n40
        p205n42
satel   .... p205n35
satfy   .... p205n37
Sat. Rev. . p205n41
Sau Ar. .. p205n43
sav.    ..... p205n46
SAVOR   .... p211n37
sax     ...... p205n50
Sax.    ..... p205n48
        p205n49
SB      ....... p015n28
        p211n48  p214n29
        p218n23
sb.     ...... p219n39
s.b.    ..... p204n43

S.B.    ..... p024n53
        p214n22
s/b     ...... p210n33
SBA     ...... p213n19
S Baruch . p222n09
sbm     ...... p219n23
        p219n24
SBT     ...... p220n45
SbW     ...... p214n23
sby     ...... p217n02
Sc      ....... p206n04
SC      ....... p208n09
        p210n02  p211n30
        p218n27  p220n24
sc.     ...... p110n21
        p157n40  p205n53
        p206n07  p206n22
        p206n25  p206n28
        p206n38  p206n45
        p206n47
Sc.     ...... p206n31
        p206n32  p206n33
        p206n34
s.c.    ..... p208n46
        p220n14
S.C.    ..... p034n42
        p204n44  p205n21
        p210n53  p213n21
        p214n24  p216n27
        p220n38
S/C     ...... p210n20
s&c     ...... p210n14
S&C     ...... p220n08
SCA     ...... p208n06
S.C.A.  ... p212n04
Scan.   .... p206n01
Scand.  ... p206n01
        p206n02
SCAP    ..... p220n37
s.caps. .. p213n21
Sc.B.   .... p024n53
scd.    ..... p206n09 .
        p206n40
Sc.D.   .... p075n50
SCE     ...... p211n33
s.c.f.  ... p216n45
s.c.f.m. . p216n46
sch.    ...... p206n08
        p206n16
sched.  ... p206n08
schem   .... p206n10
schizo  ... p206n11
        p206n12
schl.   .... p206n13
Schl.   .... p206n16
```

Ref PE1693.R94
Abbreviations

3 2551 00037125 6

REFERENCE

PE ABBREVIATIONS
1693
•R94   062260   RYBICKI

62260

Library

Auburn Community

College

Auburn, N. Y.

Reference

U.S.A.